W9-CYH-013

Here's what authors and critics are saying about the first edition of Romance Writer's Pink Pages:

All romance writers will fall in love with this book!
—Jeff Herman, author of *Insider's Guide to Book Editors, Publishers and Literary Agents*

Published and unpublished authors alike will benefit from this book, which is simply a gold mine of information.
—Rona Weisburg, *Affaire de Coeur* book reviewer (★★★★★!)

Here is a very current guide, complete with the names of editors and agents . . . It describes the market thoroughly, as well as auxiliary groups and services available to new writers.
—*Manderley* magazine

. . . the Pink Pages *is one of the most helpful tools yet to come along for the aspiring romance novelist.*
—Betty Webb, *Tribune* newspapers reviewer

Romance Writer's Pink Pages *is ideal for the novice writer since it answers many of the questions beginners don't know they should ask. It is also valuable for the experienced professional writer since it is an excellent source of information, all in one entertaining and well-written package.*
—Sharon Wagner, author of more than 70 novels

Like Chocolate Cool Whip™, I can't help but think . . . how come nobody ever thought of it before? It is concise and clever, and I wish it had been around when I was starting out.
—Judith Hill, award-winning historical author

Highly recommended for romance writers, readers, librarians, and anyone else who needs quick information about romance genre publishing.
—G. Benninger, President of Arizona Author's Association

© 1995 by Eve Paludan

All rights reserved. No part of this book may be reproduced or transmitted in any form or by any means, electronic or mechanical, including photocopying, recording, or by any information storage or retrieval system, without written permission from Prima Publishing, except for the inclusion of quotations in a review.

Production by Archetype Book Composition
Typography by Archetype Book Composition
Cover design by The Dunlavey Studio, Sacramento
Copyediting by Joan Misiewicz
Interior design by Paula Goldstein

ISBN 1-55958-581-1
ISSN 1076-9501

95 96 97 98 RRD 10 9 8 7 6 5 4 3 2 1

Printed in the United States of America

How to Order:
Single copies may be ordered from Prima Publishing, P.O. Box 1260BK, Rocklin, CA 95677; telephone (916) 632-4400. Quantity discounts are also available. On your letterhead, include information concerning the intended use of the books and the number of books you wish to purchase.

Romance Writer's Pink Pages

The Insider's Guide to Getting Your Romance Novel Published

Eve Paludan

Prima Publishing
P.O. Box 1260
Rocklin, CA 95677
(916) 632-4400

*To every romance writer who has
ever read a romance and said to
herself, "I can do that."
And then did.*

Contents

Acknowledgments

*H*ow can I ever possibly say thank you enough to the people who have made the success of this book possible?

Evan Fogelman, you are not just my agent, you're a career mentor, and a wellspring of wisdom and integrity. Thanks for returning my calls ASAP, sending copies of all correspondence, keeping me well-informed, and disbursing monies promptly. I will always be grateful for your encouragement, advice, and excellent representation.

And thank you to the staff at Prima Publishing: Jennifer Basye Sander, who believed I could do it again, Ben Dominitz, who trusts Jennifer, and Nancy Dominitz, who writes the checks promptly.

Andi Reese Brady, you are a joy to have as an editor. I hope to work with you again and again.

Jenn Nelson, you are one fabulous publicist, turbo-driven by a smile, a telephone, and what must be a very impressive Rolodex. Thanks for all your hard work.

Thanks to the Dunlavey Studio in Sacramento for a cover design that makes booksellers turn my book face out! Yes!

To all the agents, publishers, and editors who filled out questionnaires and mailed them back—I couldn't have done this without you. Thanks.

Special appreciation goes to all my new friends on GeNie's Romance Exchange (RomEx) and Writers' bulletin board. Thanks for your support and encouragement, for sharing millions of bytes of information about the romance novel and screenwriting industry, and for being there in the middle of the night.

Thank you for your input: Susan Wiggs, Jo Beverley, Anne Stuart, Pat Chandler, Judith Hill, Denise and Joan Domning, Karen Leabo, Lynn Kerstan, Rosalyn Alsobrook, Monette Cummings, Suzanne Forster, Deb Stover, Ashley McConnell, Kelsey Roberts, Alicia Rasley, Maggie Shayne, Justine Davis, Christina Dodd, Meryl Sawyer, Victoria Hinze, Hannah Rowan, Linda Hilton, Sharon and Dorothy Wagner, Casey Roberts, Sue Kearney, Laura Phillips, and many other authors and writing teachers who are recommending *Romance Writer's Pink Pages* from coast to coast. If I left out your name, I apologize.

Thanks to Romance Writers of America for your support and promotional help. Thanks to Romance Writers of Australia for helping me to go international, Jean Riva at *The Reader's Voice* for all the press, Chelley Kitzmiller at *LA Daily News* for a good review, and Rona Weisburg at *Affaire de Coeur* for five stars!

I would also like to thank Tammy Crampton of Romance Films for letting me pick her brain about Hollywood and the film industry, and also for making *Romance Writer's Pink Pages* required reading for all her scriptwriters!

A special thanks to Merline Lovelace for preparing the quick publisher reference in the appendix of this book.

Most of all, I appreciate my husband Ron for all the times he took up my slack at home so I could achieve my goals. You know someone really loves you when he says: "Forget the housework. Write!"

Introduction

*W*elcome to the second edition of *Romance Writer's Pink Pages*. This directory, which is planned to be an annual publication, was conceived to help frustrated romance writers connect with agents and publishers.

While 47% of the paperback trade is in romance, little information is available in standard publisher's directories. The romance publishing industry is a specialized one, and a kind of "Yellow Pages" was needed, just for romance authors.

The agent's section is more than just a directory: it includes specific information about agent's fees and commissions, types of romance manuscripts handled, method of contact, and much more. This edition's agent section will introduce you to 34 agents who have not graced these pink pages previously. Plus, some of your favorite agents are back, due to enthusiasm from authors who wrote to tell me they found the most wonderful agent in this book, and they are soon to be published!

In the publisher's section, many editors have given *Romance Writer's Pink Pages* permission to reprint their guidelines, as well as their tips and comments. You'll notice many new markets. Dig in! This section will save writers the expense and trouble of sending a self-addressed stamped envelope to each publisher for their individual "tip sheets."

If you are in the business of selling or buying romance manuscripts, and are not listed in this edition, you are invited to contact us for details about inclusion in the next edition of *Romance Writer's Pink Pages*. There is no charge for a listing. However, advertising copy is not accepted, and listings are at the discretion of the editor. Preference will be given to agents who do not charge reading fees. We only list book publishers who have been in business for at least one year.

This directory is as complete and accurate as possible, but if there is an error in your listing, please contact us, so we can correct it in the next edition.

Publishers, please notify us of editorial or other changes, such as adding or discontinuing a line, or new tip sheets. Agents, please send your new address and phone number if you move your office.

Efforts have been made to make sure that everyone listed is reputable, but *Romance Writer's Pink Pages* does not necessarily endorse them, nor accept liability for the results obtained from contacting anyone in this directory.

So, approach each agent or publisher in a professional manner, and don't be afraid to ask questions about contracts, fees, and pay rates. If you have a word of praise or a complaint about someone listed in *Romance Writer's Pink Pages,* please write. We'd like to know.

Whether you are a writer, an agent, an editor, or another professional involved in the romance publishing industry, we hope you will find this book to be a valuable reference. We welcome letters from readers (with SASE please) and will try to answer your questions by return mail. I want to hear your suggestions and success stories too!

Good luck!

Eve Paludan
P.O. Box 24739
Tempe, AZ 85285-4739

P.S. You can also e-mail me on the GEnie network. My e-mail address is: R.Paludan1.

1

How to Think About Literary Agency

Evan M. Fogelman

*O*nce you've completed your first manuscript, you'll need to think about *the business* of publishing. Many of you may feel intimidated by hard-core business details. The whole matter of the commercial exploitation of writing is somewhat distasteful to you, and you might want to leave those details to someone else. Whatever your own feelings on the subject may be, take responsibility for the development of your own career. Ask a lot of questions. Learn the basics of acquiring and distributing books. The quality of your decisions will rise in direct proportion to the amount of background understanding you've acquired about the topic at hand.

The right literary agent—someone who has a good understanding of the publishing business and how to help you develop your career—can be of tremendous help. In some respects publishing is an agent-driven business. The right agent can do much for a career, in dealing with money and all the other variables in a writer's professional life. Nevertheless, one great author once referred to her agent as a "benevolent parasite," and there is some merit in her characterization.

Before you begin assessing which agents or agencies are right for you, give some thought to what you want—besides that first sale—from the author-agent relationship. Much time at writers' conferences is devoted to agents, yet few authors seem to know much about the business of literary representation. Agents typically do much more than just send your manuscript to the right editors; most good agents are true career managers. You'll need to know what that entails so you can make an informed choice about what may well prove to be one of your most important career decisions.

With the exception of situations in which publishers require agented submissions, begin with the premise that agents aren't really necessary. We're not. After all, few publishers will pay you royalties as high as 15%, so you need a very compelling set of reasons to give up that much of your income to someone else. If you're the type of person who prefers to do everything yourself, you may not want to associate with a literary representative. If, however, you want to delegate some of your responsibility to a qualified professional, you'll need to explore your goals for the three areas in which agents work.

The first area is *editorial contact*. This may be the most overrated aspect of an agent's work—especially among the Romance Writers of America (RWA), where there are a manageable number of acquisitions editors and even the most novice of unpublished authors can meet editors at conferences. Also, some very savvy published authors know every bit as many editors as certain agents do. True, the martini or Perrier lunches do occur occasionally, but even the most delightful friendship between agent and editor can rarely be utilized to compel the acquisition of an unsalable manuscript. In category genre fiction there are a limited number of editors to begin with, and it certainly does not take great professional acumen to determine which editor acquires for a certain line. The mere acquaintance of editors appropriate for your manuscript does not in itself merit the compensation of an agent. You could probably hunt down the range of editors your-self and not be out the 15%.

However, the more complicated the area of editorial con-tacts becomes, the more you'll want to explore what an agent can do for you. For example, if you're writing for several lines or across genre boundaries, you may want someone to help manage your different obligations. Also, you'll need to consider the larger concerns of publishing programs. If you write more mainstream, single title books, you'll have to consider which publishers might really foster your talent and move you up the list. An agent might help you quite a bit in locating those editors whose sensibilities are in accord with your writing.

You might also consider the value of an agent's endeavors with regard to your own relationship with an editor. Many editors like working with agents because it's then clear who handles the business details and who handles the creative aspects. Thus, the author-editor relationship is freed from the encumbrances of commerce and can exist on a nurturing-of-talent level. It sounds pretty hopeful, yet it actually happens that way sometimes and is something you should think about.

Once you're comfortable with evaluating the propriety of an agent's benefit in terms of editorial contacts, you'll want to ex-plore a second area, *business management.* Business management deals with much more than advances and royalty rates; it's the area in which agents can really earn their commissions. Yes, in some cases an agent can get you more money up front and a bet-ter royalty for a first book than you could get on your own—yet that alone might not be enough to justify the relationship. Partic-ularly in the case of category works, the little extra money the agent might get for you could be more than eaten up by the agency commission you'll have to pay. Think of business manage-ment not only as a contract negotiation, but also as contract main-tenance. Signing the contract is only the very beginning.

An increasingly important part of contract maintenance is subsidiary rights management. More and more publishers look toward subrights to help their profit margins. And there's a lot more to subrights than the glamorous TV and feature film options of which we're all happy to be a part. There are also foreign rights, reprints, audio, serializations, book club sales, and other sources of potential income that may be marketed throughout the life of the title. Depending upon the publishing contract, it is often the publisher who takes primary responsibility for garnering subrights income. In the case of author-retained rights, though, it is the author's agent who seeks the subrights deals.

There is also a business management side to the author-editor relationship. During the initial submission process, this involves handling revision suggestions and informing the author about the status of any negotiations. Once your book is acquired, your agent might be the liaison between you and your editor for any pre-press information the publisher requires. At times authors feel more comfortable having their agents make inquiries about the book. Though author and editor should be able to converse as needed without the unnecessary intervention of an agent, many authors feel uncomfortable asking questions about print runs and options.

When you understand the necessity of good business management, you're able to move on to the last area you need to evaluate in your decision about an agent, *career development*. This is the most underrated, yet perhaps the most important aspect of your decision. The right agent can help your career development by associating your talent with future deals. Your agent can act as a sounding board for your ideas and provide specific input designed to keep you selling. There's a lot of value in being able to discuss your manuscripts with someone who has professional judgment. Though your first book may be a runaway bestseller, most publishers look at authors as incremental business successes. That is, your second book should be more successful than your first, your third more than your second, and so forth. Imagine how much more productive you could be if someone were guiding you along the way.

This area of career development leads us naturally to perhaps the best criterion for measuring agents: *communication*. You should feel that your agent expresses an understanding of your work and your goals. Learn as much as you can about the agents you are considering. Make an effort to find out about their backgrounds, who they represent, and their recent sales. Don't just blindly send your book to a list of agents who may or may not be receptive to your work. Look for the ones who accept unpublished authors, who have a good reputation in the romance genre, and about whom you feel generally confident.

Like most things in book publishing, finding the right agent is not nearly so easy as it sounds. Many agents do not accept unpublished authors. Since there are no particular qualifications needed to become an agent—and no certifications of any sort required—you should approach the matter cautiously. I think you'll find, though, that most agents don't run scam operations. All businesses have some measure of individuals who are dishonest, yet there's no reason to assume that in book publishing there are any more than in other places.

Here it's appropriate to mention the controversial topic of reading fees. Since some very successful agencies charge them, it would be a bit simplistic to say one should always avoid them. That's a decision you're going to have to make on your own. If you must pay a fee, make sure the agency's record merits your involvement. Inquire about the purposes of the fee. Is it designed to cover the agency's administrative costs? Is the fee used to compensate outside readers? If you're paying a fee for a critique, find out who's doing the job.

Fortunately the literary agent trade group, the Association of Author's Representatives (AAR), mandates a policy against reading fees for new members and is in the process of phasing them out altogether for existing members who wish to maintain AAR membership. (Certain agencies that do charge reading fees were grandfathered in when the ILAA and SAR merged to form the AAR.) The AAR also prescribes ethical and accounting guidelines for its members, and is thus a good place to start your search for an agent. Request their list of members and do some background checking on the ones that interest you. Cross-reference the list with the RWA's (Romance Writers of America) list in order to determine which qualified agents are active in romance fiction.

There are many fine agents who are not AAR members. Nevertheless, you've got to start somewhere, and unless you're spending a fortune attending conferences all over the country, you'll need a credible agency resource. Show respect for your career and do your homework. (Of course, there's no substitute for contacting your best friend's agent after he just got her a good contract!)

Agents have different policies about submission. Please follow them—they're designed to help agents find the best writers and writing available. As a general rule, we agents don't appreciate gimmicks. Some agents require a formal query letter before you submit a manuscript. Others are perfectly amenable to seeing sample chapters right off the bat. Some like pre-submission phone calls; some frown on multiple submissions. The best thing you can do for yourself is to follow the procedures in a professional and courteous manner.

When you and an agent are ready to come to terms, I recommend you use a written agreement in order to articulate your agent's responsibilities. Though writing is an intensely personal business, the elements of book publishing constitute business and all the relationships involved should be rooted in sound business practices.

Look for the following in writing:

1. A definition of the represented property. Are all genre or types included? What, if anything, is to be excluded?

2. An acknowledgment of the agent's commission. What about the rate for subsidiary rights and sales?

3. A clear statement of the accounting practices involved. Will the agent promptly forward to the writer all funds and statements? When? Will the agency provide accounting documentation separate from those of the publisher?

4. An unequivocal obligation to the author that the author will be informed about all offers relating to publication and licensing.

5. A clear statement of what expenses the agency will be responsible for, and which ones the author will pay. For example, what if five copies of the manuscript are needed to submit to various publishers?

6. An obligation for the agency to send to the writer copies of all correspondence related to the manuscript, and a similar requirement that the agent notify the author about all conversations concerning the book.

7. A provision of how the author-agent relationship can be terminated by either of the people involved.

Many other points may be perfectly acceptable. The main objective should be fairness to the author.

Finally, some thoughts about emerging technologies are appropriate. Publishing is going through some remarkable changes. Though retail book sales remain our taproot, computers and television possess a developmental impact that we can't ignore. Although category fiction may be the last to be affected by these changes, you should still become informed.

CD computer programs (CD-rom) make books accessible in numbers and detail previously unthinkable. (For example, did you know that 900 books can fit on one CD-rom disk?) We refer to these electronic rights as *new media* and believe the CD-I (interactive compact disk technology) may unite visual and print media for distribution to the mass-market. The entire publishing community is in the process of learning how to handle and profit from these rights.

You might also expect to see more books sold direct to buyers from television orders. What has happened to nonfiction books tied to infomercials may also be applied to direct sales of fiction. In-home shopping for all goods and services is a force to be considered.

Now you are ready. Supplied with creative property and business information, you can make good decisions about your career. It won't always be easy. A career as a published author involves a devotion that few people can really understand. You'll have to face rejection, deadlines, and all the encroachments life demands. Yet, if you're reading this, you probably suspect it'll all be worth it. When all is said and done, there's one piece of advice that may be more important than anything else in these pages: Finish your book. The starters never succeed at anything—only those who finish their manuscripts get them published.

Good luck.

Evan M. Fogelman, member of the Association of Author's Representatives and the American Bar Association Forum on Entertainment Law, owns the literary agency that bears his name.

2

Directory of
Agents

RAJEEV AGARWAL / LAWRENCE MATTIS
Circle of Confusion, Ltd.
131 Country Village Lane, Suite A
New Hyde Park, NY 11040
(212) 969-0653

Professional Affiliations: Writer's Guild of America.

Office Hours: 9:00–6:00

Fees: No reading fee.

Recent Sales/Clients
The Matrix, a screenplay sold to Warner for $1+ million
Assassins
Reptile Man
Deep Down

Submissions: Query first with SASE.

Seeking
Long Contemporary
Short Contemporary
Historical
Mystery
Romantic Suspense
Mainstream Romance
Ethnic
Fantasy
Paranormal
Time Travel

Comments: Circle of Confusion, Ltd. is primarily a film/TV agency specializing in screenplays and novels.

PAMELA G. AHEARN
The Ahearn Agency
2021 Pine Street
New Orleans, LA 70118
(504) 861-8395
FAX: (504) 866-6434

Professional Affiliations: Romance Writers of America.

Office Hours: 9:00–4:00

Fees: Charges reading fees to previously unpublished authors.

Terms: 15% on domestic rights, 20% on dramatic rights.

Recent Sales/Clients
Loving Tyler (plus 2nd untitled historical) by Susan Sawyer, Avon
2 untitled historicals by Rexanne Becnal, St. Martin's
Healing Hearts by Linda Shertzer, Berkley Homespun

Submissions: Query first with SASE.

Seeking

Historical	any time period, 100,000+ words
Mystery	75,000+ words
Romantic Suspense	100,000+ words
Mainstream Romance	100,000+ words
Ethnic	
Paranormal	
Time Travel	

Comments: No screenplays.

JAMES ALLEN

James Allen, Literary Agent
538 E. Harford Street/P.O. Box 278
Milford, PA 18337
(717) 296-6205
FAX: (717) 296-7266

Professional Affiliations: Writer's Guild of America, East.

Office Hours: 9:00–5:00

Fees: No reading fee.

Recent Sales/Clients
Veil of Fear by Judi Lind, Harlequin Intrigue
Promises by Jeanne Renick (a RITA-winning author), Harper
    Monogram

Submissions: Query by letter only.

Seeking

Long Contemporary	90,000–150,000 words
Historical	any time period, 100,000–125,000 words

Mystery	certainly, 75,000–110,000 words
Mainstream Romance	absolutely, word count is whatever's right
Fantasy	

Comments: I prefer working with people who already have their toe in the door, rather than total first timers. Initial contact should never be by phone; no multi-page first contacts by fax either. A historical has to be superlative to get my attention.

MARCIA AMSTERDAM
Marcia Amsterdam Agency
41 W. 82nd Street, Suite 9A
New York, NY 10024
(212) 873-4945

Professional Affiliations: Writer's Guild of America, Signatory to the Writer's Guild.

Office Hours: 9:30–5:30

Fees: No reading fee.

Recent Sales/Clients
Keepers of the Misty Time by Patricia Rowe, Warner

Submissions: Query first with SASE.

Seeking
Long Contemporary
Historical
Mystery
Romantic Suspense
Mainstream Romance
Time Travel
Screenplays

LYDIA R. ANNUNZIATA

Law Offices of Lydia R. Annunziata
Mailing Address:
P.O. Box 831813
Miami, FL 33283
Business Address:
Warner Place, Suite 200
111 S.W. Fifth Avenue
Miami, FL 33130–1381
(304) 324-9800
FAX: (Available to clients only)

(*Note:* Lydia R. Annunziata is a publishing lawyer, not an agent.)

Professional Affiliations: A graduate of Georgetown University Law Center in 1989, admitted to practice law in both New York and Florida. Entertainment Law Committee and Media and Communications Committee of the Florida Bar. Member of Romance Writers of America, Mystery Writers of America, Mystery Writers of America/Florida, and General Counsel.

Office Hours: 24-hour office and message service

Fees: No reading fee. Manuscript review service for historical accuracy, copyright, trademark, libel, and right of privacy clearance is $1.50 per page. These services are often needed for true crime, courtroom suspense, and historical writers.

Terms: Fees are fixed (usually under $750), or half of an agent's usual commission rate (5% to 7½%).

Recent Sales/Clients
Client list confidential, but firm represents authors from around the U.S.

Submissions: Query about *sold* manuscripts only. Representation is limited to negotiating sold works, without an agent.

Seeking
All types of romance novels. Screenplays and teleplays are also
welcome. Note that Lydia Annunziata does not sell manuscripts. She negotiates contracts for sold works from authors
without an agent.

Comments: Other legal services offered separately include litigation to reinforce contract rights or copyright, audits, recaptures,
and manuscript vetting. Experienced in matters of copyright,
trademark, and publishing litigation. Monthly legal column in
Romantic Times.

STEVEN AXELROD
The Axelrod Agency
54 Church Street
Lenox, MA 01240
(413) 637-2000
FAX: (413) 637-4725

Professional Affiliations: Association of Author's
Representatives.

Office Hours: 9:30–5:30 Monday–Friday

Fees: No reading fee.

Submissions: Query first with SASE.

Seeking
Long Contemporary
Historical
Mystery
Romantic Suspense
Mainstream Romance

JOSH BEHAR
Josh Behar Literary Agency
Empire State Building, 350 Fifth Avenue, Suite 3304
New York, NY 10118
(212) 826-4386

Professional Affiliations: Irene Goodman Literary Agency.

Office Hours: 9:00–5:00 Monday–Friday

Fees: No reading fee.

Submissions: Query first with SASE.

Seeking
Long Contemporary	110,000 words
Short Contemporary	50,000–75,000 words
Historical	any time period
Mystery	55,000–110,000 words
Romantic Suspense	
Mainstream Romance	110,000 words
Fantasy	
Time Travel	

MEREDITH BERNSTEIN
Meredith Bernstein Literary Agency
2112 Broadway, Suite 503A
New York, NY 10023
(212) 799-1007
FAX: (212) 799-1145

Professional Affiliations: Association of Author's Representatives, Sisters in Crime, Writer's Guild of America.

Office Hours: 9:00–5:30

Fees: Query first with SASE. Reading fees are charged for unpublished writers. ($50 for first three chapters and outline.)

Terms: 15% domestic sales, 20% foreign sales.

Recent Sales/Clients
Georgina Gentry, Shirl Henke, Janis Reams Hudson,
    Marilyn Campbell, Raine Cantrell

Submissions: Query first with SASE.

Seeking
Long Contemporary
Historical
Mystery
Ethnic
Mainstream Romance
Paranormal
Time Travel
(No Screenplays)

PAM BERNSTEIN
Pam Bernstein and Associates
790 Madison Avenue, Suite 310
New York, NY 10021
(212) 288-1700

Office Hours: 9:00–5:00

Fees: No reading fee.

Terms: 15% commission.

Submissions: Query first with SASE.

Seeking

Long Contemporary   word length is varied
Historical   time period is varied
Mainstream Romance   word length is varied

GREG BOYLAN
Otitis Media
1926 Dupont Avenue South
Minneapolis, MN 55403
(612) 377-4918
FAX: (612) 377-3046

Professional Affiliations: Writer's Guild of America.

Fees: No reading fees.

Submissions: Query with SASE, don't call. We prefer a chapter outline plus the first 30 pages of your manuscript, on which we base our decision.

Recent Sales/Clients
Confidential

Seeking
Historical
Romantic Suspense
Mainstream Romance
Fantasy
Time Travel
Erotic
Screenplays

RICHARD BOYLAN
Otitis Media
1926 Dupont Avenue South
Minneapolis, MN 55403
(612) 377-4918
FAX: (612) 377-3046

Professional Affiliations: Writer's Guild of America.

Fees: No reading fees.

Submissions: Query with SASE, don't call. We prefer a chapter outline plus the first 30 pages of your manuscript, on which we base our decision.

Recent Sales/Clients
Confidential

Seeking
Historical
Romantic Suspense
Mainstream Romance
Fantasy
Time Travel
Erotic
Screenplays

ANDREA BROWN
Andrea Brown Literary Agency, Inc.
P.O. Box 429
El Granada, CA 94018
(415) 728-1783

Professional Affiliations: Association of Author's Representatives, Women's National Book Association, National Association of Female Executives.

Office Hours: 9:00–5:00 Monday–Friday

Fees: No reading fees or other fees.

Terms: 15% commission.

Submissions: Query letters only with SASE.

Recent Sales/Clients
Harlequin and HarperCollins Paperbacks
Client list is confidential

Seeking
Historical   any time period, word length
                                               unspecified
Time Travel
Young Adult
(Not accepting Gothic or Contemporary at this time.)

PEMA BROWNE
Pema Browne Ltd.
Pine Road HCR, Box 104B
Neversink, NY 12765
(914) 985-2936
FAX: (914) 985-7635

Professional Affiliations: Signatory to the Writer's Guild.

Office Hours: 8:00–6:00 Monday–Saturday

Fees: No reading fees for romance, juvenile, or nonfiction manuscripts.

Recent Sales/Clients

Lost Treasure by Rebecca Robins, Avon
Lady Hope's Rules of Conduct by Cathleen Clare, Avon
Lord Grey's Marriage Mart by Cathleen Clare, Avon
Wild Sweet Ecstasy by Jo Goodman, Zebra
Sleeping Tigers by Sandra Dark, Silhouette
Message from Magan's Bay by Karen Rhodes, Harlequin
Rogue's Mistress by Jo Goodman, Zebra
Silent Cathedrals by Sandra Dark, Zebra
Garden of Love by Eileen Hehl, Zebra
Prisoner of my Heart by Paige Brantley, Zebra
4 book Contract to Zebra for Paige Brantley
Sales of nonfiction, young adult, and children's picture
    books

Submissions: Query first with SASE.

Seeking

Long Contemporary	100,000 words
Short Contemporary	word count according to publishers' guidelines
Historical	before 1890, 100,000+ words
Mystery	selective, 70,000–80,000 words
Romantic Suspense	see publishers' guidelines
Mainstream Romance	100,000 words
Ethnic	
Fantasy	
Paranormal	
Time Travel	
Screenplays	

Comments: New authors should write according to guidelines for the category imprints and should write to the various romance publishers for marketing rules of each imprint. We do not review manuscripts previously sent out to publishers.

PERRY BROWNE

Pema Browne Ltd.
Pine Road HCR, Box 104B
Neversink, NY 12765
(914) 985-2936
FAX: (914) 985-7635

Professional Affiliations: Signatory to the Writer's Guild.

Office Hours: 8:00–6:00 Monday–Saturday

Fees: No reading fees for romance, juvenile, or nonfiction manuscripts.

Recent Sales/Clients
Lost Treasure by Rebecca Robins, Avon
Lady Hope's Rules of Conduct by Cathleen Clare, Avon
Lord Grey's Marriage Mart by Cathleen Clare, Avon
Wild Sweet Ecstasy by Jo Goodman, Zebra
Sleeping Tigers by Sandra Dark, Silhouette
Message from Magan's Bay by Karen Rhodes, Harlequin
Rogue's Mistress by Jo Goodman, Zebra
Silent Cathedrals by Sandra Dark, Zebra
Garden of Love by Eileen Hehl, Zebra
Prisoner of my Heart by Paige Brantley, Zebra
4 book Contract to Zebra for Paige Brantley
Sales of nonfiction, young adult, and children's picture books

Submissions: Query first with SASE.

Seeking

Long Contemporary	100,000 words
Short Contemporary	word count according to publishers' guidelines
Historical	before 1890, 100,000+ words
Mystery	selective, 70,000–80,000 words

Romantic Suspense   see publishers' guidelines
Mainstream Romance   100,000 words
Ethnic
Fantasy
Paranormal
Time Travel
Screenplays

Comments: New authors should write according to guidelines for the category imprints and should write to the various romance publishers for marketing rules of each imprint. We do not review manuscripts previously sent out to publishers.

JULIE CASTIGLIA
Julie Castiglia Literary Agency
1155 Camino Del Mar, Suite 510
Del Mar, CA 92104
(619) 753-4361
FAX: (619) 753-5094

Professional Affiliations: Association of Author's Representatives, PEN (poets, playwrights, editors, essayists, and novelists), Society of Children's Book Writers.

Office Hours: 9:00–5:00 Monday–Friday

Fees: No reading fee.

Recent Sales/Clients
Spare Change by John Peak, St. Martin's Press
Quicksilver by Mike Dunn, Avon
Science of Desire by Dean Hamer and Peter Copeland, Simon & Schuster
Reaches of the Heart by Frances White and Anne Scott, Barricade Books

Submissions: Query first with SASE.

Seeking
Mystery
Romantic Suspense
Mainstream Romance
Ethnic

Comments: Fiction has to be special for us to take it on. It needs to have originality and strength, even in genre.

ELIZABETH CAVANAUGH
Meredith Bernstein Literary Agency
2112 Broadway, Suite 503A
New York, NY 10023
(212) 799-1007
FAX: (212) 799-1145

Professional Affiliations: Association of Author's Representatives, Sisters in Crime, Writer's Guild of America.

Office Hours: 9:00–5:30

Fees: Reading fees are charged for unpublished writers. ($50 for first three chapters and outline.)

Terms: 15% domestic sales, 20% foreign sales.

Recent Sales/Clients
Georgina Gentry, Shirl Henke, Janis Reams Hudson, Marilyn Campbell, Raine Cantrell

Submissions: Query first with SASE.

Seeking
Long Contemporary
Historical

Mystery
Ethnic
Mainstream Romance
Paranormal
Time Travel
(No Screenplays)

JACQULIN CHAMBERS
First Literary Artists International Representatives (F.L.A.I.R.)
P.O. Box 660
Coram, NY 11727
(516) 331-2438

Professional Affiliations: Tri-Star Pictures, Interscope
Communications.

Office Hours: Vary

Fees: No reading fees.

Recent Sales/Clients
Witness to Murder by Bill Johnston, Stewart Benjamin
     Productions

Submissions: Please query first with synopsis and SASE.

Seeking
Screenplays *only* of these types:
Historical   16th–18th century
Mystery
Romantic Suspense
Mainstream Romance
Fantasy
Paranormal

Comments: Only send queries for screenplays. Make sure you copyright or register your script with the Writer's Guild of America (east or west). Send synopsis first with SASE.

TED CHICHAK
Scovil, Chichak, Galen Literary Agency, Inc.
381 Park Avenue South, Suite 1020
New York, NY 10021
(212) 679-8696
FAX: (212) 679-6710

Professional Affiliations: Association of Author's Representatives.

Office Hours: 9:00–5:00 Monday–Friday

Fees: No reading fees.

Terms: 15% domestic, 20% foreign.

Recent Sales/Clients
Margaret Truman, Poul Anderson, Jack Anderson, Patricia
Gallagher

Submissions: Query first with SASE.

Seeking
Long Contemporary
Short Contemporary
Historical
Mystery
Romantic Suspense
Mainstream Romance
Ethnic
Fantasy
Time Travel
Paranormal
Screenplays

LAURA CIFELLI
Richard Curtis Associates
171 E. 74th Street
New York, NY 10021
(212) 772-7363
FAX: (212) 772-7393

Professional Affiliations: Association of Author's Representatives, Romance Writers of America, Science Fiction Writers of America, Western Writers of America, Mystery Writers of America.

Office Hours: 9:30–5:30 Monday–Friday

Fees: No reading fees.

Terms: Basic 15% commission, 20% commission foreign.

Submissions: Query first with SASE.

Seeking
Long Contemporary
Short Contemporary   (not much, but occasionally)
Historical   all time periods,
                                   100,000–150,000 words

Romantic Suspense
Mainstream Romance
Ethnic
Time Travel

Comments: We are hoping to find wonderful new authors as talented and unique as the authors we now represent. Our list is very full already.

ANDREA CIRILLO
Jane Rotrosen Agency
318 East 51st Street
New York, NY 10022
(212) 593-4330
FAX: (212) 935-6985

Professional Affiliations: Association of Author's
Representatives.

Office Hours: 9:30–5:30

Fees: No reading fee.

Terms: 15% commission on sales in U.S. and Canada.

Recent Sales/Clients
Julie Garwood, Iris Johansen, Kathryn Davis, Tami Hoag, Patricia
    Potter, Tom and Sharon Curtis, Kimberly Cates, Teresa
    Medeiros.

Submissions: Query first with SASE.

Seeking
Long Contemporary
Short Contemporary   (possibly)
Historical   all time periods
Mystery
Romantic Suspense
Mainstream Romance
Ethnic
Time Travel
(No Screenplays)

FRANCINE CISKE
Francine Ciske Literary Agency
P.O. Box 555
Neenah, WI 54957
(414) 722-5944

Professional Affiliations: Romance Writers of America, Wisconsin Romance Writers of America.

Office Hours: 9:00–5:00 Monday–Friday

Fees: No reading fee.

Submissions: Query with sample chapters and synopsis. No calls.

Seeking
Long Contemporary
Short Contemporary
Historical   all time periods
Mystery
Romantic Suspense
Ethnic
Paranormal   of the Silhouette Shadows type
Time Travel
Futuristic
Inspirational Historical Romance

Comments: Always include SASE. No "fiction novels." Target material toward a specific market.

ROB COHEN
Richard Curtis Associates
171 E. 74th Street
New York, NY 10021
(212) 772-7363
FAX: (212) 772-7393

Professional Affiliations: Association of Author's Representatives, Romance Writers of America, Science Fiction Writers of America, Western Writers of America, Mystery Writers of America.

Office Hours: 9:30–5:30 Monday–Friday

Fees: No reading fees.

Terms: Basic 15% commission, 20% commission on foreign rights.

Submissions: Query first with SASE.

Seeking

Long Contemporary	
Short Contemporary	(not much, but occasionally)
Historical	all time periods,
	100,000–150,000 words
Romantic Suspense	
Mainstream Romance	
Ethnic	
Time Travel	

Comments: We are hoping to find wonderful new authors as talented and unique as the authors we now represent. Our list is very full already.

RUTH COHEN

Ruth Cohen Inc., Literary Agent
Box 7626
Menlo Park, CA 94025
(415) 854-2054

Professional Affiliations: Association of Author's Representatives, Romance Writers of America, The Authors Guild, Mystery Writers of America.

Office Hours: 8:30–5:00

Fees: No reading fee.

Recent Sales/Clients
Confidential

Submissions: Query first with opening 10 pages of your manuscript. Enclose SASE.

Seeking

Long Contemporary	approximately 125,000 words
Historical	125,000 words
Mystery	approximately 70,000 words
Mainstream Romance	120,000 words
Ethnic	

FRAN COLLIN
Frances Collin, Literary Agent
P.O. Box 33
Wayne, PA 19087-0033
(610) 254-0555

Professional Affiliations: Association of Author's Representatives.

Fees: No reading fees.

Terms: 15% commission, 20% commission on foreign translations.

Submissions: Please query with SASE. Prefer recommendations and/or prefer previously published.

Seeking

Historical	any time period, 100,000–300,000 words (but should be tight writing)

Mystery   60,000–70,000 words
Ethnic
Fantasy

RICHARD CURTIS
Richard Curtis Associates
171 E. 74th Street
New York, NY 10021
(212) 772-7363
FAX: (212) 772-7393

Professional Affiliations: Association of Author's Representatives, Romance Writers of America, Science Fiction Writers of America, Western Writers of America, Mystery Writers of America.

Office Hours: 9:30–5:30 Monday–Friday

Fees: No reading fees.

Terms: Basic 15% commission, 20% commission on foreign rights.

Submissions: Query first with SASE.

Seeking
Long Contemporary
Short Contemporary   (not much, but occasionally)
Historical   all time periods,
                                  100,000–150,000 words

Romantic Suspense
Mainstream Romance
Ethnic
Time Travel

Comments: We are hoping to find wonderful new authors as talented and unique as the authors we now represent. Our list is very full already.

ELAINE DAVIE
Elaine Davie Literary Agency
Village Gate Square
274 North Goodman Street
Rochester, NY 14607
(716) 442-0830

Office Hours: 9:00–5:00 Monday–Friday

Fees: No reading or other fees. Authors must provide copies of manuscript for purposes of submission.

Terms: No contracts. 15% commission when book sells, 20% commission on foreign and film rights.

Recent Sales/Clients
Twilight Memories by Maggie Shayne, Sihouette Shadows
Twilight Illusions by Maggie Shayne, Sihouette Shadows
Kiss of the Shadow Man by Maggie Shayne, Sihouette Shadows
Miranda's Viking by Maggie Shayne, Sihouette Intimate
      Moments
Forgotten Vows by Maggie Shayne, Sihouette Intimate Moments
Alena by Merline Lovelace, Harlequin Historical
Siren's Call by Merline Lovelace, Harlequin Historical
Sweet Song of Love by Merline Lovelace, Harlequin Historical
Dreams and Schemes by Merline Lovelace, Silhouette Desire
Somewhere in Time by Merline Lovelace, Silhouette Intimate
      Moments
Come the Night by Christina Skye
East of Forever by Christina Skye
Hour of the Rose by Christina Skye

My Special Angel by Marcia Evanick, Loveswept
Playing for Keeps by Marcia Evanick, Loveswept
Out of a Dream by Marcia Evanick, Loveswept
Passion's Bargain by Jane Kidder, Zebra
Passion's Gift by Jane Kidder, Zebra
Hunter's Kiss by Katharine Charles, Pinnacle

Submissions: Prefers query letter with synopsis, first three chapters, and SASE. Speedy replies are given to queries, partials are responded to within a month. No telephone or fax queries. (Does *not* represent short stories, poetry, novellas, or children's books.)

Seeking
Long Contemporary
Short Contemporary
Historical
All genre romances   especially category
Paranormal
Time Travel
Women's fiction
Romantic Suspense
Ethnic
Mainstream Romance
Also handles well-written nonfiction.
(Word lengths not specified)

Comments: Elaine is a monthly columnist for *Romantic Times*.

ANITA DIAMANT
The Writers' Workshop, Inc.—Anita Diamant
310 Madison Ave #1508
New York, NY 10017
(212) 687-1122
FAX: (212) 972-1756

Professional Affiliations: Association of Author's Representatives, Overseas Press Club of America.

Office Hours: 9:30–5:30

Fees: No reading fees.

Terms: 15% commission.

Recent Sales/Clients
Ruby by V.C. Andrews, Pocket Books
Also titles by Linda Howard, Ann Major, and Lisa Jackson

Submissions: Query first with SASE.

Seeking
Long Contemporary
Short Contemporary
Historical
Mystery
Romantic Suspense
Mainstream Romance
Ethnic
Time Travel

Comments: As to word count, it depends on the manuscript.

B. J. DOYEN
Doyen Literary Services, Inc.
19005 660th Street
Newell, IA 50568
(712) 272-3300

Professional Affiliations: Romance Writers of America, and many others.

Fees: No reading fees.

Recent Sales/Clients
Confidential

Submissions: Query letter first with SASE.

Seeking
Historical   any time period
Mystery
Romantic Suspense
Mainstream Romance
Screenplays (only if we're also handling the book rights)

Comments: We represent about 50 clients and are interested in fiction and nonfiction for adults and teens.

ETHAN ELLENBERG
The Ethan Ellenberg Literary Agency
548 Broadway, #5-E
New York, NY 10012
(212) 431-4554
FAX: (212) 941-4652

Professional Affiliations: Romance Writers of America, Mystery Writers of America, Novelist's Inc., Society of Children's Book Writers and Illustrators.

Office Hours: 9:00–5:00 Monday–Friday

Fees: Never a reading fee.

Recent Sales/Clients
Frost Flower by Sonya Birmingham, Leisure
Danger's Kiss by Shary Michels, Leisure
Milord Wolf's Lady by Diane Stuckart, Zebra
One untitled novel by Diane Stuckart, Zebra

Submissions: Query first with first three chapters and SASE.

Seeking
Long Contemporary
Short Contemporary
Historical
Mystery
Romantic Suspense
Mainstream Romance
Ethnic
Fantasy
Paranormal
Time Travel

JANICE FISHBEIN
Freida Fishbein Ltd.
2556 Hubbard Street
Brooklyn, NY 11235
(212) 247-4398

Office Hours: 10:00–6:00

Fees: $80 for the first 50,000 words, then $1 per 1,000 words thereafter.

Submissions: Query only with SASE.

Seeking
Short Contemporary   50,000–70,000 words
Romantic Suspense
Mainstream Romance
Screenplays

JOYCE A. FLAHERTY
Joyce A. Flaherty, Literary Agent
816 Lynda Court
St. Louis, MO 63122
(314) 966-3057

Professional Affiliations: Association of Author's Representatives, Romance Writers of America, Mystery Writers of America, Western Writers of America, The Authors Guild.

Office Hours: 9:00–5:00 Monday–Friday

Fees: No reading fee.

Terms: 15% commission on domestic sales.

Recent Sales/Clients
Elizabeth August, Patt Bucheister, Annette Chartier, Donna Clayton, Barbara Cockrell Charlene Cross, Teresa Des Jardien, Debra Dixon, Kay Elstner, Colleen Faulkner, Amy Fetzer, Judith French, Martha Gross, Phyllis Herman, Hannah Howell, Jan Hudson, Colleen L. Johnston, Marti Jones, Mandalyn Kaye, Susan L. King, Susan Kirby, Marcia Martin, Candace McCarthy, Elizabeth Ann Michaels, Marion Oaks, Martha Schroeder, Judith Steel, Lois Stewart, Elizabeth Stuart, Elizabeth Turner, Susan Weldon, Clara Wimberly (and others)

Submissions: Either query with SASE or call.

Seeking
Long Contemporary
Short Contemporary
Historical
Mainstream Romance

Comments: Please query with SASE. We don't read unsolicited manuscripts. We are mainly taking on published authors or this year's Romance Writers of America Golden Heart finalists.

EVAN M. FOGELMAN
The Fogelman Literary Agency
7515 Greenville Avenue, Suite 712
Dallas, TX 75231
(214) 361-9956
FAX: (214) 361-9553

Professional Affiliations: Association of Author's Representatives, Romance Writers of America, American Bar Association Forum on Publishing.

Office Hours: 8:30–5:30 Monday–Friday

Fees: No reading fees.

Recent Sales/Clients
Julie Beard, Elizabeth Leigh, Lynn Bullock, Lauryn Chandler, LeAnn Harris, S. K. Epperson, Susan Macias, Judith Hill, Eve Paludan, Joni Johnston, Sally Hawkes, Victoria Chancellor

Submissions: Call. Only accepting published novelists.

Seeking
Long Contemporary	to 90,000 words
Short Contemporary	to 70,000 words
Historical	before 1800, to 110,000 words
Mystery	to 90,000 words
Romantic Suspense	to 90,000 words
Nonfiction	
Screenplays	

JAY GARON
Jay Garon-Brooke Associates
101 W. 55th Street, Suite 5K
New York, NY 10019
(212) 581-8300
FAX: (212) 581-8397

Professional Affiliations: Association of Author's Representatives.

Fees: None.

Terms: 15% domestic, 30% foreign.

Recent Sales/Clients
The Chamber by John Grisham, Doubleday
Blue Truth by Cherokee Paul Macdonald
Taboo by Elizabeth Gage, Pocket
Carpool by Mary Cahill, Random House
Arclight by Eric L. Harry, Simon and Schuster

Submissions: Query by mail only. Please do not send unsolicited manuscripts.

Seeking
Mystery	100,000–120,000 words
Romantic Thrillers	all types, 100,000–120,000 words

Comments: Mainstream only. Thorough characterization, thoroughly textured. Hardcovers and/or paperback leads. We will reject any proposals or sample chapters unless we request from a query letter. Such a query should describe the work and also include a bio and SASE.

SUSAN GINSBURG
Writer's House, Inc.
21 W. 26th Street
New York, NY 10010
(212) 685-2400

Office Hours: 9:00–5:00 Monday–Friday

Fees: No reading fees.

Recent Sales/Clients
Nora Roberts and Barbara Delinsky, clients of Agency
Jane Feather, Avon, Susan Ginsburg's client

Submissions: Query first with SASE. 6–8 weeks for response.

Seeking
Long Contemporary
Short Contemporary
Historical   Regency period preferred

AMY S. GOLDBERGER
Publishing Services
525 E. 86th Street
New York, NY 10028
(212) 535-6248
FAX (212) 988-1073

Office Hours: 9:00–5:00 Monday–Friday

Fees: No reading fees.

Recent Sales/Clients
Represents Barbara Anne Pauley

Submissions: Query first with SASE.

Seeking
Historical

IRENE GOODMAN
Irene Goodman Literary Agency
521 Fifth Avenue, Suite 1700
New York, NY 10175
(212) 682-1978
FAX: (212) 573-6355

Professional Affiliations: Association of Author's
Representatives.

Office Hours: 9:30–5:30 Monday–Friday

Fees: None.

Terms: 15%.

Recent Sales/Clients:
Garters by Pamela Morsi, Berkley
An X-Mas Short Story by Linda Lael Miller, Avon
The Man You'll Marry by Debbie Macomber, Harlequin

Submissions: Query first with SASE.

Seeking

Long Contemporary	75,000 words
Short Contemporary	55,000–65,000 words
Historical	Viking to 1900, 100,000 words
Mystery	65,000 words
Mainstream Romance	125,000 words

HANNIBAL HARRIS
Otitis Media
1926 Dupont Avenue South
Minneapolis, MN 55403
(612) 377-4918
FAX: (612) 377-3046

Professional Affiliations: Writer's Guild of America.

Fees: No reading fees.

Submissions: Query with SASE, don't call. We prefer a chapter outline plus the first 30 pages of your manuscript, on which we base our decision.

Recent Sales/Clients
Confidential

Seeking
Historical
Romantic Suspense
Mainstream Romance
Fantasy
Time Travel
Erotic
Screenplays

LINDA HAYES
Columbia Literary Associates, Inc.
7902 Nottingham Way
Ellicott City, MD 21043
(410) 465-1595

Comments: Due to a full client list, this agency is not currently accepting new clients.

YVONNE HUBBS
Yvonne Trudeau Hubbs Agency
32371 Alipaz #101
San Juan Capistrano, CA 92675
(714) 496-1970
FAX: (714) 240–1213 (call before faxing)

Professional Affiliations: Romance Writers of America.

Office Hours: 9:00–5:00 Monday–Friday

Fees: Charges an administration fee and $25 office expense fee. Editing is extra.

Recent Sales/Clients
Privileged information. I have many published writers as clients.

Submissions: Prefer a query letter first with SASE.

Seeking
Long Contemporary
Short Contemporary
Historical
Mystery
Romantic Suspense
Mainstream Romance
Ethnic
Fantasy
Paranormal
Time Travel
Screenplays (only if connected to published book)

Comments: Word length depends on category series requirements.

SHARON JARVIS
Sharon Jarvis & Co.
(A division of Toad Hall, Inc.)
RR 2, Box 16-B
Laceyville, PA 18623
(717) 869-2942
FAX: (717) 869-1031

Professional Affiliations: Association of Author's
Representatives.

Office Hours: 9:30–6:00 Monday–Friday

Fees: No reading fees.

Recent Sales/Clients
Knight's Horizon by Suzanne Barclay, Harlequin
Sea Treasure by Joanna Hailey, Zebra
Sea Witch by Sara Blayne, Zebra

Submissions: Query first with SASE. We do not look at
unsolicited manuscripts.

Seeking

Long Contemporary	up to 120,000 words
Short Contemporary	up to 90,000 words
Historical	any time period
Mystery	not over 100,000
Romantic Suspense	not over 100,000
Mainstream Romance	up to 120,000 words
Fantasy	
Paranormal	
Time Travel	
Other	

KATHERINE JENSEN
Columbia Literary Associates, Inc.
7902 Nottingham Way
Ellicott City, MD 21043
(410) 465-1595

Comments: Due to a full client list, this agency is not currently accepting new clients.

WILLIAM KERWIN
William Kerwin Agency
1605 N. Cahuenga, Suite 202
Hollywood, CA 90028
(213) 469-5155

Professional Affiliations: Writer's Guild of America, Screen Actor's Guild, Actor's Equity.

Office Hours: 11:00–7:00 Monday–Friday

Fees: No reading fees.

Recent Sales/Clients
Confidential

Submissions: Call first.

Seeking
Original screenplays with contemporary settings only for:
Mystery
Romantic Suspense
Mainstream Romance

Comments: Only represent screenplays. No books.

KATHARINE KIDDE/CHIEF ASSOCIATE; WENDY WYLEGALA, ASSOCIATE

Kidde, Hoyt & Picard Literary Agency
335 E. 51st Street
New York, NY 10022
(212) 755-9461

Professional Affiliations: Association of Author's Representatives.

Office Hours: 10:00–6:00 Monday–Friday

Fees: No reading fees.

Recent Sales/Clients

2 novels by Sally McCluskey to Bantam
A Trick of Light by Patricia Robinson, St. Martin's Press
Pirate's Kiss by Diana Haviland, Pinnacle
Many titles to Fawcett by Diana Haviland
7 titles by Helene Sinclair/Lehr to St. Martin's Press, Warner, Leisure

Submissions: Query in writing with SASE.

Seeking

Short Contemporary	word count varies
Historical	from 1088–1900, 100,000 words
Mystery	under 100,000
Romantic Suspense	word count varies, not long
Mainstream Romance	word count varies, not long
Ethnic	
Time Travel	

DANIEL P. KING

Daniel P. King, Literary Agent
5125 N. Cumberland Boulevard
Whitefish Bay, WI 53217
(414) 964-2903
FAX: (414) 964-6860
TELEX: 724389

Office Hours: 9:00–5:00

Fees: No fee to read query and sample chapters. Consultation fee may be required if (1) author has no credits and (2) editorial work must be done.

Terms: 10% on U.S. sales, 20% on foreign sales.

Recent Sales/Clients
Confidential

Submissions: Query first with SASE.

Seeking

Long Contemporary	50,000–75,000 words
Historical	50,000–75,000 words, 1700–?
Mystery	50,000–75,000 words
Fantasy	50,000–75,000 words
Mainstream Romance	50,000–75,000 words

LINDA DIEHL KRUGER

The Fogelman Literary Agency
7515 Greenville Avenue, Suite 712
Dallas, TX 75231
(214) 361-9956
FAX: (214) 361-9553

Professional Affiliations: Association of Author's Representatives, Romance Writers of America.

Office Hours: 8:30–5:30 Monday–Friday

Fees: None.

Recent Sales/Clients
Justin's Bride by Susan Mallery, Harlequin Historical (6/95)
Taking Chances by Victoria Chancellor, Audio Entertainment
Fire in the Dark (working title) by Susan Macias, Harper
    (Spring '95)

Submissions: Please call before querying.

Seeking

Long Contemporary	up to 85,000
Short Contemporary	
Historicals	time period open, up to 110,000 words
Mystery	
Romantic Suspense	
Ethnic	
Paranormal	
Time Travel	

Comments: Also interested in Regencies and works of nonfiction that target a female audience.

JAMES L'ANGELLE
Cyberstorm!
P.O. Box 6330
Reno, NV 89513
(916) 546-5974
FAX: (916) 546-5112

Professional Affiliations: Writer's Guild of America.

Office Hours: (variable) 9:00–5:00 Monday–Friday

Fees: No reading fee.

Submissions: No phone calls please! Send synopsis of one to two pages with cover letter and SASE.

Seeking

Long Contemporary	100,000 words
Short Contemporary	50,000 words
Historicals	any time period, 150,000 words
Mystery	50,000 words
Romantic Suspense	50,000 words
Mainstream Romance	50,000 words
Ethnic	
Fantasy	
Paranormal	
Time Travel	
Any Screenplays	

Comments: Focus is mainly on screenplays for film production, but queries for novels are accepted.

FRAN LEBOWITZ
Writers House
21 W. 26th Street
New York, NY 10010
(212) 685-4701
FAX: (212) 685-4702

Professional Affiliations: Co-chair of Women in Publishing, Association of Author's Representatives.

Office Hours: 10:00–6:00

Fees: No reading fees.

Recent Sales/Clients
Confidential

Submissions: Query first with SASE.

Seeking

Historical	any time period, though fond of Regency period

Romantic Suspense
Ethnic
Fantasy

Comments: Funny and lusty usually grab me. Also, a great hook.

LETTIE LEE
Ann Elmo Agency, Inc.
60 E. 42nd Street
New York, NY 10165
(212) 661-2880
FAX: (212) 661-2883

Office Hours: 9:30–5:00 Monday–Friday

Fees: No reading fee.

Terms: 15% commission.

Recent Sales/Clients
Linda Turner to Silhouette
Vickie York to Harlequin Intrigue
Carol Grace to Silhouette
Cindy Hidam (aka Elyn Day) to Silhouette
Charlotte Douglas to Zebra
Kathy L. Emerson to Harper Monogram

Submissions: Query first with SASE.

Seeking

Long Contemporary	approximately 100,000 words
Short Contemporary	50,000–75,000 words
Historical	90,000–100,000 words
Mystery	55,000+ words
Fantasy	
Paranormal	
Time Travel	
Screenplays	(limited representation)

DONALD MAASS

Donald Maass Literary Agency
157 W. 57th Street, Suite 1003
New York, NY 10019
(212) 757-7755
FAX: (212) 757-7764

Professional Affiliations: Association of Author's Representatives, Mystery Writers of America, Science Fiction Writers of America.

Office Hours: 9:30–5:30 Monday–Friday

Fees: No reading fees.

Recent Sales/Clients
Sins of the Wolf by Anne Perry, Fawcett Columbine
Traitor's Gate by Anne Perry, Fawcett Columbine
Pasquale's Angel by Paul McAuley, Morrow
Dragons of War by Christopher Rowlay, NAL/ROC
The Harp of Winds by Maggie Furey, Bantam Spectra
A Taste For Murder by Mary Stanton, Berkley Prime Crime

Prince Among Men by Robert Charrette, Warner Aspect
Outpost: The Official Strategy Guide by Bruce Balfour, Prima
    Publishing
Crossing the Distance by Amy Thomson, Berkley Ace
Hunters of the Plains by Ardath Mayhar, Berkley
The Gaia War by Mark Leon, Avon/AvoNova
Chronicles of Scar by Ron Sarti, Avon/AvoNova
The Nicholas Seafort Saga (4 volumes) by David Feintuch,
    Warner Aspect

Submissions: Query first with SASE.

Seeking

Mystery	75,000+ words
Romantic Suspense	100,000+ words
Mainstream Romance	100,000+ words

Comments: No category romance, please. We would, however,
like to hear from established romance authors who are ready to
move out of category and into the mainstream. The Donald
Maass Agency was established in 1980 and specializes in commercial fiction. Areas of special interest are science fiction, fantasy, mystery, suspense, frontier, literary, and mainstream novels.
The agency sells 50+ titles annually.

RICIA MAINHARDT

Ricia Mainhardt Literary Agency
612 Argyle Road, Suite #L5
Brooklyn, NY 11230
(718) 434-1893
FAX: (718) 434-2157

Professional Affiliations: Association of Author's Representatives, Romance Writers of America, Mystery Writers of America, Science Fiction/Fantasy Writers Association, Horror Writers of America, Children's SC Ball.

Office Hours: 9:00–6:00 Monday–Friday

Fees: No reading fee.

Terms: 15% commission.

Submissions: Query first with SASE.

Seeking
Long Contemporary
Historical
Mystery
Romantic Suspense
Ethnic
Fantasy
Mainstream Romance
Paranormal
Time Travel

DENISE MARCIL
Denise Marcil Literary Agency
685 West End Ave, #9C
New York, NY 10025
(212) 932-3110

Professional Affiliations: Association of Author's Representatives.

Office Hours: 9:30–6:00

Fees: $45.00 when agency requests manuscript.

Recent Sales/Clients
We sell books to all major hardcover and paperback publishers.

Submissions: Query with a one page letter and SASE, only.

Seeking
Long Contemporary
Short Contemporary
Mainstream Romance
Ethnic
Time Travel

EVAN MARSHALL
The Evan Marshall Agency
22 South Park Street, Suite 216
Montclair, NJ 07042-2744
(201) 744-1661
FAX: (201) 744-6312

Professional Affiliations: Association of Author's Representatives, Romance Writers of America.

Office Hours: 9:00–5:00 Monday–Friday

Fees: Small handling fee of $28 for unpublished writers who are not referred by an editor or by a client of this agency.

Terms: 15% commission on domestic, 20% on foreign.

Submissions: Query first with SASE.

Recent Sales/Clients
Confidential

Seeking
Long Contemporary
Short Contemporary

Historical   all time periods
Ethnic
Mystery
Fantasy
Mainstream Romance

ALLISON MULLEN
Howard Morhaim Literary Agency
175 Fifth Avenue, Suite 709
New York, NY 10010
(212) 529-4433
FAX: (212) 995-1112

Professional Affiliations: Association of Author's Representatives, Romance Writers of America.

Office Hours: 9:30–5:30 Monday–Friday

Fees: No reading fees.

Submissions: Query first with synopsis and first three chapters.

Seeking
Long Contemporary
Historical   all time periods
Mystery
Romantic Suspense
Mainstream Romance
Ethnic
Time Travel

Comments: We are always looking for new, talented romance writers in all areas of the genre (except short contemporaries).

KIM VAN NGUYEN, SENIOR EDITOR
The Robert Madsen Literary Agency
1331 E. 34th Street, Suite 1
Oakland, CA 94602
(510) 223-2090

Office Hours: 10:00–6:00 Monday–Friday

Fees: No reading fees.

Submissions: Query first. Keep queries brief and include SASE.

Seeking
Short Contemporary
Historical   any time periods
Mystery
Romantic Suspense
Mainstream Romance
Ethnic
Fantasy
Paranormal
Time Travel
Open to Others
Screenplays

Comments: Word counts are open.

EDWARD NOVAK
Edward A. Novak III Literary Representation
711 North 2nd Street, Suite 1
Harrisburg, PA 17102
(717) 232-8081
FAX: (717) 232-7020

Office Hours: 9:00–5:00

Fees: No reading fees.

Terms: 15% on domestic, 19% on foreign.

Recent Sales/Clients
Sweet Spanish Bride by Donna Whitfield
The Savage by Nicole Jordan

Submissions: Query first with SASE.

Seeking

Long Contemporary	120,000–150,000 words
Short Contemporary	80,000 words
Historical	no preferred time period, 100,000–120,000 words
Mainstream Romance	100,000 words

JEAN PATRICK
Diamond Literary Agency, Inc.
3063 S. Kearney Street
Denver, CO 80222
(303) 759-0291

Professional Affiliations: Novelists, Inc., Sisters in Crime, Rocky Mountain Fiction Writers.

Fees: No reading fees, but charges a $15 submission fee.

Recent Sales/Clients
Provided on request if agency offers to represent.

Submissions: Send SASE for agency and submission info *only*. No calls from writers, except contracted clients, unless the same type of project sold in the past five years.

Seeking
All that fit the current market
Occasionally represent screenplays

Comments: Not encouraging submissions from not-yet-published authors at this time.

ELIZABETH POMADA
Michael Larsen/Elizabeth Pomada Literary Agents
1029 Jones Street
San Francisco, CA 94109
(415) 673-0939

Professional Affiliations: Association of Author's Representatives, American Society of Journalists and Authors, Women's National Book Association, The Authors Guild, PEN (poets, playwrights, editors, essaysists, and novelists), National Writers' Club.

Office Hours: 9:00–5:00 Monday–Friday

Fees: No reading fees.

Recent Sales/Clients
The Last Innocent Hour by Margot Abbott, St. Martin's
Montezuma's Pearl by David Jones, Avon
The Deverry Series by Katharine Kerr, Bantam

Submissions: For fiction, send the first 30 pages with synopsis, SASE and phone number. For nonfiction, call first.

Seeking
Long Contemporary
Short Contemporary
Historical
Mystery

Romantic Suspense
Mainstream Romance
Fantasy
Time Travel
Blockbuster
Literary

Comments: To me, a book's length is like a skirt's—it should be long enough to cover the subject and short enough to keep your interest. No good book is too long; no dull book is too short. Romance is a broad topic—from *War and Peace* to *Gone with the Wind* to a Harlequin. Love conquers all.

HARRY PRESTON
Stanton & Associates International Literary Agency
4413 Clemson Drive
Garland, TX 75042
(214) 276-5427
FAX: (214) 348-6900

Professional Affiliations: Signatory to the Writer's Guild of America (West).

Office Hours: 9:00–6:00 Monday–Friday

Fees: No reading fees.

Recent Sales/Clients
TV—Movies of the Week
Feature Films

Submissions: Query first or call.

Seeking
Screenplays

Comments: Original screenplays are our main focus. We handle film and TV, but do take a novel occasionally. We will welcome romance writers who want to get into film and TV.

JEAN PRICE AND DEE PACE, SUBMISSIONS DIRECTORS

The Kirkland Literary Agency
Mailing Address:
P.O. Box 50608
Amarillo, TX 79159-0608
Physical Address:
1616 S. Kentucky, Suite A-110
Amarillo, TX 79102
(806) 356-0216
FAX (806) 356-0452

Professional Affiliations: Romance Writers of America, Romance Writers of the Texas Panhandle, Panhandle Professional Writers, Oklahoma Writer's Federation, Inc.

Office Hours: 9:00–5:00 Monday–Friday; 24-hour answering machine

Fees: A $25 reading fee is charged, but refunded if taken on as client.

Recent Sales/Clients
20 clients currently. 4 published, 16 soon-to-be, 1 sale pending with Barbour & Company's *Heartsong's Presents* line.

Submissions: Query by letter or call.

Seeking
Long Contemporary	75,000–85,000 words
Short Contemporary	55,000–70,000 words

Historical	prefer 1600–1900 A.D., 90,000–130,000 words
Mystery	60,000–75,000 words
Romantic Suspense	85,000–100,000 words
Mainstream Romance	100,000–130,000 words
Ethnic	
Fantasy	
Paranormal	
Time Travel	
Other	(representing all genres of fiction, specializing in romance and mainstream)

Comments: Jean Price is a marketing analyst who opened the agency on September 1, 1993. Her submissions director, Dee Pace, is a published author of historical romances (aka DeWanna Pace), and has run an editing service for eight years, judged more than three hundred international and national novel contests of every genre, is a former researcher for the Amarillo Professional Library, and teaches creative writing at Amarillo College.

PESHA RUBINSTEIN

Pesha Rubinstein, Literary Agent
37 Overlook Terrace #1D
New York, NY 10033
(212) 781-7845

Professional Affiliations: Association of Author's Representatives, Romance Writers of America, Society of Children's Book Writers and Illustrators.

Office Hours: 9:00–6:00 Monday–Thursday, Friday 9:00–12:00

Fees: No reading fee. Please include an SASE with enough postage to cover the return of the entire package, should that prove necessary.

Terms: 15% commission domestic, 20% foreign.

Recent Sales/Clients
3 historical romances by Tanya Crosby to Avon
4 contemporary romances by Kate Hoffman to Harlequin
The Black Prince by Karen Monk to Bantam
3 historical romances by Debra Dier to Leisure
Other clients include Jennifer Horsman, Susan Sackett, Nikki
  Rivers and various children's book authors and illustrators

Submissions: Query first with SASE.

Seeking
Long Contemporary	100,000+ words
Short Contemporary	55,000+ words
Historical	no pre-history or ancient civilizations 100,000+ words
Mystery	65,000+ words
Romantic Suspense	65,000+ words
Mainstream Romance	75,000+ words
Ethnic	
Paranormal	

Comments: Women represent the largest percentage of book buyers in America, and I want to represent books, fiction, and nonfiction for women. The writing must be high caliber, as our readers get more sophisticated and demanding, and the stories must be compelling. Modern life being the rushed affair that it is, the story must be un-put-downable, completely absorbing and convincing. Contemporary women's fiction should deal with life's major relationships (mother/daughter, father/daughter, sister/sister, woman/lover, etc.), and I think that as time goes on, the major issues affecting our times (AIDS in particular) will have to have some play in the story, without sounding like a political manifesto.

Smarter heroines in historical romances are an element that I predict, as readers clamor for more responsible stories for older teen readers. Authors will not be able to so readily create the heroine who sleeps with the hero, gets pregnant, and somehow manages to marry the reluctant father, with a happy ending for all!

The challenge to get published is greater than ever before, but the end result will be ever more talented new writers getting the coveted contract.

MEG RULEY
Jane Rotrosen Agency
318 E. 51st Street
New York, NY 10022
(212) 593-4330
FAX: (212) 935-6985

Professional Affiliations: Association of Author's Representatives.

Office Hours: 9:30–5:30

Fees: No reading fee.

Terms: 15% commission on sales in U.S. and Canada.

Recent Sales/Clients
Confidential

Submissions: Query first with SASE.

Seeking
Long Contemporary
Short Contemporary
Historical   all time periods

Mystery
Mainstream Romance

Comments: Word lengths are specific to the line you are writing for. Check the publisher's guidelines section of this directory.

KELLY ST. CLAIR
St. Clair Literary Agency
4501 Colonial Avenue
Norfolk, VA 23508
(804) 623-0288
FAX: (same phone number, but call first)

Professional Affiliations: Romance Writers of America.

Office Hours: Usually 10:00–6:00, but may vary

Fees: No reading fee.

Recent Sales/Clients
This is a new agency—we have many unpublished clients with lots of talent.

Submissions: Submissions may be sent to me directly.

Seeking
Long Contemporary
Short Contemporary
Historical
Mystery
Romantic Suspense
Mainstream Romance
Ethnic
Fantasy

Paranormal
Time Travel

Comments: I am interested in good manuscripts of all categories. If the story is good, word length doesn't matter.

MIKE SEYMOUR AND MARY SUE SEYMOUR
The Seymour Agency
P.O. Box 376
Heuvelton, NY 13654
(315) 344-7223
FAX: (315) 344-7223

Professional Affiliations: Romance Writers of America, National Outdoor Writers of America, New York State Outdoor Writers.

Office Hours: 8:00–5:00

Fees: No reading fee.

Recent Sales/Clients
Warrior Bride by Tamara Leigh, Bantam (lead title)
Virgin Bride by Tamara Leigh, Bantam

Submissions: Query with synopsis and first three chapters.

Seeking

Long Contemporary	100,000 words
Short Contemporary	70,000 words
Historical	any time period, 100,000 words
Mystery	100,000 words
Romantic Suspense	100,000 words
Mainstream Romance	100,000 words
Soft Horror	100,000 words

Ethnic
Fantasy
Paranormal

Comments: We provide an editing service for clients. We are teachers/published authors.

CHERRY WEINER
Cherry Weiner Literary Agency
28 Kipling Way
Manalapan, NJ 07726
(908) 446-2096
FAX: (908) 446-2096 (then press 3*)

Professional Affiliations: New Jersey Romance Writers of America, Western Writers of America.

Office Hours: 9:00–5:00 Monday–Friday

Fees: No reading fee.

Recent Sales/Clients
Confidential

Submissions: Full list—no queries at this time.

Seeking

Long Contemporary	100,000 words
Short Contemporary	70,000 words
Historical	any time period, 100,000 words
Mystery	100,000 words
Romantic Suspense	100,000 words
Mainstream Romance	100,000 words
Fantasy	
Paranormal	
Time Travel	

NANCY YOST
Lowenstein Associates
121 W. 27th Street, Suite 601
New York, NY 10001
(212) 206-1630
FAX:(212) 727-0280

Professional Affiliations: Association of Author's Representatives, Mystery Writers of America, Sisters in Crime.

Office Hours: 9:00–5:00

Fees: No reading fee or other fees.

Terms: 15% agency commission.

Recent Sales/Clients
Racing the Storm by Danelle Harmon, Avon
Hale's Point by Pat Ryan, Harlequin Temptation (Golden Heart finalist/Emily award)
Four Regencies to Fawcett by Michelle Martin (Reader's Choice nominee)
Too Many Cooks Spoil the Broth by Tamar Myers, Doubleday (Amish Sleuth)
Parsley, Sage, Rosemary and Crime by Tamar Myers, Doubleday (Amish Sleuth)
Several by Steve Womack (Edgar PB Mystery of the Year Award)
3 books by Victoria Thompson, (Zebra lead title)
Beauty and the Beastmaster by Carol Rusley, Silhouette Desire (Golden Heart Award)
Books by Emily Carmichael, Warner lead titles
3 female sleuth mysteries by Jan Burke, S & S
2 historicals by Emily Bradshaw, Dell
2 historicals by Rebecca Paisley
Shattered Echoes by Barbara Shapiro, Avon, (lead title)

Submissions: Query first with SASE.

Seeking

Historicals	ancient/pre-history and 1100–1900 A.D., 90,000–150,000 words
Mystery	usually with female sleuths, (except hard-boiled), 50,000–80,000 words
Mainstream Romance	80,000–120,000 words

Also interested in medical thrillers, true crime and Jean Auel-like historicals. We are especially interested in psychological suspense. No fantasy please!

Comments: I love a sense of humor, and am also looking for very sexy romances and psychological suspense. Please be sure to send a very detailed query letter and include your phone number.

(Note: Nancy Yost's authors who won Golden Hearts, Emily awards, and Reader's Choice awards did so *after* she signed them on as clients. Nancy loves to discover talented unpubs and help them fulfill their goals.)

SUE P. YUEN
Susan Herner Rights Agency
P.O. Box 303
Scarsdale, NY 10583
(914) 725-8967
FAX: (914) 725-8969

Office Hours: 9:30–6:00

Fees: No reading fee.

Terms: 15% domestic sales, 20% foreign sales.

Recent Sales/Clients
Hunter by Libby Sydes, Dell
Prince of Cups by Gayle Feyrer, Dell

Too Many Cooks by Joanne Pence, HarperCollins
Cry of the Cougar by Linda Anderson, NAL

Submissions: Query first with first three chapters and synopsis.

Seeking

Long Contemporary	100,000 words minimum
Historical	any time period, 90,000–100,000 words minimum
Mystery	80,000 words minimum
Romantic Suspense	80,000 words minimum
Mainstream Romance	100,000 words minimum
Fantasy	
Paranormal	
Romantic horror	
Regency romance	
Gothics	

Comments: Response time is 2–3 weeks, enclose SASE.

ALBERT ZUCKERMAN

Writers House, Inc.
21 West 26th Street
New York, NY 10010
(212) 685-2400
FAX: (212) 685-1781

Professional Affiliations: Association of Author's Representatives.

Recent Sales/Clients

Eileen Goudge, Nora Roberts, Barbara Delinsky, Jane Feather, Betty Receveur, Maureen Reynolds, Modean Moon, Helen Mavajakes, Carol Marsh, Janet Quinn-Harkin, Barbara Lyle, Liza Bennett

Submissions: Query first with SASE.

Comments: We are interested in experienced writers who feel they are ready to progress from category into mainstream fiction, from paperback into hardcover.

Agents Who Do Not Charge Reading Fees

Compiled from the previous listings, here are the names of 58 agents, who, to the best of our knowledge, do NOT charge reading fees:

Rajeev Agarwal, James Allen, Marcia Amsterdam, Steven Axelrod, Josh Behar, Pam Bernstein, Greg Boylan, Richard Boylan, Andrea Brown, Pema Browne, Perry Browne, Julie Castiglia, Jacqulin Chambers, Ted Chichak, Laura Cifelli, Andrea Cirillo, Francine Ciske, Rob Cohen, Ruth Cohen, Fran Collin, Richard Curtis, Elaine Davie, Anita Diamant, B. J. Doyen, Ethan Ellenberg, Joyce Flaherty, Evan Fogelman, Jay Garon, Susan Ginsburg, Amy Goldberger, Irene Goodman, Hannibal Harris, Sharon Jarvis, William Kerwin, Katharine Kidd, Daniel King, Linda Diehl Kruger, James L'Angelle, Fran Lebowitz, Lettie Lee, Donald Maass, Ricia Mainhardt, Lawrence Mattis, Allison Mullen, Kim Van Nguyen, Edward Novak, Elizabeth Pomada, Harry Preston, Pesha Rubinstein, Meg Ruley, Kelly St. Clair, Mike Seymour, Mary Sue Seymour, Cherry Weiner, Wendy Wylegala, Nancy Yost, Sue Yuen, Albert Zuckerman.

Compiled from all the agent listings, here are the names of agents, categorized by their subject interests:

Blockbuster
Elizabeth Pomada.

Contemporary, Long
James Allen, Marcia Amsterdam, Steven Axelrod, Josh Behar, Meredith Bernstein, Pam Bernstein, Pema Browne, Perry Browne, Elizabeth Cavanaugh, Ted Chichak, Laura Cifelli, Andrea Cirillo, Francine Ciske, Rob Cohen, Ruth Cohen, Richard Curtis, Elaine Davie, Anita Diamant, Ethan Ellenberg,

Joyce Flaherty, Evan Fogelman, Susan Ginsburg, Irene Goodman, Yvonne Hubbs, Sharon Jarvis, Daniel King, Linda Diehl Kruger, James L'Angelle, Lettie Lee, Fran Lebowitz, Ricia Mainhardt, Denise Marcil, Evan Marshall, Allison Mullen, Edward Novak, Dee Pace, Elizabeth Pomada, Jean Price, Pesha Rubinstein, Meg Ruley, Kelly St. Clair, Mike Seymour, Sue Seymour, Cherry Weiner, Sue Yuen.

Contemporary, Short
Pamela G. Ahearn, Josh Behar, Pema Browne, Perry Browne, Ted Chichak, Laura Cifelli, Andrea Cirillo, Francine Ciske, Rob Cohen, Richard Curtis, Elaine Davie, Anita Diamant, Ethan Ellenberg, Janice Fishbein, Joyce Flaherty, Evan Fogelman, Susan Ginsburg, Irene Goodman, Yvonne Hubbs, Sharon Jarvis, Katharine Kidde, Linda Diehl Kruger, James L'Angelle, Lettie Lee, Denise Marcil, Evan Marshall, Kim Van Nguyen, Edward Novak, Elizabeth Pomada, Dee Pace, Jean Price, Pesha Rubinstein, Meg Ruley, Kelly St. Clair, Mike Seymour, Sue Seymour, Cherry Weiner, Wendy Wylegala, Sue Yuen.

Erotic
Greg Boylan, Richard Boylan, Hannibal Harris.

Ethnic
Pamela G. Ahearn, Meredith Bernstein, Pema Browne, Perry Browne, Julie Castiglia, Elizabeth Cavanaugh, Ted Chichak, Laura Cifelli, Janice Fishbein, Andrea Cirillo, Francine Ciske, Rob Cohen, Ruth Cohen, Fran Collin, Richard Curtis, Anita Diamant, Ethan Ellenberg, Joyce Flaherty, Yvonne Hubbs, Katharine Kidde, Linda Diehl Kruger, James L'Angelle, Fran Lebowitz, Lettie Lee, Ricia Mainhardt, Denise Marcil, Evan Marshall, Allison Mullen, Kim Van Nguyen, Dee Pace, Jean Price, Pesha Rubinstein, Kelly St. Clair, Mike Seymour, Sue Seymour, Wendy Wylegala.

Fantasy
James Allen, Josh Behar, Meredith Bernstein, Greg Boylan, Richard Boylan, Pema Browne, Perry Browne, Ted Chichak,

Fran Collin, Elaine Davie, Ethan Ellenberg, Janice Fishbein, Hannibal Harris, Yvonne Hubbs, Sharon Jarvis, Daniel King, James L'Angelle, Fran Lebowitz, Lettie Lee, Ricia Mainhardt, Evan Marshall, Allison Mullen, Kim Van Nguyen, Elizabeth Pomada, Dee Pace, Jean Price, Mike Seymour, Sue Seymour, Cherry Weiner, Sue Yuen.

Futuristic
Francine Ciske.

Gothic
Allison Mullen.

Hardcover Titles
Jay Garon, Albert Zuckerman.

Historical
Pamela G. Ahearn, James Allen, Marcia Amsterdam, Steven Axelrod, Josh Behar, Meredith Bernstein, Pam Bernstein, Greg Boylan, Richard Boylan, Andrea Brown, Pema Browne, Perry Browne, Elizabeth Cavanaugh, Ted Chichak, Laura Cifelli, Andrea Cirillo, Francine Ciske, Ruth Cohen, Fran Collin, Rob Cohen, Richard Curtis, Elaine Davie, Anita Diamant, B.J. Doyen, Ethan Ellenberg, Joyce Flaherty, Evan Fogelman, Susan Ginsburg, Amy Goldberger, Irene Goodman, Hannibal Harris, Yvonne Hubbs, Katharine Kidde, Daniel King, Linda Diehl Kruger, James L'Angelle, Fran Lebowitz, Lettie Lee, Ricia Mainhardt, Evan Marshall, Allison Mullen, Edward Novak, Kim Van Nguyen, Dee Pace, Elizabeth Pomada, Jean Price, Pesha Rubinstein, Meg Ruley, Kelly St. Clair, Mike Seymour, Sue Seymour, Cherry Weiner, Wendy Wylegala, Nancy Yost, Sue Yuen.

Inspirational Historical
Francine Ciske.

Mainstream Romance
Pamela G. Ahearn, James Allen, Marcia Amsterdam, Steven Axelrod, Josh Behar, Meredith Bernstein, Pam Bernstein, Greg Boylan, Richard Boylan, Pema Browne, Perry Browne, Julie

Castiglia, Elizabeth Cavanaugh, Ted Chichak, Laura Cifelli, Andrea Cirillo, Rob Cohen, Ruth Cohen, Richard Curtis, Anita Diamant, B.J. Doyen, Ethan Ellenberg, Janice Fishbein, Joyce Flaherty, Jay Garon, Irene Goodman, Hannibal Harris, Yvonne Hubbs, Sharon Jarvis, Donald Maass, Katharine Kidde, Daniel King, James L'Angelle, Ricia Mainhardt, Denise Marcil, Evan Marshall, Allison Mullen, Kim Van Nguyen, Edward Novak, Dee Pace, Elizabeth Pomada, Jean Price, Pesha Rubinstein, Meg Ruley, Kelly St. Clair, Mike Seymour, Sue Seymour, Cherry Weiner, Wendy Wylegala, Nancy Yost, Sue Yuen.

Mystery/Suspense
Pamela G. Ahearn, James Allen, Marcia Amsterdam, Steven Axelrod, Josh Behar, Meredith Bernstein, Pema Browne, Perry Browne, Julie Castiglia, Andrea Cirillo, Francine Ciske, Ruth Cohen, Fran Collin, Elaine Davie, Anita Diamant, B.J. Doyen, Joyce Flaherty, Evan Fogelman, Jay Garon, Irene Goodman, Yvonne Hubbs, Sharon Jarvis, Katharine Kidde, Daniel King, Linda Diehl Kruger, James L'Angelle, Lettie Lee, Donald Maass, Ricia Mainhardt, Evan Marshall, Allison Mullen, Kim Van Nguyen, Elizabeth Pomada, Dee Pace, Jean Price, Pesha Rubinstein, Meg Ruley, Kelly St. Clair, Mike Seymour, Sue Seymour, Cherry Weiner, Wendy Wylegala, Nancy Yost, Sue Yuen.

Paranormal
Pamela G. Ahearn, Meredith Bernstein, Pema Browne, Perry Browne, Elizabeth Cavanaugh, Ted Chichak, Francine Ciske, Ethan Ellenberg, Yvonne Hubbs, Sharon Jarvis, Linda Diehl Kruger, James L'Angelle, Lettie Lee, Ricia Mainhardt, Kim Van Nguyen, Dee Pace, Jean Price, Pesha Rubinstein, Kelly St. Clair, Mike Seymour, Sue Seymour, Cherry Weiner.

Time Travel
Pamela G. Ahearn, Marcia Amsterdam, Josh Behar, Meredith Bernstein, Greg Boylan, Richard Boylan, Andrea Brown, Pema Browne, Perry Browne, Elizabeth Cavanaugh, Ted Chichak, Laura Cifelli, Andrea Cirillo, Francine Ciske, Rob Cohen,

Richard Curtis, Anita Diamant, Ethan Ellenberg, Hannibal Harris, Yvonne Hubbs, Sharon Jarvis, Katharine Kidde, Linda Diehl Kruger, James L'Angelle, Lettie Lee, Ricia Mainhardt, Denise Marcil, Allison Mullen, Kim Van Nguyen, Dee Pace, Elizabeth Pomada, Jean Price, Kelly St. Clair, Cherry Weiner, Wendy Wylegala.

Regency
Pamela G. Ahearn, Pema Browne, Susan Ginsburg, Linda Diehl Kruger, Allison Mullen.

Romantic Suspense
Pamela G. Ahearn, Marcia Amsterdam, Steven Axelrod, Josh Behar, Greg Boylan, Richard Boylan, Julie Castiglia, Ted Chichak, Laura Cifelli, Andrea Cirillo, Francine Ciske, Rob Cohen, Richard Curtis, Anita Diamant, B.J. Doyen, Ethan Ellenberg, Janice Fishbein, Evan Fogelman, Hannibal Harris, Yvonne Hubbs, Sharon Jarvis, Katharine Kidde, Linda Diehl Kruger, James L'Angelle, Fran Lebowitz, Donald Maass, Ricia Mainhardt, Kim Van Nguyen, Dee Pace, Jean Price, Kelly St. Clair, Mike Seymour, Sue Seymour, Cherry Weiner, Wendy Wylegala, Nancy Yost.

Screenplays
Rajeev Agarawal, Marcia Amsterdam, Greg Boylan, Richard Boylan, Pema Browne, Perry Browne, Jacqulin Chambers, Ted Chichak, B.J. Doyen, Janice Fishbein, Evan Fogelman, Hannibal Harris, Yvonne Hubbs, William Kerwin, James L'Angelle, Lettie Lee, Lawrence Mattis, Kim Van Nguyen, Jean Patrick, Harry Preston.

Soft Horror
Mike Seymour, Sue Seymour.

Thriller
Jay Garon, Allison Mullen, Nancy Yost.

True Crime
Nancy Yost.

Westerns
Elaine Davie.

Women's Fiction
Elaine Davie, Evan Fogelman, Allison Mullen, Pesha Rubinstein.

Young Adult
Andrea Brown.

Children's Fiction
Ricia Mainhardt

Nonfiction
Elaine Davie, Linda Diehl Kruger, Evan Fogelman, Ricia Mainhardt.

Literary
Elizabeth Pomada.

The Inside Track
at Putnam

Chatting with Carrie Feron,
Senior Editor

Romance Writer's Pink Pages (RWPP): Carrie, thanks for taking time out of your busy schedule to chat. Can you tell us a little about the Putnam Publishing Group?

Carrie Feron: We are a trade house that publishes commercial books, both in hardcover and paperback. Our authors include LaVyrle Spencer, Nora Roberts, Catherine Coulter, Laura Kinsale, Linda Lael Miller, Katherine Sutcliffe, Pamela Morsi, Suzanne Forster, Barbara Boswell, Judy Cuevas, and many more.

RWPP: Would you give an overview of all the publishers in the group and briefly outline the types of fiction they publish?

Carrie Feron: We publish both reprint and original fiction of all types in Berkley and Jove. Putnam is a hardcover publisher.

RWPP: What are Putnam's immediate needs for manuscripts? Are there certain areas with slots open? What kinds of manuscripts are on Putnam's wish list?

Carrie Feron: We are always looking for fresh voices in commercial fiction.

RWPP: Let's talk about the contemporary mainstreams published by Berkley. I think Suzanne Forster's *Shameless* was compelling, and a dialogically-driven page turner. Forster crossed a lot of the usual boundaries of emotional intensity, plot complexity, sexual intensity, and even language, but she crossed those boundaries very successfully. What would you say are the magic ingredients for this style of cutting edge women's fiction? Do you think *Shameless* has set a trend for Berkley's acquisitions editors?

Carrie Feron: *Shameless* is the type of book I love acquiring and publishing. I like authors who take risks, avoid clichés, and create characters that walk off the page. There is no secret formula to writing this type of book; each author must develop her own strengths and her own voice.

RWPP: What about Berkley/Jove's historicals? With many big name historical authors, such as Jill Marie Landis, Barbara Cartland, and Katherine Sutcliffe, can a new author break in here? Or would submissions to Diamond be a better shot for breaking in with a historical manuscript?

Carrie Feron: First time authors can certainly break into Berkley and Jove. Just send us a query letter if you think you have the right project for us.

RWPP: After Wendy Haley's *This Dark Paradise* was released, did you see a lot of vampire manuscripts arriving at Berkley? Are vampire romances still going strong? Are editors open to other dark romances with supernatural elements?

Carrie Feron: We are open to publishing "dark" romances with supernatural elements, but we do not have a "line" that deals exclusively with these types of stories.

RWPP: The mandatory use of pseudonyms at some publishers and the ownership of those pseudonyms has created a situation in which authors keep writing novels for the same publisher because they're fearful of losing their readership if they leave. Does Putnam (and the publishers in its group) have a company policy about pseudonym use and ownership?

Carrie Feron: We do not require that an author use a pseudonym, and usually it's the author's decision to use one.

RWPP: Another hot issue authors want to know about are their print runs. Do your authors have access to their print run info?

Carrie Feron: Authors absolutely have the right to know their print run, and we furnish the numbers upon request.

RWPP: Could you give a ball park figure of what a first time author can expect for an advance and royalty percentage for Putnam hardcover, Berkley single title historical, Jove, and the Diamond series, including Tea Rose? This is the kind of information that my readers have been asking for, and with the rumor mills grinding in writer's organizations and on the information superhighway, it would be helpful if the correct information came straight from an editor.

Carrie Feron: I'm sorry that I can't be more specific on this question, but it really is individual. Many people start out at "entry level" prices, but a truly special book deserves a "truly special" advance.

RWPP: One of the marketing strategies that differentiates Berkley romances from some of the competition are the classy covers. Is Berkley going to continue to use gorgeous flowers on the cover, then a sultry stepback illustration right inside?

Carrie Feron: We are always trying to reach readers, so watch for even better covers in the future.

RWPP: I've also noticed the folk-art covers of Diamond's Homespun books, and think they're attractive and appropriate for these types of books.

Carrie Feron: In addition to the Homespun line, we are launching a series called Harmony in 1994 that I think will appeal to fans of sweeter romances.

RWPP: Carrie, thank you for answering some tough questions. You've given authors a real insider's look at the Putnam Publishing Group.

4

Angels and Vampires and Time Travelers, Oh My!

*A*s Dorothy once said to Toto, "I don't think we're in Kansas anymore!" I think avid romance readers will agree that romance has taken an Oz-like turn into the technicolor world of wild imagination, fresh fairy tales, and twisted folklore.

What in the world has happened to romance as we once knew it? We now have elements of futuristic worlds, science fiction, time travel, angels, vampires, and fantasy in many romance lines. How did this happen? As romance writers, and as readers, we sometimes have to go beyond our own genre to see what affects the trends in romance.

Let's start with vampire romances. There's no doubt that we have Anne Rice to thank for creating Lestat, the first really sexy vampire. It took awhile for the trickle down theory to prove itself, but now almost every romance publishing house has authors who are thrilling readers with their own version of vampire romances. And readers want more. Maggie Shayne's *Twilight Memories,* in which a pair of centuries-old vampire lovers must protect a young boy from evil, is the second in her "Wings in the

Night" Miniseries for Silhouette Shadows. This sensual book was a hit, despite the awkward cover (heroine hanging upside down like a bat!). Berkley's version of the vampire romance is Wendy Haley's *This Dark Paradise*, a more emotionally uplifting novel than the title indicates.

And angels in romance? Where did they come from? This is a trend that spread from the *non*fiction side of the bestseller lists. An angel hit the cover of *Time* magazine on December 27, 1993. The accompanying article stated that 69% of Americans believe in angels and 46% believe they have their own guardian angel. Chain bookstores have had to establish angel sections. Ballantine books alone has almost twenty angel titles (nonfiction) in print. They have had to reprint one title more than twenty-five times (over half a million copies of Sophy Burnham's *A Book of Angels*) to keep up with the demand!

Numbers like that make fiction publishers sit up and take notice. Debbie Macomber's *A Season of Angels* was a Harper Monogram romance that swept America and became *the* Christmas gift of 1993. (A sequel is planned.) Anne Stuart's *Falling Angel* was about a bad boy who had just one last chance to redeem himself. Another Harlequin American angel/reincarnation romance is *One More Valentine*, which won a *Romantic Times* award for Best Harlequin American of 1993.

What about time travel romances? This trend took a little longer to develop, but is now holding strong. Kathe Robin, a reviewer at *Romantic Times* magazine says, "Probably the hottest growing subgenre is time travel."

Jude Devereaux's *A Knight in Shining Armor* was one of the first, but the more recent bestsellers by Diana Gabaldon (from *Outlander* to *Voyager*) really clinched the time travel theme for the romance industry. The success of Brenda Hiatt's *Bridge Over Time*, a Harlequin Superromance, ensures that Harlequin will be looking for more well-done time travel books that will satisfy readers. Pinnacle also publishes time travel books, and readers have a great treat in store if they haven't read Cherlyn Jac's *Shadows in Time*. (No spoiler details here!) Topaz time travel offerings treat the reader to *Timeless* by the inimitable Jasmine Cresswell, Fawcett brings us *Once in Every Lifetime* by Kristin Hannah, and Harper has more than a few time travel titles. Reruns of *Quantam Leap* on the sci-fi cable channel (Scott Bakula is a hero for all time!) and Ashley McConnell's *Quantam Leap* novels assure that additional time travel enthusiasts will be brought into the romance genre.

Leisure and Bantam are heavily into futuristics. In fact, Kay Hooper's *Wizard of Seattle*, futuristic of the year, is such a keeper that used bookstores can get thirty dollars for it, if they can find it! Kathleen Morgan's *Firestar* is also a collector's item. Melinda Helfer, a *Romantic Times* reviewer, says, "Futuristic romance is sweeping the nation."

Now, who says the Gothic is dead? Zebra may have made a mistake by ending their Gothic series with the excellent traditional Gothic, *Dark Cloister* by Sharon Wagner, but other houses are still turning out Gothics in one form or another. Though Phyllis A. Whitney and Barbara Michaels can't write 'em fast enough to suit this reader, Silhouette Shadows is keeping alive the Gothic tradition of "Don't go in the house!" with little extra twists of supernatural surprises hidden in the pages.

No one can do a better "demon lover" than Jeanne Rose in *The Prince of Air and Darkness*. And do werewolves really exist in *Waiting for the Wolf Moon* by Evelyn Vaughn? Is Jack the Ripper reincarnated in Anne Stuart's *Break the Night*? Is there really a lake monster that eats people in *What Waits Below* by Jane Toombs? Does a ghost possess a woman's lover and will history repeat itself in Carla Cassidy's *Silent Screams*? These are just a few examples of how Silhouette has revamped (pardon our pun) the traditional Gothic and brought it into the midnineties. The stories are fresh, exciting, and unputdownable. These books rarely end up in used bookstores—they are that good. So get 'em while they're hot off the press. If you are thinking of writing a Shadows book, you *must* read the current offerings.

What about science fiction and fantasy in romance? Harlequin American knows it sells. Anne Stuart's *Cinderman* stars a mostly naked hero who is the sexiest invisible man in the world and can set things on fire with his eyes. (Think about it.) And who would have believed a Silhouette Intimate Moments brings readers a nine-hundred-year-old hero (thawed out of a glacier) who brings love and desire to an archeologist with an aversion to sex? *Miranda's Viking* by Maggie Shayne gives new meaning to the phrase "the Iceman cometh."

For all of you out there who just want to write traditional romance with no "weird stuff" in it, read on. There is still plenty of opportunity for you, too!

Harper, Bantam, Signet/Dutton (formerly NAL), and other publishers are still going strong with traditional historicals. The popularity of British Isles historicals like Susan Wiggs' award-winning *The Mist and the Magic,* and the hot-seller *Winter's Heat* by Denise Domning, assure that historicals, especially British settings and Medieval Europe, are here to stay, and that publishers will want more of them.

Susan Wiggs' advice to aspiring writers is to use newspaper clippings to spark your imagination, make sure the heroine has a compelling goal, and try to figure out what the heroine would encounter in her everyday life; but Susan's secret weapon is "Come up with a *great* title."

Interested in writing mainstream romance? Romance trendsetter and *Romantic Times* Career Achievement Award winner Meryl Sawyer talks about writing "the big book." By big she doesn't mean four hundred pages of flora, fauna, and furniture. She advises writers to think big in terms of concept. As an example she uses *Bridges of Madison County.* The big concept in this novel is the fact that two people in a forbidden relationship give up each other for the greater good. Meryl advises writers to place less emphasis on romance and concentrate on one of the three basic plots:

- Hero/Heroine against a person (can even be a conflict with herself)
- H/H against society
- H/H against unbeatable forces.

Meryl Sawyer also reminds writers that conflict is the heart of the mainstream novel, truly the "mother's milk" of all fiction.

Want to write a really sexy mainstream? Suzanne Forster (the "Dr. Ruth of Romance Novels"), has paved the way for this trend with her ultra-overheated novel, *Shameless*. Carrie Feron at Berkley said she would love to acquire other risk-taking books like *Shameless*.

How does Suzanne build those dynamite love scenes that make acquisition editors say yes? First of all, she says, "Conversation is the sexiest form of foreplay . . . It's all about anticipation." She advises writers to be calculating when building love scenes, planning for it with setting, dialogue, body language, and a balance between the conflict and the attraction that the hero and heroine feel for each other. The latter is the key to romantic chemistry, and it can make or break the sale of your manuscript.

Regency authors have been complaining about the shrinking market for their manuscripts. More than five publishers in the last two years have either stopped doing Regency or cut down on their number of titles. Katherine Kingsley, *Romantic Times* award winner of the Best Historical Romance of 1993, has the answer to Regency writers' market woes. She advises writing a longer Regency and moving it over to the Historical genre where the market isn't so tight and the financial advantages are greater. She calls this writing the "Super Regency." Her advice makes good sense. It's called being flexible in a tight marketplace.

Have fun scouting out new trends that will help *you* write a romance that is exactly what editors want. Read romance novels, but also read other things, like *Time* and *Newsweek* magazines, science digests, society columns, and newspapers. One well-known romance writer reads and clips the tabloids faithfully, and uses them to help her develop story ideas. (No, I'm not telling her name!) And don't forget the bestseller lists in *Publisher's Weekly*. These can be excellent indicators of what's hot and what's not.

Whether you write Regency, Contemporary, Historical, or some new and different subgenre of romance, remember that risk-taking is the current trend. The new romances sparkle with individuality. They are still romances that fit the editor's guide-lines, but they are fresh, different, grab the reader on page one, and keep them reading through to the last page.

As Meryl Sawyer (and Mickey Spillane) once said, "The first page sells the book. The last page sells the next one."

Good luck, romance trendsetters!

(Thanks to all the authors named who shared their information and tips at romance writing workshops in Nashville, Tennessee, and on the romance exchange of the GEnie electronic network.)

5

Directory of
Publishers

ACE BOOKS
200 Madison Avenue
New York, NY 10016

Acquisitions Editors: Laura Ann Gilman, Associate Editor; Ginjer Buchanan, Executive Editor; Lou Aronica, Publisher

Media Type/Titles per Year: Paperback, 72; hardcover, 10

Submissions Policies

Don't query. Send a synopsis and first three chapters with SASE. Don't send the complete manuscript until it is requested. New authors are encouraged to send submissions. Unagented manuscripts are OK, but please, no simultaneous submissions. Agents may call. Response time is from 3–6 months and can vary widely. See Writer's Guidelines for additional information.

Pay Rate

Not disclosed. Books are normally published about 24 months after acceptance.

Actively Seeking

High Fantasy   60,000–100,000 words

Editor's Wish List

Romance must be built into the fantasy aspect—we are not looking for a romance that "might" be considered in our genre.

Tips

Read the Science Fiction/Fantasy genre before deciding that your book fits into it. The best writers are those who love the genre. It's not something you can pick up from writing courses or guidelines.

Ace Writer's Guidelines

Thank you for your interest in Ace Books. Here are a few good rules to follow when submitting a manuscript to us for consideration:

1. Be sure that you are familiar with the kinds of fiction we are currently publishing.

2. Manuscripts must be typewritten on standard-sized 8½″ × 11″ white paper, double-spaced, on one side of the paper. Please do not submit hand-written or dot matrix printed copies.

3. Do not submit a carbon copy. Clean photocopies are usually all right.

4. Be sure to keep a copy for yourself; manuscripts do occasionally get lost in the mail.

5. Include an SASE large enough to hold your manuscript should we need to return it. Also enclose a #10 envelope for our response in the event that we keep your manuscript. Do not send cash, checks, or stamp coupons.

6. The accepted length for a novel manuscript is between 60,000 and 100,000 words (about 200–400 manuscript pages).

7. Ace prefers to see only the first three chapters (about 50 pages) and a complete synopsis, rather than the entire manuscript. If we want to see the entire work, we will request it. This allows us to read our submissions much faster, and cuts down on your mailing costs.

8. Please submit your project to only one publisher at a time.

9. Allow at least 2 months for a reply; after 3 months you might politely inquire as to the status of your submission.

10. Ace does not accept computer submissions. Please do not send disc, fax, or on-line submissions. They will not be read.

Thank you for your interest in our company, and the very best of luck to you.

Ace (Sci-fi and Fantasy) Books is an imprint of Berkley Publishing Company.

ARCHWAY PAPERBACKS
1230 Avenue of the Americas
New York, NY 10020

Acquisitions Editor: Patricia MacDonald, Young Adult Editor

(Did not respond to questionnaire in time for this edition.)

ATHENEUM CHILDREN'S BOOKS
866 Third Avenue
New York, NY 10022

Acquisitions Editors: Marsha Marshall/Jean Karl, Young Adult Editors

(Did not respond to questionnaire in time for this edition.)

AVALON BOOKS (THOMAS BOUREGY CO.)
401 Lafayette Street, 2nd Floor
New York, NY 10003
(800) 223-5251

Vice President/Publisher: Marcia Markland

Media Type/Titles per Year: Hardcover, 60

Submissions Policies

Query first or send first chapter and two- to three-page synopsis. Don't send complete manuscripts unless requested. New authors are encouraged. We publish many first novels. Unsolicited or un-agented manuscripts are OK. Please tell us if it is a simultaneous submission. Agents may call. Response time is about 3–6 months.

Actively Seeking
Contemporary	40,000–50,000 words
Mystery/Suspense	40,000–50,000 words
Ethnic	40,000–50,000 words
Inspirational	40,000–50,000 words

Tips

We prefer career-oriented heroines dealing with today's problems. Also looking for good mystery series and ethnic romance, well-written with believable characters and no explicit sex or graphic violence. Please, no amnesia, ghosts, paranormal experiences, or cruise ship romances.

Thomas Bouregy & Company Writer's Guidelines

Under its Avalon Books imprint, Thomas Bouregy & Co., Inc., publishes hardcover secular romances and westerns for the library market. Our books are wholesome adult fiction. No profanity or graphic sex.

We publish 60 books a year in bimonthly cycles of 10. A cycle consists of two career romances, two mystery romances, four general romances, and two westerns. All the romances are contemporary; all the westerns are historical. Books range in length from a minimum of 40,000 words to a maximum of 50,000 words (usually about 160 to 210 manuscript pages).

ROMANCES

General Information: We do not want old-fashioned, predictable, formulaic books. We are looking for contemporary characters and fresh plots and storylines. Supporting characters and subplots should be interesting and realistic and should add an extra and interesting dimension to the book.

Heroines: Every Avalon heroine should be an independent young woman with an interesting profession or career. She is equal to the stresses of today's world and can take care of herself.

Heroes: Avalon heroes should be warm, likable, realistic, sympathetic, understanding men who treat the heroine as an equal, with respect for her intelligence and individuality.

Mysteries: The heroine does not have to be the protagonist in a mystery, nor does the work have to be a romance. (Just keep in mind that we do not publish explicit sex or violence.) We are interested in how the mystery is unraveled, i.e., through clues, red herrings, and logical deductions from the evidence.

Career Romances: The only difference between a romance and a career romance is that the plot of the career romance is centered around the heroine's job. We want these novels to explore the many exciting professions open to women today. They must be carefully researched so that all the background information is authentic. It is all right for a career romance to straddle categories and have a mystery plot.

WESTERNS

General Information: All westerns are historical novels, and it is important that they be placed in time and that the background be carefully researched. Avoid using words and phrases that were not part of the language at the time your western is set. Plots should be suspenseful and action packed, but vivid descriptions of gory violence are to be avoided.

AVON
1350 Avenue of the Americas
New York, NY 10019
(212) 261-6800
FAX: (212) 261-6895

Acquisitions Editors: Ellen Edwards, Senior Editor; Lyssa Keusch, Assistant Editor; Christine Zika, Assistant Editor

Media Type/Titles per Year: Paperback, 48–62 (romance)

Submissions Policies

Agents may call. Authors, a query will get you the quickest response, but you may send a synopsis and sample chapters or the entire manuscripts plus a one- to two-page synopsis. New authors are always encouraged. Avon is constantly on the lookout for new talent. Unsolicited manuscripts are OK. All submissions, unsolicited and agented, are given fair consideration. Simultaneous submissions are OK. No electronic submissions. The usual response time for agented submissions is 6–8 weeks. Usual response time for unsolicited and unagented submissions is about three months. See Writer's Guidelines for additional information.

Pay Rate

Books are normally published about 12 months after acceptance.
Average advance varies.

Actively Seeking

Historical	100,000 words, 1100–1899
Contemporary	100,000 words
Women's fiction	100,000 words
Mystery/Suspense	60,000 words; psychological suspense, women in jeopardy, straight mysteries, cozies

Anything *except* category romances.

Turn-offs/Taboos

Avon novels are sexy. No rape, except in rare instances, when
handled with extreme sensitivity.

Tips

Read current Avon novels. Endings are always happy. Also see
guidelines below.

Avon Books Writer's Guidelines

At the heart of Avon's romance program are some of the most talented, well-respected, and creative individuals in the world of romance today. We are proud of our authors and the fact that we publish the best writers in the romance genre. We continue to help our authors grow and expand in their chosen profession. And we are always on the lookout for the fresh, exciting, new voices of tomorrow.

We've recently expanded our romance program. A quick glance will show you how we position each of our stellar authors in the best possible way to help them reach their full potential.

Each month, Avon publishes several romance titles:

The Lead position is reserved for well-established authors whose substantial sales allow them to compete against non-romance titles on national bestseller lists. Avon publishes one lead historical romance almost every month.

The Avon Romantic Treasure is a program designed for authors whose previous historical romances have shown exceptional promise and whose sales have earned them a degree of recognition within the romance-buying community. Treasure authors are carefully selected by Avon's editorial staff to join this prestigious program. Some Treasure writers are Avon authors who have "moved up," others come to this program with established track records at other houses. We publish one Romantic Treasure a month.

The Avon Romance program, now over 10 years old, was created for new or almost new writers of historical romance. Avon Romances take place in any time period from the Middle Ages to the end of the 19th century (1100–1900). We publish two Avon romances each month.

The Avon Regency Romance rounds out Avon's overall romance program and provides another good place for new writers to start. Avon Regencies are 50,000–55,000 words long and follow the conventions of this specialized genre. We publish one Regency each month.

In addition, Avon Books publishes mainstream contemporary women's novels by established writers. Avon does not publish short contemporary category romances (such as Harlequins, Silhouettes, and Loveswepts).

If you love romances, have an active imagination, enjoy writing, and are willing to work hard to become a published writer, we encourage you to try your hand at writing a historical romance for Avon. Here are some helpful hints to get you started:

1. Avon Romances are 100,000–125,000 words long (400–500 manuscript pages) and take place in any time period from the Middle Ages to the end of the 19th century (1100–1900). Avon will consider "Viking" romances that are set earlier than the Middle Ages, but we advise new authors to stick with more traditional time periods. We will not consider (historical) romances set after 1900.

2. Hook the reader with a strong opening that makes her want to keep reading.

3. The hero and heroine should meet early in the book (by page 30 at the latest) and once they've met, they should not be separated for lengthy periods.

4. Do careful research. Historical accuracy is a must. Try to capture the flavor of the time and place you're writing about.

5. Start by creating an appealing and memorable hero and heroine who interact in exciting, original, sexy, and romantic ways. Know your characters thoroughly. Know why, besides sexual attraction, they're drawn to each other and fall in love.

6. The hero and heroine should make love in sensual, tastefully described love scenes—but not before you've established a degree of emotional intimacy between them.

7. The heroine shouldn't make love with anyone but the hero. (I'm afraid the double standard still applies; it's OK for the hero to make love to other women, but preferably *not* after he makes love with the heroine.)

8. Make sure the focus of your book is the romantic relationship between the hero and heroine. Everything you include should contribute to the development of that relationship in some way.

9. Be original. Read other historical romances to know what story ideas have been overused. Do something different; find variations on the tried and true themes.

10. Master the technique of writing well. A good story will only come alive for the reader if you tell it skillfully and energetically.

11. Be critical of your work. Make sure it's your very best work.

12. Keep asking yourself, Will a "jaded" romance reader who's read dozens of historical romances find my manuscript entertaining?

13. Keep in mind who your audience is and why she reads historical romances.

14. Avon will consider time-travel romances in which a major contemporary character travels back in time to a previous era.

15. Ghosts and other supernatural elements are acceptable if handled skillfully; science fiction and fantasy elements—as found in the fantasy genre—are not acceptable (for example, no talking animals, please.) However, here too, we advise new writers to stick with more traditional storylines.

16. Make sure your book ends "happily ever after."

WRITING A REGENCY ROMANCE
Avon publishes traditional Regencies with an emphasis on romance. There should be lots of romantic interaction between the hero and heroine. These are not sensual books, but the best Regencies do have strong sexual tension. In Regencies, taking off a glove and caressing a wrist can be as sexy as a far more graphic scene in a full-length historical romance. Accurate period detail is essential. Be sure to include the wit and sparkle that makes the Regency period so popular. Clever, romantic dialogue is an important part of a good Regency, in which the characters woo each other with words.

HOW TO SUBMIT
All manuscripts should be neatly typed on plain bond paper, double-spaced with generous margins. Please include a cover letter briefly describing who you are, what your book is about, and your background as a writer. Include a stamped, self-addressed envelope big enough to contain your manuscript in case we have to return it to you.

Please send with a query letter *or* the first three chapters (or 50–100 pages) and a five to ten page synopsis of the whole story (rather than sending the complete manuscript). Mention in your cover letter if the complete manuscript is available, and if not, when you intend to finish it. If we like the partial, we will ask to see the complete manuscript.

Send your manuscript to any of the Avon editors at the top of this listing. It takes 4–6 weeks for response to a query letter and 4–6 months to read an unsolicited manuscript. If you haven't heard from us after that time, please drop us a postcard with your name, address, phone number, title of manuscript, whether is is partial or complete, when you originally sent it, and to whom. We'll get it back to you.

Have fun writing your romance! We look forward to receiving your submission at Avon Books.

AVON FLARE BOOKS
1350 Avenue of the Americas
New York, NY 10019
(212) 261-6800
FAX: (212) 261-6895

Acquisitions Editor: Ellen Kreiger, Young Adult Romance

(Did not respond.)

BALLANTINE
Columbine/Girls Only Books
1265 Aerowood Drive
Missisauga, Ontario L4W 1B9
CANADA

(Did not respond to questionnaire in time for this edition.)

BALLANTINE/DEL REY/FAWCETT/IVY

A Division of Random House
201 E. 50th Street
New York, NY 10022
(212) 751-2600

Acquisitions Editor: Barbara Dicks

Media Type: Paperback

Submissions Policies

Unagented manuscripts are OK. Submit complete manuscripts or
partials (synopsis and first three chapters) with SASE. Manuscripts should be double-spaced with no blank lines between
paragraphs, except scene breaks. Paragraphs are indented five
spaces. Don't bind manuscript. Response time is several months.
Reads all manuscripts. Printed form rejections are usual, due to
volume of submissions.

Pay Rate

"Competitive" advances and royalties. Contracts are individually
negotiated.

Actively Seeking

Historicals	100,000–125,000 words
Regencies	70,000–75,000 words
Adult Fantasy	60,000–100,000+ words
Science Fiction	60,000–100,000+ words

Tips

No UFO or occult works. No coincidence solutions. Read
McCaffrey, Foster, and Chalker to see what kind of fantasy is
published. Romance is usually light and sweet when it is a plot
element.

BALLANTINE/DEL REY/FAWCETT/IVY
Women's Fiction Books
201 E. 50th Street
New York, NY 10022
(212) 751-2600

Acquisitions Editor Pam Strickler is no longer buying romance, and sent a letter to *Romance Writer's Pink Pages* requesting to be deleted from the mailing list.

BANTAM/DOUBLEDAY/DELL BOOKS
Bantam Fanfare
1540 Broadway
New York, NY 10036
(212) 354-6500
FAX: (212) 782-9523

Acquisitions Editors: Wendy McCurdy, Senior Editor; Beth de Guzman, Senior Editor; Shauna Summers, Assistant Editor

Media Type/Titles per Year: Paperback and hardcover, approximately 36

Submissions Policies

Please query first with SASE. Authors, only send synopsis and sample chapters if requested after query letter. No complete manuscripts at initial contact, except from agents. New authors are encouraged. Simultaneous submissions are OK, but include this info in the cover letter. Agents may call. Response time is usually 2 months.

Pay Rate

Confidential advances and royalties.

Actively Seeking

Historical   any time period or setting
Contemporary
Mainstream
Ethnic
Mystery/Suspense
Time Travel
Paranormal
Word counts are flexible.

Editor's Wish List

A gripping story of human emotion and relationships with very real, likable, and interesting characters.

Turn-offs/Taboos

No incest; no hero raping the heroine.

Tips

Our romances are sweet, spicy, sensual, or sexy. Read our books to know what we want. We publish a wide variety of women's fiction, so be sure to study a variety of our books.

    Some of the Bantam Editors' favorite romances are *The Beloved Scoundrel* by Iris Johansen; *Blue Willow* by Deborah Smith; *Whisper of Roses* by Teresa Medeiros; and *Dark Paradise* by Tami Hoag.

Bantam Writer's Guidelines

At Bantam Books there are no guidelines for Women's Fiction because the stories and styles of our books cover the entire spectrum of the genre. If you wish to submit your work for consideration by Bantam and are unagented, send us a query letter. The query letter should be no more than three pages covering the basics of who your characters are, what the conflict is that they face, and how your plot develops. It usually takes eight weeks to receive a response from us. Please don't submit sample chapters or a complete manuscript until we request them. Unfortunately, we cannot give comments on many submissions. Be sure to include a self-addressed stamped, envelope; we cannot respond to queries that are not accompanied by return postage.

We advise you to review the titles we have published during the last several years by such bestselling authors as Sandra Brown, Amanda Quick, Iris Johansen, Deborah Smith, Tami Hoag, Teresa Medeiros, Roseanne Bittner, Susan Johnson, Kay Hooper, Lynda Robinson, and Jessica Bryan.

We're constantly searching for the stars of tomorrow, the new authors who are the genre's life blood. If you write a great book, we'll buy it!

(Fanfare is the showcase for Bantam's popular women's fiction, with spectacular covers and even more spectacular stories. Fanfare presents three novels each month, ranging from historical to contemporary, all with great human emotion and great love stories at their heart, all by the finest authors writing in any genre.

BANTAM/DOUBLEDAY/DELL BOOKS

Bantam Loveswept
1540 Broadway
New York, NY 10036
(212) 354-6500
FAX: (212) 782-9523

Acquisitions Editors: Beth de Guzman, Senior Editor; Shauna Summers, Assistant Editor

Media Type: Paperback

Submissions Policies

Please query first with SASE. Authors, only send synopsis and sample chapters if requested after query letter. No complete manuscripts at initial contact, except from agents. New authors are encouraged. Simultaneous submissions are OK, but include this info in the cover letter. Agents may call. Response time is usually 2 months. See Writer's Guidelines for additional information.

Pay Rate

Confidential advances and royalties.

Actively Seeking

Contemporary   60,000 words

Editor's Wish List

A great story with intelligent, interesting heroines and sexy heroes. The focus must be on the hero and heroine's developing relationship.

Turn-offs/Taboos

Loveswept is a category romance line—no historical books within Loveswept.

Tips

Our romances are sweet, spicy, sensual, or sexy. Read a lot of our books to know what we want. Our books are varied—funny, intense, suspenseful, and sweet.

Some of the Bantam Editors' favorite romances are *Midnight Hour* by Deborah Dixon, *Avenging Angel* by Glenna McReynolds, and *Surrender, Baby* by Suzanne Forster.

Bantam Loveswept Writer's Guidelines

Thanks for your interest in our Loveswept line. Here are some pertinent facts about our romances:

Loveswepts run about 60,000 words and are set in the present. The books are wonderfully written and feature sparkling dialogue rather than long narrative. Quickly paced, our Love-swepts are page turners!

The characters are deftly crafted, well-rounded people who readers care about and root for. They should meet as close to page one as possible and never be apart for more than 8 to 10 manuscript pages. The sexual tension and attraction between the hero and heroine should be apparent from their first encounter on, but their love for each other should be based on emotions and feelings, not simply on sexual attraction.

We expect mystery/intrigue/adventure/paranormal and other elements to be kept to a minimum and that the romance remain the focus of the story at all times. Secondary characters should also be limited in number and in importance. More valuable than any "tip sheet" or "guideline," the books themselves are your best tools for learning what we're looking for in a Loveswept. Read as many as possible before you submit to us.

Send us a query letter if you don't have an agent. The query should be no more than two or three pages, but it should cover the basics of who your characters are, what the conflict is that they face, and how your plot develops. It usually takes 8 weeks to receive a response from us. Please don't submit sample chapters or a complete manuscript until we request them. Unfortunately, we cannot give comments on any submissions. Be sure to include an SASE; we cannot respond to queries that are not accompanied by return postage.

We're constantly searching for the stars of tomorrow, the new authors who are the genre's life blood. Write a great book, and we'll buy it!

BANTAM/DOUBLEDAY/DELL BOOKS

Bantam Spectra
1540 Broadway
New York, NY 10036
(212) 782-9187

Media Type/Titles per Year: Paperback, hardcover, and audio-cassette, 60

Acquisitions Editors: Jennifer Hershey, Executive Editor; Tim Dupree, Senior Editor; Janna Silverstein, Editor; Heather McConnell, Assistant Editor

Submissions Policies

AGENTS ONLY. Please query first. Agents, it's easier if correspondence is by mail (versus a phone call). OK to send a short synopsis of three to five double-spaced pages and three sample chapters. Don't send the complete manuscript unless it is requested. New authors aren't encouraged. No unsolicited manuscripts. Simultaneous submissions are OK from agents. Response time is 1–12 weeks.

Pay Rate

Confidential advances. Royalties are 8% for paperback and 10% for hardcover. Books are normally published about 12 months after acceptance.

Actively Seeking
Science Fiction/Fantasy
Romance elements are *not* the main focus of Spectra.

Editor's Wish List

We like to see solid, well-researched Science Fiction and well-written Science Fiction and Fantasy. Our standards are very high and we aren't interested in any author who isn't willing to work hard to meet those standards.

Turn-offs/Taboos

Imitations of other writers. We like authors who create original new worlds and ideas.

(Note from *Romance Writer's Pink Pages:* Although Spectra Books is in the broad spectrum of fiction and not really romance genre, this listing is here because of many requests by romance authors who want to write cross-over books with romantic sub-plots. For romance info, see previous listings for Bantam Fanfare and Bantam Loveswept.)

BARBOUR AND COMPANY, INC.

Heartsong Presents
P.O. Box 719
1810 Barbour Drive
Uhrichsville, OH 44683
(614) 922-6045
FAX: (614) 922-5948

Vice President Editorial: Stephen Reginald

Acquisitions Editor: Rebecca Germany

Media Type/Titles per Year: Paperback, 48+

Submissions Policies

Send synopsis and three or four random chapters. New authors are encouraged to send submissions. Unsolicited manuscripts are OK, as are unagented manuscripts. Simultaneous submissions are OK. Agents may call. Usual response time is 3 months.

Pay Rate

Average advance is $500; average royalties are 10% of net.

Actively Seeking

Historical   45,000–50,000 words
Contemporary   45,000–50,000 words
All of our books are Christian.

Heartsong Writer's Guidelines

The Basics: All manuscripts in the Heartsong Presents inspirational line should have a conservative, evangelical, Christian world view. Manuscripts that do not reflect this position will be returned to the author(s).

Specifics: Heartsong Presents will consider contemporary and historical manuscripts of 45,000–50,000 words. A historical manuscript, for our purposes, is any time period covering the years prior to and during World War II. A contemporary manuscript would be any time period after or post World War II, although strictly speaking, we would probably not consider a manuscript set in the 1950s as contemporary. Since all of the contemporaries we have published thus far have been set in the 1990s, your best bet for acceptance is the present time period.

Things to Consider: The underlying theme in all of our romances is the belief that a true and honest faith in God is the foundation for any romantic relationship. Although we are not looking for "sermons in novel form," the importance and need for a personal relationship with Jesus Christ should be apparent.

Our readers are primarily women who consider themselves born again Christians. One of the reasons they choose Heartsong Presents books over other reading material is because our books confirm their values and beliefs. As a writer/editor, you must take this into consideration.

Things to Avoid: Avoid the truly controversial. Although conflict is important for any storyline, certain matters should be avoided at all costs. Stay away from language that could be considered foul. Avoid euphemisms like heck or darn. To many of our readers these words are substitutes for profanity, and in their minds as bad, or worse. Main characters should be Christians (or Christians by the end of the book) and should act accordingly. They need not be "saints," but their actions should be consistent with Christian teaching.

The hero and the heroine should not be divorced. This is acceptable for secondary and non-Christian characters. The idea of divorce and remarriage is a problem for most of our readers. Most of our readers also find a woman as pastor, or even assistant pastor, unbiblical. If your heroine is a pastor or youth pastor, etc., we will not consider your manuscript.

While drinking is unacceptable for Christian characters, for non-Christians this conflict can be explored. In handling drinking in your novel, it is important that the reader understand that this behavior is not acceptable. Exceptions, such as may be found in historical novels, will be evaluated individually. The same is true for dancing.

Avoid controversial doctrinal issues. We will not list these (there are too many); however, if you keep in mind that we are appealing to a broad range of Christian evangelical readers, we believe you will be on the right track. Controversial items to steer clear of include Spirit baptism, water baptism (meaning of), time of Spirit baptism, time of water baptism, gifts of the Spirit (e.g. tongues), end times (setting dates), Lord's Supper (ordinance vs. sacrament), women's ordination, Christian perfection, transferring qualities of Jesus or Mary to heroes/heroines.

Physical tension between characters should not be overdone. Do not be overly descriptive when describing how characters feel when kissing, embracing, and so on. Characters, especially women characters, should be modestly dressed. They should never appear outside their bedrooms in nightgowns, underwear, and other private garments. No matter how innocent some of this may seem, we will edit questionable scenes out of manuscripts.

Summary: One particular biblical message should be threaded throughout if possible. This can be presented through many different characters, through symbols, and so on. The main element of the books is the romance and to that end characters must be perceived as appealing and capable of finding each other attractive. Conflict within the relationship will draw hero and heroine closer and involve readers more personally.

Few would doubt the breathless appeal of a love story, but a Christian love story combines the elements of enchantment and inspiration to produce a tale that is unforgettable.

How to Submit
If you believe that you have an inspirational romance that would fit Heartsong Presents guidelines, please send a summary of the story along with three to four randomly selected chapters to our Editorial Department.

Computer Preparation of Manuscripts: If you will be typing your manuscript on a computer, it would save us a great deal of time if you send us the manuscript on disks along with a printout. This simplifies production and prevents errors in typesetting. This can only be done if you have an IBM or IBM-compatible computer using an MS-DOS operating system (no Apples). The word processing program you use generally doesn't matter.

If your manuscript has already been typed into your computer, do the following: 1. Print out the manuscript (double-spaced). 2. Label disks with your name and the correct order of the disks. 3. Enclose in your cover letter the brand of computer you used and the name and version of your word processing program. 4. package everything carefully, by using disk mailers or protecting disks with heavy cardboard. Mail the disks together with the manuscript to avoid mixups.

If you haven't typed in the manuscript yet, do the following: 1. *As* you type, only hit RETURN at the end of a paragraph, never at the end of a line. Let the computer wrap the text itself until you reach the end of a paragraph, then use one RETURN to indicate a new paragraph. 2. Use no tabs, no indents, no centering, no flush right, no boldface, no italics. 3. You may use underlines to indicate italics. 4. Single space the manuscript. 5. Use the number 1 rather than the letter l for the number one. 6. Be sure to include dedications and/or acknowledgements on disk. 7. The result will look terrible to you! When you print it out, everything will be flush left. This is exactly what we want. 8. Print out the manuscript, then follow the directions listed above for labeling and mailing. This is not the natural way to type, but you'll get used to it after a page or two and find the typing goes much faster. If you want, you can indicate on the manuscript such things as sub-heads, extracts, etc. Manuscripts typed like this zip right into our computer and come out just right. Thanks for your help.

(Note from *Romance Writer's Pink Pages:* This flush left printout format may be unacceptable to other publishers. FYI, cover price is $4.95, about 186 pages. Mass-market format. Read *Drums of Shelomoh* to get a feel for what the HP editors are buying.)

BERKLEY
(See PUTNAM BERKLEY PUBLISHING GROUP and ACE BOOKS.)

BETHANY HOUSE
11300 Hampshire Avenue, South
Minneapolis, MN 55438
(612) 829-2500
FAX: (612) 829-2768

Acquisitions Editor: Carol A. Johnson, Editorial Director

(Did not fill out the questionnaire in time for this edition, but did send writer's guidelines.)

Bethany House Writer's Guidelines

We are happy to share these guidelines with you, but they come with this note of caution: We have discovered that the publishing commitments we already have made to Bethany House Publishers' authors and to other writers whom we have commissioned make it very unlikely that there will be room in our publishing program in the foreseeable future for additional projects.

Bethany House is an evangelical publisher of books in a broad range of categories, and the leading publisher of religious fiction (besides Bible Study References, Personal Growth Books, Devotionals, Contemporary Issues, and Marriage and Family Principles Books). We are seeking a series of fictional historical novels for adults and children that offer a strong and clear spiritual truth. The following are some of the fiction categories in our list.

Prairie Romance: Our bestsellers in this category are the Janette Oke novels. Attempting to actually copy her style is not likely to work, but we will consider other manuscripts in the general category (such as the "Starlight Trilogy" series by Marian Wells).

Historical Fiction: This category includes stories in a historical setting, such those in the following series: "Stonewycke" by Michael Phillips and Judith Pella, "Zion Chronicles" by Bodie Thoene, and "House of Winslow" by Gilbert Morris.

Young Adult Fiction: See the "Cedar River Daydreams" series by Judy Baer for examples of style, etc.

Juvenile Fiction: See "Mandie" and "An American Adventure" series.

We do not publish formula romance, but are instead looking for:

1. An intriguing, well-written story with strong characterization, and complex and colorful description.
2. One main scriptural teaching, skillfully incorporated into the story without being preachy or too obscure.
3. Historical/geographical/social accuracy without sacrificing plot or characterization.
4. A romantic relationship that usually is not essential to the resolution of the plot. The work should portray the true

meaning of love—commitment and responsibility, rather than only the emotional and physical attraction.

5. Series possibilities with same characters or historical setting.
6. Adult manuscripts should be 60,000 words or longer.

HOW TO SUBMIT
Send a synopsis and three sample chapters. (Keep your original.) Manuscript must be typed, double-spaced. Photocopies and quality dot matrix are acceptable. Include a brief description of your qualifications. Compare your book with other Christian novels (e.g., my book is like title/author/brief description, but is different because . . . ") SASE is required for return of your material. Address submissions to the Editorial Dept. Response in 2–9 weeks. Sorry, we do not provide critiques.

Once a contracted manuscript satisfies our editorial requirements, we assume all costs of production and distribution . . . The author receives a royalty for each book sold, the rate being comparable to that paid by other publishers.

Our books are promoted through our trade catalog, dealer mailings, and ads in bookseller's journals and leading Christian magazines. Bookstore sales are by a nationwide network of sales representatives, by major American and Canadian distributors, and by distributors in over 20 foreign countries.

BOOKS IN MOTION AUDIOBOOKS
9212 E. Montgomery #501
Spokane, WA 99206
(509) 922-1646
FAX: (509) 922-1445

Acquisitions Editor: Gary D. Challender, President

Media Type/Titles per Year: Audiocassette books, 120

Submissions Policies

It is not necessary to query first. Send synopsis and sample chapters, but don't send the complete manuscript until it is requested. New authors are encouraged to send submissions. Unagented manuscripts are OK, but not unsolicited manuscripts. Simultaneous submissions are permitted. No calls from agents, please. Response time is "slow."

Pay Rate

No advance. Average royalty rate is 10%. Audiobooks are normally published about 6 months after acceptance.

Actively Seeking

Historical	30,000–120,000 words
Contemporary	30,000–120,000 words
Action Adventure	30,000–120,000 words

Our romances are conservative.

Editor's Wish List

Well written, moderately intellectual, minimum of profanity, full of mystery, suspense, action and adventure, with a minimum of sex. As few characters as possible and a solid plot.

Turn-offs/Taboos

Unnecessary profanity, gratuitous sex.

Tips

The listener *must* be hooked in the first chapter. We record the entire story—no abridgements.

COGSWELL
(See listing in Chapter 8, Non-Book Markets.)

DARE TO DREAM BOOKS

5062 S. 108th Street, #112
Omaha, NE 68137
(402) 455-4946

Acquisitions Editor: Tony McCawley

Media Type/Titles per Year: Paperback, 8

Submissions Policies

Don't query first. Send synopsis and first three chapters, but not the whole manuscript, unless it is requested. New authors are encouraged to send submissions. Unsolicited, unagented, and simultaneous submissions are all OK. Agents may call. Usual response time is 4–8 weeks. See Writer's Guidelines for additional information.

Pay Rate

Average up front payment is $1,500 plus an average royalty of fifty cents per book. Books are normally published about six months after acceptance.

Actively Seeking

Historical	50,000 words, no preferred time period, but prefer U.S. settings
Contemporary	50,000 words, prefer characters with desirably unique circumstances
Mainstream	50,000 words
Mystery/Suspense	50,000 words
Time Travel	50,000 words

Dare to Dream Books are sensual.

Tips

Main character has only one lover, and no past lover is introduced into the story. We attempt to personalize all characters within the book, the exception being we don't always personalize the antagonist characters. Thus, we like novels with ten or fewer characters to be personalized.

Editor's Wish List

Main characters are very appealing role model type people. Whatever it is that our main characters do or accomplish, it must be so extremely exciting or fun that a potential purchaser wants to "put" themselves or their friend or loved one as a personalized character in that book.

Turn-offs/Taboos

1. Main character is an author writing a novel.
2. Main characters are extremely traumatized or die in the book.

Dare to Dream Writer's Guidelines

Dare to Dream Books is a 21st century publisher, and we're taking a leap into the future style of novel publishing. It's an approach in which every novel we print is personalized.

We customize our books with names and personal information as provided by each purchaser of a novel. No two novels will be the same. However, the basic story and plot within the novel will remain intact. The character's names and descriptions will be changed to reflect the personal information provided by the purchaser of the book.

A personalized approach has been used in publishing children's books, new and more affordable technologies now make it possible to publish full length novels in this personalized fashion. We at Dare to Dream Books feel this may revolutionize the way in which many novels are sold and published.

Dare to Dream Books is now accepting manuscripts of exciting novels. We like keeping our readers up late at night, till they've read the last page of the last chapter. The following is an outline of the type of novel that is of interest to us:

We like contemporary stories in which the main characters are CEOs of large corporations, powerful government officials, movie stars, superstar sports figures, etc. We are very picky about what our main protagonists accomplish in our books. We demand that they perform in a very big or unique way that would have massive appeal to a potential purchaser.

The main character is a respectable person that anyone could fantasize being. They must be monogamous, and no past lover is a character in the book.

The only family relatives introduced into the book are the main character's husband or wife, and their parents and/or grandparents. Preferably no other characters are family related. Not everybody has a sister, brother, or nephew. Our books must be somewhat generic in that the story and characters within can apply to the broad general public.

Nothing dealing with race, religion, or any topic that is controversial. We want happy stories with happy endings.

Third person narrative only.

Romance, comedy, mystery, adventure, old western, sports, and science fiction are all welcome.

Adult books of about 50,000 to 60,000 words, teen books of about 40,000 words, and children's (fourth grade and up) of about 20,000 words.

Interested authors whose finished novel(s) fit our qualifications may send the first three chapters of their printed manuscript. Enclose an SASE of sufficient postage if you would like your manuscript returned. No query necessary. Mail your submissions to the address above, to the attention of Tony McCawley. We normally respond within 8 weeks upon receiving your manuscript.

Authors of novels published by Dare to Dream Books will be compensated by $1,500 up front payment for adult, $1,000 for teen, and $750 for children's. This is not an advance on royalties. This payment is totally separate from royalty pay, and has nothing to do with how many copies of your novel are sold. There is a 50¢ royalty for each copy printed, beginning with the very first copy. Your up front payment check will be promptly mailed upon our receiving a signed contract from you. Royalty checks will be paid on a semiannual basis. Payments will be made on or around March 15 and September 15, for all copies printed in the prior 6 months.

The author retains copyrights to their manuscript. We require exclusive publishing rights to your manuscript for three years. The contract automatically renews every year thereafter, unless either party chooses not to renew.

Normally it will take about 6 months for a newly accepted novel to reach the market. Our first novels may take longer. Dare to Dream Books would like to begin advertising and have our sales catalogs printed mid 1995.

DAW BOOKS
375 Hudson Street
New York, NY 10014

No romance novels, per se—only publishing Science Fiction and Fantasy. (Romance may be a subplot.) Submissions should be addressed to Peter Stampfel.

DEL REY
201 E. 50th Street
New York, NY 10022

Acquisitions Editor: Shelly Shapiro

(Did not respond.)

DUTTON/SIGNET (FORMERLY NAL)

Topaz, Signet, Onyx
375 Hudson Street
New York, NY 10014
(212) 366-2000
FAX: (212) 366-2888

Acquisitions Editors: Audrey LaFehr, Executive Editor; Jeanmarie LeMense, Senior Editor; Hilary Ross, Senior Editor

Media Type/Titles per Year: Paperback and hardcover, 1,000+ (company-wide)

Submissions Policies

Agents, please query first by phone. Send complete manuscripts after query. New authors are encouraged, but should only send submissions through agents or personal contacts. No unsolicited manuscripts. Simultaneous submissions are permitted, as long as author/agent calls *before accepting* any offer. Usual response time is 4–6 weeks.

Pay Rate

No such thing as an average advance. Average royalties are 6–8%. Books are normally published about 14 months after acceptance.

Actively Seeking

Historicals   100,000 words
Contemporary
Mainstream
Ethnic
Suspense
Big thrillers with female protagonists
(For supernatural stories submit to Dreamspun)
Our romances range from sweet to spicy to sensual to sexy.

Tips

Read the new authors who are selling well. Read outside the genre. Study good writing. Read current titles to see what editors are buying. *Winter's Heat* and *Summer's Storm* by Denise Domning, for example, are the first two medievals of a Topaz quartet.

Editor's Wish List

Great writing, something fresh and extraordinary about the plot, believable characters who are *not* ordinary.

M. EVANS & COMPANY

216 E. 49th Street
New York, NY 10017-1502

(Did not respond.)

FAWCETT/JUNIPER/IVY

(See BALLANTINE BOOKS. Editor Barbara Dicks.)

GOODFELLOW PRESS, INC.

7710 196 Avenue, N.E.
Redmond, WA 98053
(206) 868-7323

Acquisitions Editors: Sharon Plowman, Sally Astridge, Kay Morison, C. J. Wycoff, Pamela R. Goodfellow

Media Type/Titles per Year: Quality trade paperback, 12–24

Submissions Policies

Query first. New authors are encouraged to send submissions. Unagented manuscripts are OK, as are simultaneous submissions. Agents may call. Usual response time is 3 months. See Writer's Guidelines for additional information.

Pay Rate

Average advances not disclosed. Average royalty is 6–10%. Books are normally published about 8–12 months after acceptance.

Tips

Write the book you want to write—forget rules and guidelines. Polish to the best of your ability and find an editor who believes in you and your project.

Editor's Wish List

Quality polishing, grounded characters, and well-written scenes.

Turn-offs/Taboos

Goodfellow Press looks at all/any projects. We have no taboo subjects except where characters, good or evil, are not treated in a respectful manner. Goodfellow Press is an advocate of humanity.

Goodfellow Press Writer's Guidelines

The intention of Goodfellow Press is to publish fiction that is smooth and seamless, peopled with characters who will live beyond the confines of the book covers. To that end characters should always be believable. We appreciate diversity in interests and background. By the time you finish sketching your principle players, you should know what makes them laugh and cry, their ambitions, their fears. Today's reader is more likely to appreciate a heroine who can stand up for herself.

It is our contention that a well-crafted book is founded in five major scenes: the first meeting, which is self-explanatory; the sensual scene; a fight or confrontation scene, in which the characters display other aspects of their personalities; a tender moment, when we see that they respect each other; and the resolution, which should leave the reader wanting more. We place considerable emphasis on the importance of respect.

Conflict is integral to every book that will sustain the reader's interest. This conflict may be physical or emotional, internal or external, but it will always arise from the unique interaction of your hero and heroine.

The target length of a manuscript should be 85,000 to 120,000 words. However, your work need not be completed to send a proposal. Please submit detailed character profiles of the protagonists, one polished major scene, as outlined above, and synopses of the other four scenes. Please enclose an SASE, and send submissions to the attention of Pamela R. Goodfellow at the above address.

(Note from *Romance Writer's Pink Pages:* Goodfellow Press publishes romances in quality trade paperback, which is the same cover size as *Romance Writer's Pink Pages.* Bookstores do not practice cover stripping of quality trade paperbacks, as with mass market books. Goodfellow has long-lasting bindings with heavier paper than mass-market, and print is easy to read. We use recycled paper and soy-based inks. Cover price is about $7.99. GP covers have tasteful mainstream-type illustrations, not "clichés." To see what GP editors are buying, read *Hedge of Thorns* by Sally Ash and *This Time* by Mary Sharon Plowman.)

HARCOURT BRACE TRADE DIVISION
Odyssey Paperbacks, Voyager, Jane Yolen Books, Gulliver Books
525 B Street, Suite 1900
San Diego, CA 92101-4495
(619) 699-6810
FAX: (619) 699-6777

Media Type/Titles per Year: Paperback, 75+

Submissions Policies
AGENTS ONLY. Send query letter/manuscript. No phone calls.

Tips
Read current releases to determine what editors are buying. Unsolicited manuscripts are not being accepted by Gulliver Books or Jane Yolen Books. Address envelope Attn: Manuscript Submissions at above address. For picture books, submit entire manuscript; for novels and longer nonfiction, send an outline/synopsis and two to four sample chapters. No simultaneous submissions. Do not send originals. For artwork, separate black and white and color art into two distinctive selections. All samples should be rendered in one style, no larger than legal size. Ten to fifteen samples are sufficient. SASE a must for responses. Art samples should be addressed Attn: Art Director at the above address. We prefer samples with children and animals, all rendered in one style. Response time is about 4–8 weeks.

HARLEQUIN AMERICAN ROMANCE
300 E. 42nd Street, 6th Floor
New York, NY 10017
(212) 682-6080

Acquisitions Editors: Debra Matteucci, Senior Editor and Editorial Coordinator; Mary Ellen O'Neill, Associate Editor; Julianne Moore, Associate Editor; Bonnie Crisalli, Assistant Editor

Media Type/Titles per Year: Paperback, 48

Submissions Policies

Please query first. Published authors may send synopsis and sample chapters at initial contact. Send the complete manuscript if we request it. Published authors may send complete manuscript. We prefer no unsolicited manuscripts. New authors are encouraged. Unagented manuscripts are OK. Absolutely no simultaneous submissions. Agents may call. Usual response time is about 12 weeks. See Writer's Guidelines for additional information.

Pay Rate

Advances and royalty rates are confidential. Publishing schedule not disclosed.

Actively Seeking

Contemporary spicy to sensual romances of 70,000 words.
Preferred topics are marriages of convenience, secret babies,
    mail-order mates, classic hooks with a twist.
Fast-paced, upbeat stories only.
No melodrama please.

Tips

Familiarize yourself with the series—read the books and the guidelines.
    Editor's Favorite Romance Novel is *A Wish . . . and a Kiss* by Margaret St. George.

Editor's Wish List

A clean, crisp writing style, and a well-focused, well-written plot. A fresh approach to classic romantic conflicts and hooks.

Turn-offs/Taboos

Wordy, overly narrative and descriptive manuscripts. Characters with a lot of emotional baggage, written by authors who appear to have read too many self-help books. Manuscripts with a plot focused on any particular political issue/cause.

Harlequin American Romance Writer's Guidelines

These novels are bold, brash, exciting romantic adventures that tap the pulse of America.

Plot: Show, don't tell! We want lively, upbeat, action-packed material that is not problem-based or introspective. Aim for fictional credibility, not realism, looking to your imagination and dreams for inspiration, rather than to everyday life. Above all, we look for a strong hook or premise: the conflicts that grow out of this initial situation lead to a big "payoff," in which everything comes out right in the end. The focus is tightly on the relationship between the hero and heroine, so subplotting is kept to a minimum.

Hero: He's not the boy next door! This 90s man is a man no woman can resist. Whether he's rough around the edges, or earthy, or slick and sophisticated, every reader will fall in love with him. He is so dynamic, he may even be the focus in a hero-led story.

Heroine: She is sassy, strong, and full of spunk, and never wimps out to her hero. In fact, this highly contemporary woman occasionally bests him, which fuels his desire, as so few women have.

Setting: Anywhere.

Sensuality: These stories are intense, passionate, and filled with *all* the emotions of falling in love.

TIPS ON PROFESSIONAL PRESENTATION

Title Page: The author's real name and address, the title and the approximate number of words should be stated. Also indicate pseudonym if applicable.

Manuscripts: Should be typewritten, error-free, double-spaced, and on one side of the paper only. Leave a 1 1/4" margin around the entire page, and be sure to use a good grade of white bond.

In the upper right-hand corner of each manuscript page, include the author's last name and the page number (e.g., Smith - 12, Smith - 13, etc.).

If you use a computer printer, the print must be letter-quality. Dot matrix is unacceptable.

Be sure to make a complete copy for your files.

Do not bind or staple your manuscript. Use an envelope or box large enough to contain your manuscript flat.

HARLEQUIN HISTORICALS

300 E. 42nd Street, 6th Floor
New York, NY 10017
(212) 682-6080
FAX: (212) 682-4539

Senior Editor: Tracy Farrell

Media Type/Titles per Year: Paperback, 48

Submissions Policies

Query first or synopsis and sample chapters from published writers. First time authors, please send the complete manuscript. Include a cover letter with information about your writing experience. New authors are encouraged. Unsolicited manuscripts and unagented manuscripts are OK, but not simultaneous submissions. Agents may call. Usual response time is 6–8 weeks.

Pay Rate

Advances vary. Average royalty is in-house information. Books are normally published about 18 months after acceptance.

Actively Seeking

Historicals   over 95,000 words, before 1900,
no preferred settings

Editor's Wish List

A good story with well-developed characters and a strong emotional feel.

Harlequin Historicals Writer's Guidelines

The primary element of the Harlequin Historical novel is romance. The story should focus on the heroine and how her love for one man changes her life forever. For this reason, it is important that you have an appealing and believable hero and heroine, and that the relationship that builds between them is a compelling one. The conflicts they must overcome and the situations they face can be as varied as the setting, but there must be romantic tension—some spark between your hero and heroine that keeps your reader interested.

Heroine: The reader's main identification is with the heroine. Therefore, it is imperative that she be a sympathetic character. She should be strong willed, independent, and intelligent, but she should also be emotionally vulnerable. Though she is in circumstances unfamiliar to readers, she should react in a familiar and believable way.

Hero: The hero must be appealing. He should be strong, both physically and emotionally, though he should not be physically dominating or abusive.

Plot: The historical setting—time period, place, culture and events—is vital and should be well developed and authentic. But it is your characters who must make history come alive. Your writing should be rich and evocative. Be sure to avoid textbook and travelogue descriptions. Your story will be much more meaningful if your readers see your historical setting as it is seen and experienced by the characters about whom they care.

We're looking for stories with depth and complexity; sub-plots and secondary characters are important. The overall tone may vary. Some stories may be more humorous and entertaining; some more adventurous; others more dramatic or emotional.

Sex: Your story should be sensual, though the level of sensuality will be determined by your characters. The emphasis should be not only on the sensual, but on the emotional aspect of your hero and heroine's relationship.

Setting, Time Frame: We rarely accept books set after 1900. We are looking primarily for books set in North America, England, and France between 1700 and 1900 A.D. We are flexible, however, and will consider most periods and settings.

HARLEQUIN INTRIGUE
300 E. 42nd Street, 6th Floor
New York, NY 10017
(212) 682-6080

Acquisitions Editors: Debra Matteucci, Senior Editor and Editorial Coordinator; Mary Ellen O'Neill, Associate Editor; Julianne Moore, Associate Editor; Bonnie Crisalli, Assistant Editor

Media Type/Titles per Year: Paperback, 48

Submissions Policies

Please query first. Published authors may send synopsis and sample chapters at initial contact. Send the complete manuscript if we request it after you query. Published authors may send complete manuscript. We prefer no unsolicited manuscripts. New authors are encouraged. Unagented manuscripts are OK. Absolutely no simultaneous submissions. Agents may call. Usual response time is about 12 weeks.

Pay Rate

Advances and royalty rates are confidential. Publishing schedule not disclosed.

Actively Seeking

Mystery/Suspense   75,000 words
Open to paranormal and time travel elements.
Intrigues range from spicy to sensual.

Tips

Familiarize yourself with the series—read the books and the guidelines.

Editor's Favorite Intrigue Romance Novel is *What Child is This?* by Rebecca York.

Editor's Wish List

A manuscript with a perfect mix of romance and suspense. Intrigues are at their best when the romance and intrigue intertwine and play off of each other. Classic romantic conflicts with intrigue and suspense folded in.

Turn-offs/Taboos

Manuscripts about witchcraft or devil worship. Excessive violence on-page. Treasure hunts and stories involving actors, movies, or the theater are not taboo but generally do not sell.

Harlequin Intrigue Writer's Guidelines

These taut, edge-of-the-seat contemporary romantic suspense tales of intrigue and desire are so involving you can barely believe they're told in a mere 70,000–75,000 words! Kidnappings, the stalkings of personal ad applicants, or fiancés wrongly accused of murdering their brides-to-be are examples of storylines we love most. Whether a murder mystery, psychological suspense, thriller, espionage tale, or a woman in jeopardy, the love story must be inextricably bound to the mystery at the level of the novel's premise. Gripping plots twist, turn, and thicken, ever leading toward a final resolution where all loose ends are neatly tied up, while shared dangers lead right to shared passions. Our hero and heroine's lives are on the line and so are their hearts.

Plot: Both the romantic element and the intrigue or mystery must be introduced early in the book and be maintained throughout. During this complex, realistic, quickly paced story, the romantic relationship must grow and develop as the mystery develops. Provide enough red herrings and twists and turns of plot and to avoid a predictable ending; tie up all clues.

Sensuality: Intrigues involve the highest stakes imaginable—life and death; thus passion is naturally heightened. In an atmosphere of suspense and danger, the desire for love is strong. The emotions of love—and the physical expression of it—are more important than ever.

Hero: Whether he works in tandem with the heroine, or whether his presence in her life plants "seeds of doubt," he's active in the resolution of the story and rarely separated from the woman he's coming to love. He's sexy, mature, and of any nationality.

Heroine: Like the hero, she possesses knowledge and skills that will contribute to the final resolution of the mystery. Mature, and of any nationality, this woman is an equal partner.

Setting: The story may be set anywhere in the world. An interesting setting may serve to enhance the mystery, suspense, and romance.

HARLEQUIN PRESENTS
(See MILLS & BOON.)

HARLEQUIN PRIVILEGES
(See MIRA BOOKS.)

HARLEQUIN REGENCY
225 Duncan Mill Road
Don Mills, Ontario M3B 3K9
CANADA
(416) 445-5860
FAX: (416) 445-8655

Acquistions Editor: Paula Eykelhof, Regency Editor

Media Type/Titles per Year: Paperback, 4

Submissions Policies

Unpublished authors should query first. Don't forget Canadian postage on SASE, or enclose International Reply Coupons. Published authors may send synopsis and three chapters or query and full manuscript. New authors are encouraged. Unagented manuscripts are OK. No simultaneous or electronic submissions. Agents may call. Usual response time to a query is 6–8 weeks on queries (if possible), 4–6 months on manuscripts.

Pay Rate

Advances are variable. Royalties are standard. Books are normally published about 24 months after acceptance.

Actively Seeking

Regency romances   50,000–60,000 words, set between 1811 and 1820 in England, Scotland, etc.

Tips

Read current Regency books to see what the editor is buying.

HARLEQUIN ROMANCE
(See MILLS & BOON.)

HARLEQUIN SUPERROMANCE
225 Duncan Mill Road
Don Mills, Ontario M3B 3K9
CANADA
(416) 445-5860
FAX: (416) 445-8655

Acquisitions Editor: Paula Eykelhof, Senior Editor

Media Type: Paperback

Submissions Policies

Query first or query and full manuscript. SASE must have Canadian postage or International Reply Coupons. New authors are encouraged. Unagented manuscripts are OK. No simultaneous or electronic submissions. Agents may call. Usual response time to a query is 6–8 weeks on queries (if possible), 4–6 months on manuscripts.

Pay Rate

Advances are variable. Royalties are standard. Books are normally published about 24 months after acceptance.

Actively Seeking

Contemporary Mainstream
    Romance   85,000 words

Tips

Read current Superromance books to see what the editor is buying.

Harlequin Superromance Writer's Guidelines

Provocative, passionate, contemporary stories that celebrate life and love!

The only requirements for today's Superromance novels are page-turning stories of 85,000 words strongly focused on believable heroines and heroes. Their quest to find love and to shape their lives must take place in a dynamic plot and conclude with a satisfying resolution.

The characters should define and drive the plot through their actions and reactions. The heroines are intelligent, warm, and motivated women with a clear idea of their own strengths. Whether they desire to make their mark in the world or in the fabric of the family, their values reflect their dreams of true partnership. The heroes are sexy, passionate men. Their strengths may emanate from their knowledge of who they are and what they want from life.

For the rest, let your imagination be your guide . . . .

The choice of components can be diverse, as can the level of sensuality and scope of time frame. And the locale? Anywhere from Paris, Texas, to Paris, France. The tone is up to you. It can range from comic to intense, provocative to emotional. You can choose multiple or central points of view. Whatever the story elements and issues, they should be explored within the context of the central romance. The range of possibilities is endless: fun, moving, exciting, heartwarming, sensuous, imaginative, humorous, innovative, suspenseful, or adventurous.

Your responsibility is to summon your own distinctive voice to harness the kind of story that only you can tell.

The *essence* of Superromance lies in emotionally compelling characterization.

The *excitement* of Superromance vibrates in the scope, variety, and complexity of the story you want to tell.

The *excellence* of Superromance is its authors.

HARLEQUIN TEMPTATION
225 Duncan Mill Road
Don Mills, Ontario M3B 3K9
CANADA
(416) 445-5860
FAX: (416) 445-8655

Acquisitions Editor: Birgit Davis-Todd, Senior Editor

Media Type: Paperback

Submissions Policies

Query first with SASE (Canadian stamps or IRC's) or query and full manuscript. New authors are encouraged. Unagented manuscripts are OK. No simultaneous or electronic submissions. Agents may call. Usual response time to a query is 6–8 weeks on queries (if possible), 4–6 months on manuscripts.

Pay Rate

Advances are variable. Royalties are standard. Books are normally published about 24 months after acceptance.

Actively Seeking
Contemporary Romance   60,000 words

Tips

Read current Temptation books to see what the editors are buying.

Harelquin Temptation Writer's Guidelines

Sensuous, bold, sometimes controversial, Harlequin Temptation stories focus on contemporary relationships between adults. These fast-paced books may be humorous, topical, adventurous or glitzy, but at heart, they are pure romantic fantasy.

Heroine: She is an attractive North American woman age 23 or older, who may be single, divorced, or married. A contemporary woman of the nineties, the heroine is involved with a career she cares about and has a strong sense of her own individuality. She'd like to meet the right partner in order to fulfill herself emotionally and sexually and to make a lifetime commitment.

Hero: He is compatible in age to the heroine and may or may not be North American. Handsome, successful at his job, he's sexier than any man has a right to be! The Temptation hero should be strong, compelling, larger than life, and play an active role in the story. Beyond that, he may be characterized as a self-assured, strong-willed, new alpha man, the unpredictable bad boy or the highly appealing and sometimes humorous nineties man.

Plot: In a Harlequin Temptation novel, the plot is the developing romance between the hero and heroine. The plot must be fresh, original, complex enough to sustain 60,000 words and action-oriented rather than introspective. A good blend of sparkling dialogue and minimal narrative is important. Strong, believable conflicts are also essential in a Temptation. Secondary characters and minor subplots may be included to enrich the plot. Temptation books cover a range of plots: humorous, fantasy (both romantic and sexual), topical, adventurous, emotional, glitz and glamor. Truly innovative stories may be designated "Editor's Choice."

Sex: Temptation is Harlequin's boldest, most sensuous series, mirroring the lives of contemporary women. A high level of sexual tension is required throughout the story in order to maintain the necessary edge and arousing feel. The hero and heroine should have several sensuous encounters and should consummate their relationship at a point appropriate to the plot. Love scenes should be highly erotic, realistic and fun, but above all, emotional. Let your imagination be your guide!

Setting: The stories are written from a North American viewpoint, but may take place anywhere in the world. A feeling for the setting should be subtly evoked without overwhelming the romance.

HARPERCOLLINS/HARPER PERENNIAL
10 E. 53rd Street
New York, NY 10022
(212) 207-7000

Acquisitions Editor: Tracy Behar, Editorial Manager

Media Type/Titles per Year: Paperback and hardcover, 600

Submissions Policies

AGENTS ONLY. Agents must query first. Do not send unsolicited manuscripts. Agents may not call. No electronic submissions. Simultaneous submissions are OK. New authors are encouraged, but only through agents. Usual response time is 6–8 weeks.

Pay Rate

Advances and royalty figures are confidential. Books are normally published about 9–12 months after acceptance.

Actively Seeking
Women's Fiction
Ethnic
Gothic
Mystery/Suspense

Tips

For best results, submit only through an established, qualified literary agent.

Editor's Wish List

Looking for women's fiction that is "literary fiction," not genre-type romances.

HARPER PAPERBACKS
Monogram Imprint
10 E. 53rd Street
New York, NY 10022
(212) 207-7752
FAX: (212) 207-7759

Acquisitions Editor: Carolyn Marino, Executive Editor

Media Type/Titles per Year: Paperback, 78+

Submissions Policies

Authors may send synopsis and sample chapters. New authors are encouraged. Unsolicited manuscripts and unagented manuscripts are OK. Simultaneous submissions are OK, but please inform us. New authors are encouraged. Agents may call. Usual response time is 2 months.

Pay Rate

Not reported.

Actively Seeking
Historical
Time Travel

Tips

The best way to learn what we're looking for is to read our books. Harper Monogram does not have formal guidelines, but offers the following tips.

Harper Monogram is a new imprint of HarperPaperbacks that was launched in September 1992. In addition to authors with proven track records, we have room for new talent and love to build writers for the future. Many Monogram authors go on to write multiple books for us.

There's no formula for a Monogram romance. We publish historicals and contemporaries, including time travel, historicals with American and European settings, romantic suspense, and much more. Though we're open to practically any kind of romance, we're especially eager for strong historicals.

We're also starting to publish Regency romances on a regular basis and welcome submissions in this area. Works should follow the traditional Regency format, with an emphasis on strong characterization. Length should be 60,000–75,000 words.

If you've read some Monograms, you'll see how original and varied they are. Many of our romances are traditional American or British historicals, including those set in the West, but we also publish more detailed and descriptive historical novels. In the contemporary area, we've had great success with relationship-centered family stories.

One thing we always look for is strong emotional tension between the hero and heroine. The romantic relationship should be the heart of the book, though of course an exciting plot, lively dialogue, and believeable characters are also crucial. Humor can work well, too.

If you have an idea for a romance we might like, please send us a brief synopsis and three sample chapters. Please be sure to include an SASE with your submission. We promise to respond promptly.

Some of our major authors include Constance O'Banyon, Debbie Macomber, and Susan Wiggs. The best way to learn more about us is to check out your local bookstore and pick up a Monogram.

HEARTSONG PRESENTS
(See BARBOUR AND COMPANY, INC.)

HERALD PRESS
616 Walnut Avenue
Scottdale, PA 15683

Comments: Herald Press did not respond by filling out a questionnaire, but they did send guidelines. Herald Press is a division of Mennonite Publishing House, Inc. Their goals include publishing books which are consistent with Anabaptist/Mennonite traditions and scriptural teachings (recommend NSRV of the Bible). They invite book proposals from Christian authors.

Herald Press Writer's Guidelines

Send to the book editor:

1. A one page summary of your book.
2. A one or two sentence summary of each chapter.
3. The first chapter and one other; doublespaced, separated pages. Note which Bible version was used.

4. Statement of the significance of the book.

5. Description of targeted audience.

6. Brief statement of educational, publishing, religious, professional, etc. involvements.

7. SASE. (Response time is about 2 months.)

KENSINGTON PUBLISHING, INC.

Zebra/Pinnacle/Kensington/Z-Fave
850 Third Avenue
New York, NY 10022
(212) 407-1500
FAX: (212) 935-0699

Executive Editors: Ann LaFarge (Zebra); Sarah Gallick (Kensington); Paul Dinas (Pinnacle); Elise Donner (Z-Fave)

Senior Editors: Denise Little, Beth Lieberman, Monica Harris, Pat Lo Brutto, Jennifer Sawyer, Tracey Bernstein, John Scognamiglio

Media Type/Titles per Year: Paperback and Kensington hardcover, 480

Submissions Policies

Don't query. Send synopsis and complete manuscripts with SASE. New authors are encouraged. Unsolicited manuscripts are OK. Simultaneous submissions are OK, as are unagented manuscripts. Agents may call, but it is better to send material, with a good submission letter. Response time varies.

Actively Seeking

Arabesque—Multicultural romances. 115,000 words. Submit to Monica Harris at Pinnacle.

Contemporary—115,000 words

Denise Little Presents—Very, very special books by authors who
are already published but new to Zebra. Submissions to
Denise Little.

Erotic Women's Fiction—Plans for this line are on hold.

Futuristic—Submissions to Beth Leiberman, Senior Editor. No
tip sheets.

Glitz and Glamor—Contemporary romance of 115,000 words,
depicting life and love of the rich and beautiful. Submissions
to John Scognomiglio, Senior Editor.

Gothic—This line was discontinued.

Heartfire—This historical line was discontinued.

Historicals—Sometimes overinventoried, but always accept-
ing especially good manuscripts of about 115,000 words.
No formulaic misunderstandings between the hero and
heroine. Submissions to Senior Editors: Beth Leiberman,
Tracy Bernstein, Jennifer Sawyer, or Monica Harris
(Pinnacle).

Horror—Scary tales, two per month, of about 100,000 words,
especially vampire fiction, for both Zebra and Pinnacle.
Submissions to any editor.

Magnolia Road—Antebellum South historicals of 120,000 words.
Setting is real or fictional plantation. Read *Southern Fire* by
Ashley Snow.

Mainstream—115,000 words.

Married Couples Romances—Send query letter/synopsis to
Jennifer Sawyer at Pinnacle.

Mystery—These are cozy mysteries, not hard-boiled. Prefer a series with repeating characters. Recommend you read Carol
Finch's mysteries. Full list until 1995. Will look at whole
manuscript and synopsis. 75,000 words (series only).

Paranormal—Submissions to Beth Leiberman, Senior Editor. No
tip sheets. 115,000 words.

Regency—Seeking completed Regencies of 60,000–75,000 words
or 120,000+ in an English setting. Query first with cover

letter, 3–5 page synopsis, and sample chapters. Submit to Jennifer Sawyer, Senior Editor at Pinnacle.

Romantic Suspense/Woman in Jeopardy—Modern-day Gothics of 100,000 words that feature the heroine in terrible danger.

Saga—Hard to buy and publish. Not recommended at this time.

Sleuth Series—Female amateur detective teams up with the hero to solve mysteries in all time periods. Send complete manuscripts with synopsis and short proposals of books planned for a series.

Time Travel—Submissions go to Beth Leiberman, Senior Editor. No tip sheets. 115,000 words.

To Love Again—A woman strives to carve out a new life for herself in this line of reality-based novels targeted at readers 45 years of age and older. There should be a complete renewal and a satisfying ending. 110,000 words. Send synopsis/query to Ann LaFarge, Senior Editor.

True Crime—Paul Dinas is Pinnacle's Executive Editor of this line of eight true crime novels per month.

Westerns—Senior Editor Patrick LoBrutto is seeking big western novels of the *Lonesome Dove* type.

Woman in Jeopardy—100,000 words. Submissions to any Pinnacle editor.

Women's Fiction—Contemporary stories of 100,000+ words.

Z-Fave—This is the Young Adult division of Kensington Books, which includes a Mystery series with a sealed final chapter (send for guidelines), Girlfriends (multicultural teen books), Scream/Nightmare Club (kid/teen horror novels), and Middle Readers (6–9 year olds with varied subjects). Submissions should go to Elise Donner, Senior Editor.

Tips

Write from the heart. Don't listen to what others tell you about what does or doesn't work. Push the envelope.

For tip sheet, send SASE to any Zebra editor.

Comments

There are four divisions of Kensington Publishing:

Kensington Hardcovers (15–20 per year)—only top selling paper-
    back authors should submit here

Zebra Books, which include historicals and Denise Little Presents

Pinnacle, which includes varied single title releases, both fiction
    and nonfiction

Z-Fave, for kids/teen/YA.

KEYSTONE ENTERTAINMENT
(See Chapter 6, Romancing the Hollywood Connection.)

LEISURE BOOKS/DORCHESTER PUBLISHING
Leisure Books and Love Spell
276 Fifth Avenue, Room 1008
New York, NY 10001
(212) 725-8811
FAX: (212) 532-1054
TELEX: 238198

Acquisitions Editors: Kim Mattson, Sharon Morey

Media Type/Titles per Year: Paperback, 100

Submissions Policies

Send synopsis and sample chapters. SASE a must. New authors
are encouraged. Unsolicited manuscripts are OK, as are unagented manuscripts. No simultaneous submissions. Agents may

call. Usual response time is 2 months. See Writer's Guidelines for additional information.

Pay Rate

Average advance is negotiable. Average royalty not given. Books are normally published about 12 months after acceptance.

Actively Seeking

Historicals	115,000 words
Time travel	100,000 words
Paranormal	100,000 words
Futuristic Romance	100,000 words

Leisure Books and Lovespell Books are sensual.

Tips

Read a romance before you try to write one. Do your research— read the guidelines that follow. Keep writing and rewriting (practice makes perfect).

Editor's Wish List

A plot that is interesting and well thought through; strong conflict between the hero and heroine; something new and interesting.

Leisure and Love Spell Writer's Guidelines

The following are the *only* categories of original fiction we are currently acquiring.

Historical Romance: Sensual romances with strong plots and carefully thought-out characterizations. Spunky heroine whose love for the hero never wavers; he's the only one she makes love with and she's as passionate as he, although he may have to instruct her in the ways of love, since she's almost invariably untouched before she falls in love with the hero. Hero is often arrogant, overbearing; heroine often can't stand him at first, but discovers that beneath the surface lies a tender, virile, and experienced lover. It helps if both the heroine and hero have a sense of humor—a certain amount of wit leavens the heavy-breathing passion. Hero and heroine are constantly separated by misunderstandings, jealousy, Acts of God, war, etc., but in the end they overcome the barriers between them and live happily ever after.

We don't want a heroine who sleeps around, or a hero who's sadistic, although if there's a villain or villainess, he or she can be as nasty as possible.

Historical background, details of costume, etc,. should be accurate; however, we don't want endless descriptions of battles, the political climate of the period, or a treatise on contemporary social history. Our readers are more interested in the trials, tribulations, and love life of the heroine than in how many men Napoleon lost at the battle of Waterloo.

Futuristic Romance: Futuristic Romances contain all the elements of Historical Romances—beautiful heroine, dashing hero, some conflict that separates them, a happy ending, etc.—but they are set in lavish lands on distant worlds. Avoid science-fiction-type hardware, technology, etc.

Time Travel Romance: A modern-day hero or heroine goes back in time and falls in love. Traditional guidelines for Historical Romances apply. The challenge here is to maintain credibility during the transition between the present and the past. The fun is seeing history and another way of life through the eyes of someone from our own time. The conflict and resolution of the romance arise from the fact that the hero and heroine are from different eras.

Beware of a lot of philosophizing about fate, the meaning of time, and how the past affects the present. No time machines please.

How to Submit
Please query or submit synopsis and first three chapters only—no complete manuscripts unless specifically requested. Include a

stamped, self-addressed envelope (of sufficient size) for possible return of proposal or manuscript. No material will be returned without SASE.

Synopsis, sample chapters (and manuscript if requested) must be typed, double-spaced. Word processors are OK, but letter quality only. Please retain a copy of all material sent in case the original gets lost in the mail.

For a free catalogue of Leisure Books, please send a self-addressed stamped envelope (#10) to the above address.

MILLS & BOON/HARLEQUIN ENTERPRISES LTD.

Harlequin Presents (NA)
Eton House, 18-24 Paradise Road
Richmond, Surrey, TW9 1SR
UNITED KINGDOM
(081) 948-0444
FAX: (081) 940–5899

Acquisitions Editors: Address to The Editorial Department

Media Type/Titles per Year: Paperback, 72

Submissions Policies

Query with a one or two page synopsis. If you wish, you may also send the first 10 pages of your manuscript.

Pay Rate

Confidential.

Actively Seeking
Contemporary Romance   50,000–55,000 words

Harlequin Presents Writer's Guidelines

This series features exciting, emotionally-intense stories. A passionate love affair is played out between a spirited, independent woman and a strong, charismatic man.

Heroine: She is the character with whom readers want to identify. Therefore, she should be modern, intriguing, and definitely her own woman. Her age and professional status will vary according to her role in the plot; she may or may not be career-oriented. She can be sexually experienced—but of course, she is never promiscuous.

Hero: He is usually older than the heroine and often more worldly and sexually experienced—though again, he should not be promiscuous. He is the man with whom all our readers want to fall in love, so make him attractive, powerful, and compelling—and never the boy next door. He's a real fantasy figure!

Plot: The story line doesn't need to be complicated, and the emphasis should be on the developing romance. A good romantic plot contains conflict—enough to sustain the whole novel—plenty of emotion, but also a generous dose of escapist fantasy. While grounded in reality, your story should not dwell on harsh or downbeat elements; this is the romance of a lifetime, and the reader wants to be left feeling good.

Sex: Our readers have come to expect a high degree of sensual tension from this series. But remember that clinical descriptions have no place in a Presents story, so the focus must very definitely be on the emotional relationship that develops between your hero and heroine. Above all, the art of sexual description is to include as much as you personally feel comfortable with.

Setting: Our audience is global, and craves backgrounds that can be interpreted as magical and glamorous by any culture. Be sure that the setting you choose is integral to the mood and the plot, and as accurate as you can make it; mistakes can spoil the reader's enjoyment of a book. Fictional backgrounds are acceptable, but they must feel real.

Minor Characters: These should be included in your story only when they serve to enhance the central romance, or if they move the action along. A cast of characters will crowd out the all-important central romance, and sap its intensity.

Style: This should reflect the powerful emotions that your hero and heroine feel for each other—which means plenty of dialogue and a fast pace. The reader should be left in no doubt that, by the last page, these two are made for each other!

MILLS & BOON/HARLEQUIN ENTERPRISES LTD.

Harlequin Romances (NA)
Eton House, 18-24 Paradise Road
Richmond, Surrey, TW9 1SR
UNITED KINGDOM
(081) 948-0444
FAX: (081) 940–5899

Acquisitions Editors: Address Submissions to Editorial Department

Media Type/Titles per Year: Paperback, 72

Submissions Policies

Query plus synopsis of one to two pages. If you wish, you may also submit the first 10 pages of your manuscript.

Pay Rate

Confidential

Actively Seeking
Contemporary   50,000–55,000 words

Harlequin Romance Writer's Guidelines

This series features traditional, heartwarming romances between attractive, sympathetic women and strong, confident, successful men.

Heroine: She will probably be aged between 17–28 and a little younger than the hero. She must be likable, warm, proud, and hold traditional moral values. She may be a career woman or a homemaker, but she enjoys what she is doing; she isn't just sitting around waiting for Mr. Right!

Hero: He is somewhere between his late twenties and mid-thirties. Compellingly attractive, dynamic, and with natural authority, he's definitely not Mr. Average; his status reflects what he's achieved in life. But he needs to balance strength with gentleness.

Plot: A story simply told can form the basis of a most successful romance, if it is woven around a strong sustainable conflict and also some happy times. Your plot can contain original themes, but they should be retold with sincerity, freshness, and originality.

Sensuality: Though lovemaking can take place between your hero and heroine, explicit sexual description does not belong in a Harlequin Romance. The accent is on warm, tender emotion, rather than on the physical.

Setting: These must be romantic and magical, and have appeal for an international audience. Be sure to be accurate with your research and keep background details to a minimum—although the Romance reader likes to visit faraway places, she does not want a travelogue.

Minor Characters: These should be included in your novel only when they serve to enhance and highlight the central romance, or if they move along the plot. Secondary characters should never feature so much that they overshadow the hero and heroine and their all-important romance. If in doubt, leave them out!

Style: Exchanges between the hero and heroine are the lifeblood of a Harlequin Romance, so use plenty of them to convey feelings and developments in the plot. Humor plays a part in the Romance series, but it should never be at the expense of either your hero or heroine, so farce or slapstick is probably best left to other genres. Try to look for the funny side of relationships—the humor that can always be found even in the most challenging emotional situations.

MILLS & BOON/HARLEQUIN ENTERPRISES LTD.
Legacy of Love and Love on Call
Eton House, 18-24 Paradise Road
Richmond, Surrey, TW9 1SR
UNITED KINGDOM
(081) 948-0444
FAX: (081) 940–5899

Acquisitions Editors: Tessa Shapcott, Senior Editor; Alison Coles, Senior Editor; Sheila Hodgson, Senior Editor; Elizabeth Johnson, Senior Editor; Sue Curran, Editor; Sam Bell, Editor; Cath Laing, Editor; Gillian Green, Editor; Karin Stoecker, Editorial Director

Media Type/Titles per Year: Paperback, 240+

Submissions Policies

Query first with SASE. Return postage should be in International Reply Coupons (IRCs) for submissions from outside England. OK to send synopsis and sample chapters, or the complete manuscript. New authors are encouraged to send submissions.

Although unsolicited and unagented manuscripts are OK, simultaneous submissions are not acceptable. Agents may telephone. Usual response time is 8 weeks.

Pay Rate

Average advances and average royalties are confidential. Books are normally published about 24 months after acceptance.

Actively Seeking

Historical	75,000–85,000 words, prefer Regency period
Contemporary	50,000–55,000 words
Medical Romances	50,000–55,000 words

Our romances include a range of sensuality. See Legacy of Love and Love on Call guidelines below.

Legacy of Love Writer's Guidelines

We are looking for born story tellers with a love of history who have the ability to bring a period vividly to life, and create characters who involve and absorb the reader from page one.

It goes without saying that the historical detail should be well researched and accurate. You should incorporate enough detail to allow the reader to almost taste and smell the life and times, but do not convey so many facts that the reader feels lectured to and overwhelmed. Don't forget to add "color," such as clothing descriptions, necessities of daily life, facial expressions, tones of voice, and body language/movement, all of which create a visual picture.

There must be a good central plot, into which the actual historical happenings of people may or may not be woven (obviously this decision will depend upon the type and complexity of your main plot). Bear in mind that the general reader is not likely to be familiar with the more esoteric periods, and if you choose to tackle something particularly unusual, its acceptance will depend very much on your ability as a writer. For instance, Oriental, Ancient Egyptian, and similar settings are difficult to convey successfully. As well as British history, you might also consider European history.

Look at and incorporate aspects other than royalty, such as politics, industry, the arts (examples might be the gem trade of Amsterdam, the money markets of Bruges, or the arts sponsored by Lorenzo the Magnificent, Borgia). All of these can be used as the background of good plots.

Whatever character type you choose to create, it is important that the heroine be lovable and the hero charismatic. Please note that actual historical characters do not usually feature as either the hero or the heroine of storylines. Should you wish to do this, you should first discuss your ideas with the editor. Strive to create fully rounded characters within the conventions of your chosen period. Look at all layers and facets of human behavior—mental, physical, emotional—and use tension as well as rapport.

Alongside these aspects you must employ a variety of pace, so that with the highs and lows of emotion the reader is enthralled, rather than bored by a telegraphed plot and flat, even writing.

The development of the hero and heroine and the growth of their relationship (which must have a happy ending) are vital strands threaded through the plot. Your characters are the means by which the reader is emotionally caught up into the story and should never be neglected.

There is no bar to the use of sensuality if it seems appropriate to both characters and plot, but we are not in the market for "bodice-rippers." The emotional responses are as important as any physical response, because the emotions generate the overall romantic aura. Avoid long absences by the hero and, when he is with the heroine, they must communicate.

Good use of dialogue can lift a book out of the crows, but aim for clarity and simplicity. Regency dialogue is a specific skill (beware of overusing slang expressions), but with other periods it is generally wiser not to overdo period language (Medieval, for example). The effect can create a stiff and stilted feeling that holds your characters at a distance from the reader. It is always better to allow your characters to "show" themselves through dialogue, rather than have you explain them through narrative.

Your skill and enthusiasm, warmth, and conviction, will imbue a book with that extra special "something."

Love on Call Writer's Guidelines

The theme for this category is present day medicine. Hospital settings are, of course, welcome, but the tree of medicine has many branches—general practice, district nursing, private nursing, physiotherapy, occupational therapy, and specific divisions such as children's, handicapped, and casualty, to name but a few. The range of medical themes to be featured and explored within these settings is just as wide.

Of equal importance is the development of the central relationship and the depth of characterization. The practical details of medicine are interesting, but ultimately it is the people who bring a story to life. Subsidiary characters (such as patients) are obviously valuable, but the hero and heroine should carry the story. They are the driving force within your plot, and your success (or lack of it) in developing the chemistry and charisma between them can make or break an otherwise satisfactory story.

More specifically, both hero and heroine will be medical professionals. As such, they will usually work together. If they don't, then opportunities for contact should be wide. Their communication, through action and dialogue, should naturally involve rapport as well as conflict, humor as well as sadness. The world of medicine is rich in human drama—both joys and tragedies—and the emotional ranges should be *fully* explored. If appropriate to both character and plot, the incorporation of sensuality is welcomed—but not if used gratuitously.

Above all, there should be a happy balance between all strands of the plot, between the love affair and the medical detail, and between the characters and their emotions. This way, we can absorb and involve readers into hours of good reading.

Medical Detail: Ideally, you will have a thorough knowledge of up-to-date methods and use of drugs. However, convincing use of medical detail in storylines can also come from a lively interest in the subject matter combined with adequate research skills. When creating their medical scenarios, our authors draw upon "secondary" medical experience, gained from talking to family, friends, and other contacts working in the medical profession, and "desk research," using information from medical journals and textbooks. Your local reference library may subscribe to medical journals that can aid you in researching your book.

You may also try consulting the following books: *The Concise Medical Dictionary, Watson's Medical Surgical Nursing and Related Physiology, Family Medical Adviser,* and *Reader's Digest.*

(Note from *Romance Writer's Pink Pages:* When writing for Mills & Boon, *The London Almanac* and *Anglophile's Dictionary* are two indispensible references. For info, contact Kristine Hughes, 6774 Buckingham Ct., Naples, FL 33942.)

MIRA BOOKS
225 Duncan Mill Road
Don Mills, Ontario M3B 3K9
CANADA
(416) 445-5860
FAX: (416) 445-8655

Acquisitions Editor: Dianne Moggy, Senior Editor and Editorial Coordinator

Media Type/Titles per Year: Initially, the majority of MIRA Books will be produced in paperback—although some titles will be hardcover, and a few will be both! 12 titles per year are planned at this time.

Submissions Policies

Please send a query letter with SASE at initial contact. A query letter will get you the quickest response. Remember, Canadian postage or IRCs will be required for return postage.

Pay Rate

Advances and royalty rates were not disclosed, but are "competitive."

Actively Seeking
Women's Fiction   100,000+ words

Tips

Editor Dianne Moggy emphasized that this is a very difficult market to break into. Although MIRA Books has contracted with one previously unpublished author, initially the editorial department hopes to attract well-established historical authors, as well as contemporary authors with proven track records. Later, when the program expands, other authors, both established and new-but-talented, will be added to the list.

Editor's Wish List

Really entertaining reads. We are primarily looking for contemporary novels, although we will be doing some historicals, too. MIRA Books is looking for contemporary and historical dramas, family sagas, romantic suspense, glitz and glamor—almost anything goes in women's fiction. The romantic element doesn't have to be the central focus of the story, and stories don't necessarily have to have the traditional happily ever after ending, with the hero and heroine riding off into the sunset together, but they must have "satisfying" endings.

Turn-Offs/Taboos
None.

A Letter from the VP of Retail Marketing and Editorial

Dear Romance Authors,

Harlequin Enterprises Ltd. is delighted to announce the most exciting publishing event of 1994—the launch of MIRA Books, an imprint destined to become "the brightest star in women's fiction." Starting this October (1994), MIRA will offer outstanding, single-title fiction from the world's most popular authors.

The name defines our new imprint: "mira" means "wonderful" in Latin. And mira is also one of the brightest stars in the southern constellation.

Initially, MIRA will publish one lead title per month. The frontlist will also be supported by an active backlist program. The number of original titles offered each month will increase as the program develops.

MIRA Books will publish novels of 100,000 words plus, ranging from contemporary and historical dramas to romantic suspense, political intrigue, and family sagas. Our October launch title is *Slow Burn,* an original novel by the *New York Times* bestselling author Heather Graham Pozzessere. Heather is an award-winning author who has over ten million books in print around the world.

In addition to Heather Graham Pozzessere, upcoming authors with books slated for publication include Barbara Bretton, Penny Jordan, Elise Title, JoAnn Ross, and Jasmine Cresswell. Also in the MIRA list are eagerly-awaited reprints by Sandra Brown, Jayne Ann Krentz, and many others.

From the outset, MIRA Books' promotion and advertising campaigns will emphasize author recognition. Our message to the consumer and trade alike is that we are publishing outstanding books by outstanding authors for outstanding readers.

You will find that contracts and packaging are fully competitive with the marketplace both domestically and internationally. The plan is for every title to be published in North America, France, Germany, Italy, and the United Kingdom, and later in many global regions.

In choosing manuscripts for MIRA Books, we have only one requirement: each book should be a compelling story that will satisfy readers worldwide. If you have questions, please contact Dianne Moggy, Senior Editor and Editorial Coordinator at 416-445-5860, extension 268. We look forward to hearing from you!

> Sincerely,
> Candy Lee
> Vice President, Retail
> Marketing and Editorial

(Note from *Romance Writer's Pink Pages:* The planned Harlequin Privileges line evolved into MIRA Books, a totally new program. Do not address any queries to the Privileges line, which no longer exists.)

THE NAIAD PRESS, INC.
P.O. Box 10543
Tallahassee, FL 32302
(904) 539-5965
FAX: (904) 539-9731

CEO: Barbara Grier

Acquisitions Editor: Katherine V. Forrest

Media Type/Titles per Year: Paperback, 24

Submissions Policies

Always query first, no exceptions! Send synopsis or precis; no sample chapters. Never send complete unsolicited manuscripts. We have readers around the U.S. and we delegate. New authors receive much encouragement. No simultaneous submissions. No discussions of manuscripts with agented authors. Electronic submissions are OK. Usual response time to queries is 7 days maximum. Often 48 hours is enough. SASE is a must. See Writer's Guidelines for additional information.

Pay Rate

Advances are very flexible. We use standard 15% recovery contract 99% of the time. Books are normally published 18–24 months after acceptance.

Actively Seeking

Historical	52,000 words, time period is variable
Contemporary	52,000 words, various topics
Women's Fiction	52,000 words, all topics
Mystery/Suspense	52,000 words, variable topics

Tips

All of our books are lesbian. Romances range from conservative to sweet to spicy to sensual to sexy. These are books by, for, and about lesbians, but we work in every sub-genre. Self-serving authors win the prize. Know the books already done by the company. Think slim and well-done books. Our advantages are that we keep books in print permanently and we market to a very hungry and fast growing audience. Reader loyalty to name of author is incredible and increases rapidly with each book. We like to publish a new book by an author every 18–22 months, sometimes more often than that.

Editor's Wish List

As is probably true of all publishers, we want books that will do as well as some of our historical best sellers. Books such as *Curious Wine* by Katherine V. Forrest, *Horizon of the Heart* by Shelly Smith, and *Cherished Love* and *To Love Again* by Evelyn Kennedy are examples of the contemporary love stories we publish.

Turn-offs/Taboos

Any sado-masochistic involvement is a definite no-no. Our readers tend to be conservative, at least in terms of adventurous sexuality. No ménage à trois, no multiple girlfriends. Characters need to end up happily "wed" to the girl of their dreams. The same requirements apply to lesbian romances as apply to heterosexual romances.

Naiad Press Writer's Guidelines

As you read this please consider that we receive about 750 inquiries and/or wholly unsolicited novel length manuscripts each year. Following the suggestions below is your only chance of consideration or acceptance.

    Any unsolicited manuscript received without a stamped return mailer will be discarded. There are no exceptions.

1. Write (type) a single page letter on 8½″ × 11″ paper. Ask permission to submit a manuscript by identifying it by type (i.e., novel, nonfiction, etc.). Give a single brief statement that inclues your name, address, and day and evening telephone number (and the times you can best be reached as well). Please do not include any personal information that is not directly related to your ability to create a book suitable for publication (a possible exception to this would be your movement status). Always include all publication information.

2. We accept no simultaneous query letters or submissions. If you are interested in being published by the oldest, largest, and by far the most successful of the lesbian publishing companies, please direct your query to us. If not, please do not include us in a list of possible publishers.

3. Do not submit poetry or poetry queries. Do not submit queries on autobiography unless your name is a household word in the lesbian movement.

4. Include a one page precis of the plot. No testimonials about its quality from your friends, your family, or any famous writer are helpful to your cause, and may, in fact be damaging. Include the word count of the book (the best way to do this is to count the words on 10 pages, divide by 10, and multiply by the number of pages in the manuscript). Be sure your precis includes the conclusion of your book, as well as what happens, why, when, where, and how. We will not read any novel in excess of 60,000 words. There are no exceptions. Manuscripts in the 52,000 word length range are considered ideal.

5. Be very sure before you begin the process that you have completed your end of the book. It has been written (and rewritten and revised and rewritten), neatly typed (consult many writing manuals in any public library), and edited by you to the limit of your ability. It is a finished product from your point of view.

6. Know our works. Be sure you understand that you are submitting a manuscript to The Naiad Press and that our publishing program is unique. We do books by, for, and about lesbians and we emphasize popular fiction sub-genres, such as romances, mysteries, spy themes, ghost themes, fantasy and science fiction, erotica, westerns, regencies.

If your book is to be read, you will be instructed on how and whom it is to be sent. Good luck!

NAL/DUTTON PUBLISHING, A DIVISION OF PENGUIN USA
(See DUTTON SIGNET.)

NEW VICTORIA PUBLISHERS
P.O. Box 27
Norwich, VT 05055
(802) 649-5297

Acquisitions Editor: Claudia Lamperti

Vice President: Beth Dingman

Media Type/Titles per Year: Paperback, 6

Submissions Policies
Query first. If requested, send synopsis and sample chapters. Do not send complete manuscripts. New authors are encouraged. Unsolicited manuscripts are OK. Unagented manuscripts are preferred. Simultaneous submissions are OK, if the editor is made aware of the other submissions. Claudia Lamperti prefers to read hard copy, but is happy if it is on disk as well. Prefers letter queries from agents. Usual response time is 2–3 weeks.

Pay Rate
We usually do not give advances. Average royalty is 10%. Books are normally published 12–18 months after acceptance.

Actively Seeking
Historical
Contemporary
Women's Fiction
Ethnic
Mystery
(Word counts not specified)

Tips
New Victoria Romances are sensual. No heterosexual sex. Be sure to enclose SASE or we will not respond. See Writer's Guidelines section for more information.

Editor's Wish List

Strong female protagonists, preferably lesbian. Complex exciting plot. Intelligent writing.

Turnoffs/Taboos

We are not interested in heterosexual sex, pornography, or typical, cliché-ridden romances (even if it is lesbian).

New Victoria Writer's Guidelines

New Victoria is interested in fiction with a clear narrative story line. We are primarily looking for well-written novels using mystery, adventure, romance, science fiction (speculative fiction), or fantasy as a vehicle to discuss important issues in lesbian and feminist lifestyles and relationships. Stories should contain strong, active protagonists and transformation in the characters. Humor and passion are always vital ingredients.

We will consider stories with strong feminist heroines, "woman-identified" journeys into and out of the self, as long as the material investigates real alternatives or models for living.

In addition we are interested in well-researched lesbian and feminist history or biography that would appeal to a general as well as an academic audience.

Please send your inquiry with an outline and a sample chapter. If you would like it returned, enclose a self-addressed stamped envelope.

NOTABLE NOVELLETTES
(See COGSWELL PUBLISHING in Chapter 8, Non-Book Markets.)

POCKET/POCKETSTAR
Simon & Schuster Consumer Group
1230 Avenue of the Americas
New York, NY 10020
(212) 698-7000

Acquisitions Editors: Claire Zion, Executive Editor; Ruth Ashby, Young Adult Senior Editor; Carolyn Tolley, Romance Editor

Media Type/Titles per Year: Paperback, hardcover, 300+

Submissions Policies

AGENTS ONLY. Query first to appropriate editor with detailed synopsis and sample chapters. SASE for return of material.

Actively Seeking
Contemporary Romance
Historical Romance
Archway—young adult novels, especially romantic comedies and
    suspense/thrillers of 35,000 words or 160 pages.

Pocket Books Writer's Guidelines are free with an SASE sent to the above address.

PUTNAM BERKLEY PUBLISHING GROUP
200 Madison Avenue
New York, NY 10016
(212) 951-8830
FAX: (212) 545-8917

Acquisitions Editors: Judith Stern, Senior Editor; Hillary Cige, Senior Editor; Melinda Metz, Editor; Gail Fortune, Associate Editor

Media Type: Paperback and hardcover

Submissions Policies

Query first with SASE. Only send synopsis and sample chapters after querying. The complete manuscript should not be sent unless requested. New authors are encouraged to send submissions. Query first rather than send unsolicited or unagented manuscripts. Simultaneous submissions are OK, but please tell us in your letter. Usual response time is 6 weeks. Agents may call. See Writer's Guidelines for additional information.

Pay Rate

Books are normally published about 9–12 months after acceptance. Average advance varies. Average royalty not disclosed.

Actively Seeking

Historical	90,000–100,000 words
Contemporary	90,000–100,000 words
Ethnic	90,000–100,000 words
Mainstream	word count is open
Mystery/Suspense	60,000–90,000 words
Time Travel	90,000–100,000 words
Paranormal	90,000–100,000 words

Our romances are sweet, spicy, sensual or sexy.

Berkley Writer's Guidelines

At Putnam Berkley Group we pride ourselves on the diversity of our women's fiction program. With our three imprints (Berkley, Jove, Diamond) we publish a minimum of four romances a month. Our novels range from historical romance, contemporary mainstream, and romantic suspense to women-in-jeopardy, prehistory novels, and Regencies.

We are open to publishing historical romances in any setting and time period. In addition, we have these ongoing lines: Homespun, Wildflower, and Tea Rose. Homespun romances are sweeter historical romances set in nineteenth century American small towns and countrysides. The focus of these books is the love story but they also feature family relationships. All Homespuns have a child worked into the storyline. Wildflower romances are highly sensual romances set in the American West and capture the ruggedness of the frontier during the late 1800s. Presently we are also looking for strong sensual romances, taking place between the years of 1300 and 1900 in any setting.

We prefer agented submissions, but if you are unagented, please send a query letter to a specific editor including a brief description of the plot, previously published works, if applicable, as well as any other pertinent information. Please allow 8 weeks for replies to manuscripts requested by an editor.

ST. MARTIN'S PRESS

Mass Market Division
175 Fifth Avenue
New York, NY 10010
(212) 674-5151
FAX: (212) 677-7456

Acquisitions Editors: Jennifer Weis, Senior Editor; Christey Bahn, Editor

Media Type/Titles per Year: Paperback

Submissions Policies

Query or send synopsis and sample chapters. Send completed manuscripts if available. Agents may call. New authors are encouraged. Unagented and unsolicited manuscripts are OK. No electronic submissions. Usual response time is 3 months.

Pay Rate

Advances and royalties are confidential. Books are normally published about 9 months after the acceptance of a full manuscript.

Actively Seeking

Contemporary   75,000–100,000 words (submit synopsis and sample chapters to Editor Christey Bahn)

Historical
Women's Fiction
Suspense
Woman-in-Jeopardy

SERVANT PUBLICATIONS

Vine Books
P.O. Box 8617, 840 Airport Boulevard
Ann Arbor, MI 48107
(313) 761-8505
FAX: (313) 761-1577

Acquisitions Editors: Ann Spangler, Beth Feia

Media Type/Titles per Year: Paperback, 40

Submissions Policies

Query first with SASE. OK to send synopsis and sample chapters, but not the complete manuscript, unless it has been requested. New authors are only encouraged if they have published in magazines and journals. No unsolicited or unagented manuscripts.

Simultaneous submissions are OK. Agents, please write instead of calling. Usual response time is 60–90 days.

Pay Rate

Average advances and royalty rate was not given. Books are normally published about twelve months after acceptance.

Actively Seeking
Historical	80,000–120,000 words, prefer 17th–19th century rural America
Religious Romance	80,000–120,000 words

Editor's Wish List

Manuscripts must be from a Christian point of view, displaying Judeo-Christian values, but not preachy. Historical research must be accurate; fast-moving plots work best. Strong writing ability a must.

SILHOUETTE DESIRE
300 East 42nd Street
New York, NY 10017
(212) 682-6080

Acquisitions Editors: Lucia Macro, Senior Editor (all Silhouette editors can acquire for all Silhouette lines)

Media Type/Titles per Year: Paperback, 72

Submissions Policies

First time authors must query first. Only send synopsis, sample chapters, or complete manuscripts if requested. New authors are encouraged, but query first. Prefer no unsolicited manuscripts. Unagented manuscripts are OK, but query first. No simultaneous submissions. Usual response time is 3 months. Agents may call. See Writer's Guidelines for additional information.

Pay Rate

Average advance was not disclosed. Publishing schedule not given.

Actively Seeking
Contemporary   55,000–60,000 words
Silhouette Desires are sensual.

Tips

Remember that these are emotional love stories. They can be serious or humorous, but they must have an emotional pull, a strong hook, and a salable concept. For example, no one cares if you save an old inn, but they care if you save a baby. Read and see what is selling!

Editor's Wish List

A well-written story with excellent dialogue, fast pacing, and an emotional hook to draw in readers. Editor's favorite romance novel is *Rebecca* by Daphne DuMaurier.

Turn-offs/Taboos

Heroes who are in the arts; land development ("save the inn!"); politicians; sports figures; travelog.

Silhouette General Writer's Guidelines

Thank you for your interest in Silhouette Books. We do not accept unsolicited complete or partial manuscripts, but ask instead that you submit a query letter. Please indicate what Silhouette series you think your project is appropriate for, if it is completed, what you think makes it special, and previous publishing experience (if any). Also include a synopsis of your story that gives a clear idea of both your plot and characters and is no more than two single-spaced pages. A self-addressed envelope (SASE) will ensure a reply. Should your manuscript be requested, please note the following information:

1. We publish only category romances! Please do not submit any other type of fiction or nonfiction. Your manuscript should take place in the present and be told in the third person, primarily from the heroine's point of view. However, the hero's perspective may be used to enhance tension, plot, or character development.

2. All material should be the author's own original work. Stories that contain scenes or plot lines that bear a striking resemblance to previously published work are in breach of copyright law and are not acceptable.

3. All material must be typewritten, double-spaced and on 8½″ × 11″ paper. No disk submissions. Computer generated material is acceptable, but must be letter quality, and pages must be separated. Any material received on computer reams will be returned without evaluation.

4. *Do not* submit your material bound in binders, boxes, or containers of any kind. Secure material with rubber bands. You may enclose a postcard if you wish acknowledgment of receipt. Cover sheets must have your complete name, address, and phone number. Each page should be numbered sequentially thereafter. Please type your name and title in the upper left-hand corner of each page. If we ask to see your manuscript, please include a complete synopsis.

5. All material will be evaluated in as timely a fashion as volume allows. Please do not call regarding the status of your manuscript. You will be notified by mail as soon as your work has been reviewed.

6. *Do not send any material that is being considered by another publisher.*

7. A literary agent is not required in order to submit.

8. You must enclose a SASE with all submissions to ensure the return of your material. Please send an envelope large enough to accommodate your work and adequate postage.

9. This sheet is designed as a guide to aid you in understanding our requirements and standards. However, there is no better way to determine what we are looking for then reading our books.

(All Silhouette Writer's Guidelines are copyrighted property of Silhouette Books, and are reprinted here with permission.)

Silhouette Desire Writer's Guidelines

Sensual, believable, and compelling, these books are written for today's woman. Innocent or experienced, the heroine is someone we identify with; the hero is irresistible. The conflict should be an emotional one, springing naturally from the unique characters you've chosen. The focus is on the developing relationship, set in a believable plot. The characters don't have to be married to make love, but lovemaking is never taken lightly. Secondary characters and subplots must blend with the core story. Innovative new directions in storytelling and fresh approaches to classic romantic plots are welcome.

SILHOUETTE INTIMATE MOMENTS
300 East 42nd Street
New York, NY 10017
(212) 682-6080

Acquisitions Editor: Leslie Wainger, Senior Editor and Editorial Coordinator

Media Type/Titles per Year: Paperback, 72

Submissions Policies

If you have an unsolicited manuscript or are unagented, send a
query letter first. Only send synopsis and sample chapters if requested or if agented. No unsolicited manuscripts. Unagented
manuscripts are OK if we have requested them. No simultaneous
submissions. Usual response time is about 3 months. New authors
are encouraged. Agents may call. See Silhouette General Writer's
Guidelines on pages 165–167 for more information.

Pay Rate

Books are normally published about 18–24 months after acceptance. Average advance and royalty rate was not disclosed.

Actively Seeking
Contemporary romance   80,000–85,000 words
May include elements of mystery/suspense, time travel or para-
      normal.
This is a sensual line.

Tips

Read! Read everything in the line that you can get your hands on,
analyze what works and what doesn't, then write the best book
you can.

Editor's Wish List

Strong characters, a strong story, and lots of compelling emotion.

Turn-offs/Taboos

If you, as a reader, have seen a lot of a particular topic, rest as-
sured that other readers have noticed its frequent appearance as
well, so you'll have to try harder to make any story on that topic
unique. Subjects that seem unpopular include the worlds of theater and the ballet.

Silhouette Intimate Moments Writer's Guidelines

Believable characters swept into a world of larger-than-life romance, such is the magic of Silhouette Intimate Moments. These books offer you the freedom to combine the universally appealing elements of a category romance with the flash and excitement of mainstream fiction. Adventure, suspense, melodrama, glamor— let your imagination be your guide as you blend old and new to create a novel of emotional depth and tantalizing complexity, a novel that explores new directions in romantic fiction, a novel that is quintessentially Intimate Moments.

SILHOUETTE ROMANCE
300 East 42nd Street, 6th Floor
New York, NY 10017
(212) 682-6080
FAX: (212) 682-4539

Acquisitions Editors: Isobel Swift, Editorial Director; Anne Canadeo, Senior Editor

Media Type/Titles per Year: Paperback, 72

Submissions Policies

Query first. Agents may call. New authors are encouraged. No unsolicited manuscripts. Unagented manuscripts are OK, but query first. No simultaneous submissions. No electronic submissions. Usual response time is 6–12 weeks. See Silhouette General Writer's Guidelines on pages 165–167 for additional information.

Pay Rate

Average advance is variable. Standard royalty starts at 6%. Books are normally published about 12–24 months after acceptance.

Actively Seeking
Contemporary Romance   53,000–58,000 words

Tips

Our romances are conservative. Silhouette Romances are contemporary, warm, and dynamic, with a solid base of traditional family values. Stories can be powerfully emotional or humorous and charming, but all must be believable, compelling love stories at heart.

Editor's Wish List

Strong, believable characters and conflict. Emotional, believable *romance*.

Turn-offs/Taboos

Stories must be fresh and contemporary, even when using classic storylines such as marriage of convenience.

Silhouette Romance Writer's Guidelines

Silhouette Romance requires talented authors able to portray modern relationships in the context of romantic love. Although the hero and heroine don't actually make love unless married, sexual tension is a vitally important element. Writers are encouraged to try new twists and creative approaches to this winning formula. Our ultimate goal is to give readers a romance with heightened emotional impact—books that make them laugh or cry, books that touch their hearts.

SILHOUETTE SHADOWS
300 E. 42nd Street
New York, NY 10017
(212) 682-6080

Acquisitions Editor: Leslie Wainger, Senior Editor and Editorial Coordinator

Media Type/Titles per Year: Paperback, 24

Submissions Policies

Authors, send query letter, synopsis and sample chapters, *or* complete manuscript. Agents may call. New authors are encouraged. Unsolicited manuscripts are OK. Unagented manuscripts are OK. No simultaneous submissions. Usual response time is about three months. See Silhouette General Writer's Guidelines on pages 165–167 for additional information.

Pay Rate

Average advance and royalty rate was not disclosed. Books are normally published about 18–24 months after acceptance.

Actively Seeking
Contemporary "dark" romance   70,000–75,000 words, including soft horror and elements of time travel mystery/suspense and paranormal

Shadows novels are sensual.

Tips

Read! Analyze everything you read in the line, the books you like as well as those you don't, then find your own voice and tell your story.

Editor's Wish List

It must be both strongly romantic and "dark," spooky, chilling, "shadowy" (as the title of the line suggests).

Turn-offs/Taboos

None so far, but bear in mind that if the book is too graphically violent, it will be hard to achieve and maintain the necessary level of romance.

Silhouette Shadows Writer's Guidelines

"In an empty house, the air thick with darkness, a woman waits alone. Her heart beats faster as she hears the creaking of the front door, and then a man's voice, soft with menace, call out, asking if anyone is there. Is the threat in his voice for her? Or will the danger turn to passion when he finds her waiting for him? Her heart begins to pound, and the blood runs hot through her veins as she prepares to confront her fate . . . "

We at Silhouette Books invite you to join us as we embark on an exciting new publishing venture, the creation of Silhouette Shadows. These are tales from the dark side of love, designed to keep the reader on the edge of her seat as she, like the heroine, steps into the unknown, risking everything in a search that can lead to the fulfillment of love or the edge of madness—even the possibility of death. Behind every door lies danger, down every curving corridor the embodiment of fear, and even the heart of the man she loves may hide a fatal passion in place of the enduring romance she craves. The possibilities, like your imagination, are limitless.

The heroine is a strong, contemporary woman, capable of confronting and conquering the dangers that threaten her, whether physical or psychological, of the world as we know it or from beyond. She is always a match for the hero as they play out a compelling romance in the midst of a plot that may range from Gothic in tone to a woman in jeopardy story, even incorporating elements of the paranormal and moving into soft horror. The hero may represent—even personify—the dangers she faces, or he may provide support and comfort in the midst of a dark and menacing world.

Always, though, their ending must be a happy one, with lasting romance her reward for triumphing over darkness.

Silhouette Shadows novels are contemporary romances that explore the dark side of love, that send shivers up the spine and make the heart beat faster—both from passion and from fear.

These novels are atmospheric, dark, sensuous in the fullest sense of the word, and always frightening. Black humor and occasional comic relief may play a role, but these are not ghostly romps or spoofs of the genre.

Classic examples that capture the tone and types of stories we envision, even if not the contemporary setting, include Mary Stewart's *Nine Coaches Waiting*, Victoria Holt's *Menfreya in the Morning*, and Daphne DuMaurier's *Rebecca*.

These contemporary romance manuscripts should generally be written in the third person, though first person is acceptable.

SILHOUETTE SPECIAL EDITION
300 E. 42nd Street, 6th Floor
New York, NY 10017
(212) 682-6080

Acquisitions Editor: Tara Gavin, Senior Editor

Media Type/Titles per Year: Paperback, 72

Submissions Policies

Authors, send query letter first plus outline of story. Send synopsis and sample chapters only at editor's request after query letter. Agents may call. New authors are encouraged. No unsolicited manuscripts. Unagented manuscripts are OK, but query first. No simultaneous submissions. No electronic submissions. Usual response time is 6–8 weeks. See Silhouette General Writer's Guidelines on pages 165–167 for additional information.

Pay Rate

Average advance is variable. Standard royalty starts at 6%. Book publishing schedule varies.

Actively Seeking

Contemporary category
75,000 words with a strong focus
on romance; topics vary

Tips

A Silhouette Special Edition has a broad range—sensuality
depends on the author and what works for the story. Read the
line and study the market! Keep in mind who you are writing
for, and what subjects will be meaningful and entertaining to
them.

Editor's Wish List

Our readers look to us to provide stories with a strong focus on
the developing romance. The longer length of the Silhouette
Special Editions offers authors the opportunity to create a more
in-depth characterization and a broader concept, in order to connect with the reader in a unique and meaningful way.

Turn-offs/Taboos

Too much reliance on contrivance, misunderstanding—or the
other woman/other man chestnut.

Silhouette Special Edition Writer's Guidelines

Sophisticated, substantial, and packed with emotion, Special Edition demands writers eager to probe characters deeply, to explore
issues that heighten the drama of living and loving, and to create
compelling romantic plots. Whether the sensuality is sizzling or
subtle, whether the plot is wildly innovative or satisfyingly traditional, the novel's emotional vividness, depth, and dimension
should clearly label it a very special contemporary romance. Subplots are welcome, but must further or parallel the developing romantic relationship in a meaningful way.

THE WRITTEN WORD

Silhouette/Harlequin/Mills & Boon
Silhouette Books
300 E. 42nd Street
New York, NY 10017
    or
Harlequin Books
225 Duncan Mill Road
Don Mills, Ontario M3B 3K9
CANADA

Acquisitions Editors: Melissa Senate, Editor & Special Projects
Coordinator, Silhouette Books; Malle Vallik, Editor, Harlequin
Books

Actively Seeking
Contemporary Romance   50,000 words

Tips

Tone should be very contemporary, fast-paced, fun, flirtatious,
hip, sassy, and upbeat. Storylines can range from zany comedies
to emotional heart-tuggers. Can be sexy, but no requirements.

Turn-offs/Taboos

Paranormal stories are not encouraged.

The Written Word Writer's Guidelines

Silhouette, Harlequin, and Mills & Boon are pleased to announce
this exciting new line, and we're looking for submissions. Short
and sassy, these contemporary novels are about men and women
encountering romance in unexpected ways. What's different
about this line? See the two unique twists below.

1. A celebration of the written word. The story and romance must begin with a form of written communication. Start with a snappy opening using a personal advertisement, a love letter, an invitation, divorce papers, or an on-line computer network—just to name a few of the intriguing possibilities. Hook your readers and let your imagination soar.

2. A celebration of the chase. The story will sweep readers into the character's romantic adventures on the hunt for love. The story doesn't have to focus on a single romance (but it can) and doesn't have to end in marriage, though a satisfying, upbeat ending is required.

For example, a personal ad placed by a heroine may result in several humorous dates with several Mr. No-Way—until Mr. Wonderful is found. Their commitment to each other may be their happy ending. Touch readers' hearts and tickle their funnybones as your characters explore the trials, tribulations, and triumphs of the hunt.

Examples of movies that capture the tone and types of stories we envision—if not exactly the "written communication" thread—include *Working Girl, Crossing Delancy,* and *Green Card.*

Stories should be told in the third person, primarily through the main character's point of view, but multiple points of view are acceptable, if done well.

SINGER MEDIA CORPORATION
Seaview Business Park
1030 Calle Cordillera, Unit #106
San Clemente, CA 92672
(714) 498-7227
FAX: (714) 498-2162

President: Kurt Singer

Acquisitions Editor: Helen J. Lee

Media Type/Titles per Year: Paperback, hardcover, and video, 100+

Submissions Policies

We handle published books and features for the foreign market. Query first by brief letter. Do not send synopses or sample chapters. No new authors. No unsolicited manuscripts. No unagented manuscripts. No simultaneous submissions. Agents may call. Average response time is 2 weeks. See Writer's Guidelines for additional information.

Pay Rate

Average advances of $500–$100,000. Average royalty of 6%–10% Publication is about 12 months after acceptance.

Actively Seeking
Contemporary
Mystery/Suspense
Mainstream
Business
Computer

Tips

Especially interested in reprints of previously published books for which the author holds foreign rights. Also anything new, different, and not run of the mill.

Editor's Wish List

Must already be published.

Turn-offs/Taboos

Pornography, historical romance, anything of local interest only.

Singer Media Corporation Writer's Guidelines

Singer Media Corporation is an internationally oriented syndicate and, as such, we must produce multiple sales by reaching as many places as possible. Much of our income (40–50%) comes from foreign countries where television is limited and people read more. We have been on the international scene for decades and many of our staff have been active by watching the needs and changes for over 50 years.

The problem we face as we review incoming submissions is that the bulk of the material—features, comics, cartoons, books, and manuscripts—deals primarily with the author, interviewer, or artist's locale and its problems, interests, or uniqueness. The submission may be stunning and well presented, but it is of no value to us unless it will hold the readers' interest in such places as Stockholm, Hong Kong, Cape Town, or Sydney. From the standpoint of those who submit material to us, it is clear that the greater the global appeal, the greater the number of sales and renumeration.

We must reject material that:

1. Relies on U.S. statistics.
2. Is filled with local terms or vernacular.
3. Relies on products that are not available in other countries.
4. Has words that rhyme or statements which have no meaning if translated from English, as in riddles and poetry.

Because of the time gap between our acceptance of material and its publication abroad, we look for a timeless approach to writing. For instance, John Doe may be 35 at the time the author writes about him, but he may be 40 by the time the piece is released or re-released. Therefore if his birthdate is given rather than his age, the material is still correct and not outdated.

We are especially interested in seeing reprints of previously published books and features. They are easier for us to process and are more impressive to foreign editors. For legal reasons, however, we need written assurance that the author controls his/her reprint rights. When submitting manuscripts of any length, we encourage the author to include a short synopsis of the work.

We also prefer a letter of query from those who wish to submit. If we see possibilities, we answer immediately and request to see the material. If not, we frankly say so, thus saving postage, time, and inconvenience for all concerned. In keeping with professional etiquette, we expect all submissions and queries to be accompanied by addressed stamped envelope or proper return postage.

At the present we are in search of:

1. Published books, both fiction and nonfiction, for which the author holds foreign rights.

2. Interviews with people in the international public eye, preferably with accompanying color photographs.

3. Published short stories or feature articles, published cartoons, comic strips, and juvenile activity features, puzzles, and games.

4. Anything new, different, and not run-of-the-mill.

5. Columns and cartoons to run for at least 52 weeks.

Write for the world, and not only for home consumption. Milk your good old literary properties for a new run. We like out of print books and features published by leading magazines for second, foreign, and subsidiary rights sales.

These guidelines are not meant to infer that we concentrate only on foreign markets. To the contrary, we have a business that is healthy and growing in the United States, but because so few people look no farther than their own local or national boundaries, we have emphasized how to search for global sales in an effort to broaden your scope.

We look forward to hearing from you. We take every possible care in handling your material, but cannot be responsible for loss or damage.

SOUND PUBLICATIONS

10 E. 22nd Street, Suite 108
Lombard, IL 60148
(708) 916-7071 (but please, no phone calls)

Acquisitions Editor: Address submissions to "Fiction Editor"

Media Type/Titles per Year: Audiocassette (1994 is our first
year of producing fiction. That, along with the fact that we are a
small company, limits us to a small number of audio books per
year.)

Submissions Policies

We prefer to see queries or a synopsis with sample chapters.
Always include SASE. New authors are absolutely encouraged
to send submissions. Unsolicited submissions are OK, as are
unagented manuscripts and simultaneous submissions. Please
no phone calls from authors or agents. Our usual response
time is 1–2 months. See Writer's Guidelines for additional
information.

Pay Rate

No advance presently. Royalties are negotiable. Audio books are
normally published about 6–9 months after acceptance.

Actively Seeking
Historical
Contemporary
Mainstream
Mystery/Suspense
Time Travel
Paranormal
Word count is anywhere between 30,000–100,000.

Editor's Wish List

Our audiobooks are read in the format of old-time radio plays, with various characters. We use sound effects and original music. We like to see a fast-moving plot with a lot of dialogue.

Sound Publications Writer's Guidelines

Thanks for your interest in Sound Publications! We're a small audio publishing company that has been publishing educational and children's audiotapes; however, we have recently begun producing original, never-before-published fiction on tape.

Material must be typewritten, double-spaced, letter-quality (or near), on 8½" × 11" white paper. No disk submissions. We would like to see the first two or three chapters of your work, plus a detailed synopsis. Please include your publishing credentials and any other relevant information. If you wish to have the material returned, a self-addressed, stamped return envelope is a must. We will contact you (generally within one month) if we wish to see your complete manuscript. Please do not send originals of your work.

We are interested in adult fiction of any genre—mystery, romance, action/adventure, techno-thrillers, etc. We're open to any level of sensuality, but we don't want to see anything violent or that which borders on pornography. Because the work will be performed on audiotape, it is very important to us that the manuscripts contain a great deal of dialogue and fast moving action, rather than long descriptive narratives. Our novels are produced in the form of radio plays, complete with multiple actors, sound effects, and original music.

THIN ICE PUBLISHING

The Romantic, Heart to Heart, Romantic Adventures
6001-0 Lomas NE #124
Albuquerque, NM 87110
(505) 255-7672

Co-Owner/Director, Romance Division: Sandy M. Jacob (Please direct submissions to the correct department or line, rather than a specific editor.)

Media Type/Titles per Year: Paperback, 12–120; magazine stories, 48–72; illustrated romance, 4–12

Submissions Policies

Always query first. OK to send synopsis and sample chapters but the complete manuscript should only be sent at our request. New authors are very strongly encouraged to send submissions. Unagented manuscripts are OK. Simultaneous submissions are OK, except for Romantic Adventures. Agents may call. Usual response time is 1–3 months.

Pay Rate

The average advance varies. (See our guidelines below.) Average royalty rate is 5%. Books are normally published about 6 months after acceptance.

Actively Seeking
Historical
Contemporary
Mainstream
Ethnic
Mystery/Suspense
Time Travel
Paranormal
Adult
No young adult.

Tips

We don't reject without telling the author why. We critique good stories that don't quite meet industry standards to help authors become publishable.

We are on line with Prodigy (FMUY26A), Z-Talk (Sandy Jacob), America On-Line, and GeNie for the sole purpose of communication and to assist authors with questions. We have an internal Q & A Department for authors who are not on line, to write questions and receive answers by mail. (Write to Thin Ice Publishing, c/o Q & A Department.)

A very detailed set of guidelines (of about 15 pages) is also offered for $1.25 postage/handling, $1.75 Canada/Mexico (send a check in U.S. dollars). The detailed guidelines (besides the ones reprinted here) give information about submission, contracts, how we pay, rights we buy, and much more. When you request these guidelines, you are automatically put on our mailing list and will receive regular updates and our T.I.P. Club packet about once every four weeks. We strongly recommend these additional guidelines, as two of our products are fairly new to the market and we want everyone to get in on the fun and understand what we are doing. Send requests for expanded guidelines (with check) in care of the Romance Division.

Editor's Wish List

Solid characters and plot. Well-written.

Turn-offs/Taboos

Spanking stories, gay/lesbian, religious, young adult, first person (true confession, true romance).

Thin Ice Writer's Guidelines

Thin Ice Publishing was established in 1983 as Thin Ice Creative and focused on Games and Comic Magazines. In July 1993 our name changed to Thin Ice Publishing and three divisions were born; Comics, Games, and Romance. Although romance is a new endeavor to our company, it is not new to the many people who are working in our Romance Division. The division currently publishes *The Romantic*, a monthly, full color magazine of short romantic fiction; *Heart to Heart,* our paperback book line for romance; and *Romantic Adventures,* illustrated romance.

THE ROMANTIC

We are looking for short romance stories of up to 20,000 words. We do not restrict sub-genre as long as your submission is romance. Payment is 4–6¢ a word. We ask that writers submit a query, synopsis, and three to five pages of the manuscript. Very short stories of up to ten pages can be submitted in full. Please be sure to include an SAE with enough postage for return. Do not send original manuscripts, since we mark them up as we read. Our response time on queries and manuscripts is generally 4–6 weeks.

We are happy to look at unpublished authors and try to print at least one unpublished writer per month. We work with both agented and unagented writers.

The Romantic will be available by subscription and on sale in many major book/magazine stores. First release is July 1994. Direct queries to *The Romantic* at the above address.

HEART TO HEART

We are looking for romance stories over 50,000 words. We do not restrict sub-genre as long as your submission is romance. Payment is approximately 5% royalty of American cover price. We ask that writers submit a query, synopsis, and three sample chapters of the manuscript. One sample chapter should include either the first kiss or the first love scene. Please be sure to include an SAE with enough postage for return. Don't send original manuscripts, since we mark them up as we read. Our response time on queries is generally 4–6 weeks, and on manuscripts 1–2 months.

We are happy to look at unpublished authors and will publish a new writer when the work is good. We work with both agented and unagented writers.

Heart to Heart will be available through our T.I.P. Club and on sale in many major bookstores. First release is August 1994. Direct queries to *Heart to Heart* at the above address.

ROMANTIC ADVENTURES

With *Romantic Adventures* we are bringing back an art form from the 30s, 40s, and 50s, using 90s technology. The results are romance novels in beautiful, full-color illustrated format. Although we do not restrict sub-genre, submissions must be high action/adventure and no more than 75,000 words. Manuscripts should be submitted in standard narrative format. Payment is 4–5% royalty of the American cover price. We ask that writers submit a query, synopsis and three sample chapters of the manuscript. One sample chapter should include either the first kiss or the first love scene. We will also be looking for the action/adventure, so make sure it is described in at least one chapter as well. Please be sure to include an SAE with enough postage for return. Don't send original manuscripts, since we mark them up as we read. Our response time on queries is generally 4–6 weeks, and on manuscripts 1–2 months.

Since not many writers are used to this format, we are especially happy to critique good stories that may not be quite up to standard (at no charge to the writer). We are happy to look at unpublished authors and will publish a new writer when the work is good. We work with both agented and unagented writers. As this is basically a "new" format, we suggest you talk to your agent about it before submitting a manuscript.

Romantic Adventures will be available through our T.I.P. Club and on sale in many major bookstores. First release is approximately October 1994. Direct queries to *Romantic Adventures* at the above address.

TOR BOOKS
Forge Imprint
175 Fifth Avenue, 14th Floor
New York, NY 10010
(212) 388-0100

Acquisitions Editors: Melissa Ann Singer, Senior Editor; Natalia Aponte, Assistant Editor

Media Type: Paperback and hardcover

Submissions Policies

Don't query. Send a one-page synopsis and sample chapters or complete manuscripts with SASE. Agents are invited to call. New authors are encouraged. TOR accepts unsolicited and unagented manuscripts. Simultaneous submissions will not be considered. No electronic submissions (paper only). Please do not fax anything! Usual response time is 2–3 months.

Pay Rate

Average advances and standard royalty rates remain confidential. Books are normally published about 12 months after acceptance.

Actively Seeking

Historical	60,000 words minimum, any time period
Contemporary	60,000 words minimum, wide range of topics
Women's Fiction	60,000 words minimum, wide range of topics
Mystery/Suspense	60,000 words minimum, hard-boiled featuring a woman; cozies

Editor's Wish List

We don't really do too much in the way of category-type romances. We are looking for more women's fiction and will consider almost any plot. Writing must be strong, plot handled in a fresh way, and the heroine must be strong.

Turn-offs/Taboos

We'll consider almost anything that's handled well.

WARNER BOOKS

1271 Avenue of the Americas
New York, NY 10020
(212) 522-5054
FAX: (212) 522-7990

Acquisitions Editor: Jeanne Tiedge, Senior Editor

Media Type/Titles per Year: Paperback, hardcover, and audio-cassette, 21 romance, 250+ total

Submissions Policies

Authors, please query first by letter with SASE. A synopsis may be sent, but please don't send unsolicited manuscripts. As a rule, I believe an author should have an agent, but I will consider un-agented writers' query letters. New authors are not encouraged. We publish very few first novels. Agents may call with queries. Simultaneous submissions are acceptable from agents, if we are informed. Usual response time is 2 months.

Pay Rate

Advances and royalties vary. Books are normally published about 10–18 months after acceptance.

Actively Seeking

Historical	125,000 words, 17th–19th century, prefer American or English settings
Contemporary	120,000 words, prefer contemporary mainstream romantic fiction

Tips

Warner Books specializes in publishing and promoting authors who have already published two or more titles and are looking for more personalized and targeted publishing programs. We do not have any "lines" which, by nature, can help expose/publicize a first time author in the marketplace. Warner does not have tip sheets. Warner romances are sensual.

Editor's Wish list

A book that is romantic and has interesting subplots and minor characters offering scope and depth to the story are Warner's favorites. Sensual scenes should never be gratuitous.

Turn-offs/Taboos

Glitz and glamor; Hollywood settings; period settings (anywhere from 1900–1960).

DANIEL WEISS ASSOCIATES, INC.
33 W. 17th Street, 11th Floor
New York, NY 10011
(212) 643-3865
FAX: (212) 633-1236

Acquisitions Editors: Ann Brashares, Senior Editor; Liz Craft, Editorial Assistant

Media Type/Titles per Year: Paperback, 120

Submissions Policies

Query first. OK to send synopsis and sample chapters, but not the complete manuscript (unless requested). New authors are encouraged to send submissions. Unagented manuscripts are OK, as are simultaneous submissions. Agents may call. Usual response time is 6–10 weeks.

Pay Rate

Average advance and average royalty percentage varies.

Actively Seeking
Contemporary Romances
for young adults   45,000 words

Tips

Our romances are conservative, sweet, or sensual.

ZEBRA/PINNACLE/KENSINGTON/ Z-FAVE PUBLISHING CORP.
(See KENSINGTON PUBLISHING.)

6

Romancing the Hollywood Connection

Some writers think of screenplays as golden tickets to fame and fortune. And they can be. The one screenplay in about forty thousand that actually gets produced by a Writer's Guild Association (WGA) signatory film company can net the author about five times (or more) the amount of the average romance novel advance. (Not all film producers pay WGA union wages.)

Although the odds are against an unknown ever succeeding as a screenwriter, it happens often enough, and the rewards are great enough to make writers eager to get a foot in the door.

An agent is really a must for your Hollywood connection, unless you live in LA, subscribe to all the trades, know which producer is looking for what, can effectively pitch your idea, can negotiate for B.O. (box office points), and understand labyrinthine contracts.

Seventy percent of screenwriters are unemployed at any one time, and the ones that are employed may be writing dialogue for cartoon characters, doctoring other people's scripts, or writing scenes for industrial safety films, while they work on their own "spec" screenplays in stolen moments.

The world of book publishing is a kind and considerate place in comparison to the world of film and television. In the book industry, acquisitions editors often answer their own telephones and will patiently listen to an agent pitch a manuscript and agree to read it. Hollywood studios have a much shorter attention span—it comes with the territory. In fact, the majority of the film/cable/TV production companies contacted for this reference did not even respond to an invitation for a free listing. Not to worry, though—agents know where they are.

One warning about the film industry. While plagiarism is rarely heard of in the book publishing industry, it happens often enough in the film industry that WGA has a registration service for scripts and screen treatments.

Here's what usually happens to a screenplay after it has been written:

Registration: The WGA will register for you any written materials for film, TV, radio, or theater. WGA will also register manuscripts for novels, short stories, lyrics, and poetry. (The latter is a new service.) The registration lasts for five years and can be renewed. Call one of the registration information numbers below for instructions. (Note: Titles are not protected by registration, nor are they copyrightable.)

How to Decide What's Next: There are three ways to get someone to read your screenplay:

1. An agent pitches and submits it through connections he/she has previously established.

2. You have done business with someone inside the studio and can rely on them to get you a read.

3. You have a personal referral from *somebody* (for example, Meryl Streep has read your script and wants the lead). Realistically, getting an agent should be the next step.

Getting an Agent: There are agents in this reference who handle screenplays, and WGA also has a list. If you already have an agent for your romance novels, ask about possible screenplay representation. Your agent may want to represent your screenplay, or may refer you to someone he/she trusts. (This method beats picking an agency by its zip code!) Besides writing, getting an agent is the hardest part.

Pitching: What this boils down to is the agent convincing a studio executive in five minutes or less that your idea is unique, has mass-market appeal, and will net them millions of dollars if produced. Pitching is a skill that gets your screenplay a read, and that alone is worth the 10% your agent will earn if the property is acquired.

The Read: The story analysts will decide *yes, no,* or *maybe.* If the answer is "yes," congratulations—you (and your agent) are on your way!

There are other ways authors have broken into Hollywood—there is a back door or two.

Maggie Davis (who writes as Katherine Deauxville and Maggie Daniels), author of *A Christmas Romance,* had her agent sell an option for her very successful novel. The film producer hired screenwriters to adapt a screenplay from the book. It did not get produced. When the option ran out, Maggie saw the screenplay for the first time. The screenwriter had made her heroine into an awful shrew! Maggie and Jeff Davis, her collaborator, wrote a much better screenplay, and again an option for TV and film rights was picked up, this time by Sondra Locke's company Caritas Productions. We are crossing our fingers for Maggie, as she waits to see whether her screenplay will be produced.

(For those who are wondering if an author gets money for an option on a screenplay, whether or not it is produced, yes, you may, depending on the terms and assignments of rights specified in your book contracts. So read those book contracts carefully before you sign away specific rights! And do ask your agent about film options on your books.)

Anne Marie Duquette, another romance author, made a sale to Paramount and was *invited* to pitch more of her ideas!

Ashley McConnell, who writes romantic sci-fi, has found that Hollywood has made its way to *her* door. She's written several Quantam Leap novels for Ace; her books are so hot that more offers are sure to come!

What kind of screenplays have the best chance?

Linda Stuart says, "As a story analyst at Paramount, I knew that the studio was primarily interested in commercial screenplays with mass audience appeal. So I steered clear of small, arty scripts that were too limited in scope, even though the writing may have been strong." (Quoted from *Getting Your Script Through the Hollywood Maze*, 1993.)

Although everyone wants to write screenplays for Paramount, Touchstone, or Warner, these are tough markets to crack, even with a fabulous screenplay and an agent who can pitch in his sleep. So *Romance Writer's Pink Pages* has narrowed down the markets to just a few "best bets" that might be more receptive to romance writers. Good luck!

KEYSTONE ENTERTAINMENT
930 N. Doheny Drive, Suite 304
Los Angeles, CA 90069
(310) 278-1203
FAX: (310) 437-7343

Send submissions to:
P.O. Box 411831
Los Angeles, CA 90041
(310) 259-8115

Production Executive: Judith Abarbanel

Media Type: Paperback, Hardcover, Screenplay

Submissions Policy

No need to query first. Submission of published materials and screenplays is fine. New authors are encouraged to send submissions. Unsolicited manuscripts are fine, as are unagented manuscripts. Simultaneous submissions are OK and agents may call. Usual response time is 8–12 weeks.

Actively Seeking
Historical
Contemporary
Mainstream
Religious
Ethnic
Mystery/Suspense
Time Travel
Paranormal
We are happy to look at a variety of offerings.

Producer's Wish List

We are looking for stories from all genres, time periods and locales that feature strong characterization, colorful locations, and storylines complex enough to sustain a one-hour or longer TV, mini-series, or feature presentation.

Turn-offs/Taboos

We are open to just about anything.

MARTIN MORRIS PRODUCTIONS, INC.
4256 Camellia Avenue
Studio City, CA 91604
(818) 761-0046

Production Executive: Ralph Michaels

Media Type: TV Series, Made-for-TV movies, Cable, Feature Films

Submissions Policy

It doesn't matter if scripts are WGA-registered or not. We consider spec scripts from unagented writers. We prefer a query letter before the phone pitch, however. OK to send story ideas or screen treatments. We are not looking for published novels for which film options are available.

Actively Seeking
Action Adventure
Erotic
Suspense Thrillers
Westerns
Family Relations

Producer's Wish List

Good dialogue, good backstory, strong conflict.

Turn-offs/Taboos

We don't want Comedy or Science Fiction.

ROMANCE FILMS
c/o Tammy Crampton
115 W. Morten Avenue
Phoenix, AZ 85021
FAX: (602) 944-0579

Contact Person: Tammy Crampton, President

Media Type: TV Series, Made-for-TV Movies, Cable, Feature Films, Video

Submissions Policies

Screenwriters should register their work with WGA before submitting. We will consider spec scripts from unagented writers. We prefer a screen treatment by letter, rather than a story idea via phone pitch. Although it is OK to send a story idea, we prefer a screen treatment (synopsis of several pages) that fleshes out the characterization, motivation, conflict, and plot.

We do not require or encourage script form for authors who are unfamiliar with it. Screen treatments may be submitted in the form of a traditional book synopsis. If author is not familiar with traditional script formats, we will also look at stories in manuscript format. We do not want to hinder an author's creativity, or discourage talented writers from submitting to us just because they are new to screenplay or screen treatment format.

We also want to see published novels for which the author owns the rights, for possible film option.

We charge *no* reading fees whatsoever. We are strong advocates of romance authors and want to encourage the positive messages of the romance genre.

Actively Seeking
Story ideas, screen treatments and screenplays.
Also seeking options on published novels for which the author
    owns the rights.
We are primarily interested in mystery and action adventure
    where romance is the primary moving force of the story, and
    there is a strong conflict challenging that romance. Romance should not be a background element, but should be
    important and running as a theme through the entire story.
    We do want to see stories that are highly sensual (not porn)
    with lots of emotional motivation for the leads to fall in love

with each other. If you send us a story that is not mystery or action adventure, but it's still a great story and a great romance, we might be interested. We also have a general film division, in addition to romance films, and will refer you if you have a good story that would better fit the needs of the general film division.

Producer's Wish List

Our goal is to make films that are written, developed, directed, and produced by women. These movies will be produced primarily for a female audience and will contain positive female role models and upbeat stories that will make you laugh, cry, and cheer. We want strong female characters (heroines), as well as strong male characters (heroes). The supporting leads (secondary characters) need to be well thought out. No two dimensional supporting leads, please. All characters should have strengths and also vulnerabilities that translate well to the screen. If the lead (heroine) has a best friend, that character should have a life of her own, with her own problems and personal characteristics that make her different from the lead. Relationships between people should be believable. Think character-driven, motivation-driven, with the plot well planned and well paced.

Turnoffs/Taboos

We do not want to see anything with excessive violence, especially domestic violence toward women.

Although we would eventually like to do some historicals, we currently focus primarily on contemporary settings. If you have a historical setting that could be modernized and you still have a great story, we'll be glad to look at it.

Some of our favorite films include old Cary Grant pictures, *When Harry Met Sally,* and *Broadcast News.* There are a lot of pictures we like, but had they been our projects, we would have emphasized the romance more. Romance is the most important aspect of any film.

Romance Writer's Pink Pages'
Mini-Guide to Hollywood

Here is some advice to get you closer to a Hollywood Connection:

1. B.O. is something you want. It means box office points (a percentage of the box office net. It is what screenwriters can get if they have a great script and a great agent who starts a bidding war over the script!)

2. Do not move to L.A. until you sell your first screenplay, and even then be prepared to be out of work for a year before you sell the next one.

3. If your agent asks for a photo of you for the producer, know that this is about age discrimination, not because they want to cast you for a part. The younger you look, the better. Try to get as close to thirty-something as possible in your photo.

4. Get your hands on a real script, so you can learn. If you join the GEnie electronic network, you will find a very good Northern Exposure script in the library of the "writers" bulletin board. Download it.

5. Do not put camera angles (etc.) in your own script, unless you have been to film school.

6. Dress upscale casual (not suit and tie) for in-person pitches to agents or producers. No safety pins through nose or noisy jewelry, either.

7. Have at least two backup pitches ready, in case the agent/producer says no thanks. It's hard to get an audience, so while you're there, you might as well take advantage of the opportunity. Be prepared to expound on your idea. And don't take rejection personally.

8. Be realistic. Unless you are Arnold, Clint, or Sly, producers are really tired of these themes: Defy authority, destroy property, get naked for no reason, swear a lot.

9. You do not have to sleep with anyone to get ahead as a screenwriter, unless you are married to the producer!

The following related resources may be useful in getting you started on your way to Oscardom:

WGAw

8955 Beverly Boulevard
West Hollywood, CA 90048
(310) 205-2500 (registration information) or (310) 205-2540

WGAe

555 W. 57th Street, Suite 1230
New York, NY 10019
(212) 757-4360 (registration information) or (212) 767-7800

Publications of WGAw:

WGA Directory. $17.50. Contains names, credits of people in the
   film industry, and their contact phone numbers.
The Journal. $40/yr for 11 issues. Single/back copies $5.

List of WGA Agents: Send SASE and check for $2.
Informative Pamphlets are $3.50. Specify "Creative Rights,"
"Plagiarism," or "Working With Writers."

Other helpful publications include:

Daily Variety
P.O. Box 7550
Torrance, CA 90504
(800) 552-3632

$145/yr, $97/6 months,$39/3 months. This trade magazine carries
all the daily news about the film industry.

Hollywood Scriptwriter
1626 N. Wilcox #385
Hollywood, CA 90028
(818) 991-3096

Monthly newsletter of about 10 pages per issue. 12 issues for $44. Recommended for advice from pros and market listings. Also excellent yearly screenplay agent's survey.

Screenwrite Now!
P.O. Box 7, Long Green Pike
Baldwin, MD 21013-0007
(410) 592-3466

$48 (USA) includes highly recommended bi-monthly magazine and membership benefits in the Forum. Dedicated to helping you write better screenplays and professional advice on approaching the Hollywood market.

Variety
5700 Wilshire Boulevard, Suite 120
Los Angeles, CA 90036

Weekly B.O. reports, Film production listings, reviews and industry news. Sunday home delivery is available in L.A., N.Y., and other areas. Call (800) 323-4345. (Single copies are $3.50 at newsstands.)

Helpful Books

The Complete Book of Scriptwriting by J. Michael Straczynski
The Elements of Screenwriting by Irwin R. Blacker
Feature Filmmaking at Used Car Prices by Rick Schmidt
Getting Your Script Through the Hollywood Maze by Linda Stuart
How to Make It in Hollywood by Linda Buzzell
How to Write for Television by Madeline DiMaggio
Madison Avenue Handbook by Peter Glenn Publications
    (800) 223-1254
The New Screenwriter Looks at the New Screenwriter by William
    Froug
Successful Scriptwriting by Jurgen Wolff and Kerry Cox

Screenwriting Courses, Contests, Fellowships, and Internships

American Film Institute
2021 N. Western Avenue
Los Angeles, CA 90027
(213) 856-7600

American Film Institute Minority Screenwriting Contest
P.O. Box 69799
Los Angeles, CA 90069

Creative Sreenwriters Group
518 9th Street N.E., Suite 308
Washington, D.C. 20002

GEnie On-Line
(800) 848-8199

This is the cheapest (on-line charges only) and best source of information available from experienced screenwriters. Once you're on line, type WRITERS to get to the writer's bulletin board. The screenwriting category is number 33 (subject to change) and contains on-line help, workshops, message board, agent advice, and even a few downloadable scripts in the writers library.

Hollywood Scriptwriting Insitute
1605 Cahuenga Boulevard, Suite 211
Hollywood, CA 90028
(213) 461-8333

Michael Hauge's Screenwriting for Hollywood or Hilltop Productions
P.O. Box 55728
Sherman Oaks, CA 91413.
(800) 477-1947

Traveling weekend seminar, approximately $200.

Nicholl Academy Fellowships
Academy of Arts and Sciences Foundation
8949 Wilshire Boulevard
Beverly Hills, CA 90211

Sundance Film Institute
Columbia Pictures Entertainment
10202 W. Washington Place
Culver City, CA 90232

UCLA
Attn: Diane Thomas Awards/Extension Writers #313
10995 LeConte Avenue
Los Angeles, CA 90024

Universal Studios/Chesterfield Writers Film Project
100 Universal City Plaza
Universal City, CA 91608

Walt Disney Studios Fellowships
Attn: Ms. Brenda Vangsness, Program Director
Walt Disney Studios
500 S. Buena Vista Street
Burbank, CA 91521

Screenwriting Software

Is the screenwriting software advertised in writer's magazines too expensive? The author of this book has a PC-shareware version she'd love to share. It is only for IBM PC or compatible computers. (Sorry no MAC version available.) Virus tested and easy to use. Manual prints out from disk. Program operates from DOS. Windows not necessary. Send $1, one formatted disk (5 1/4" or 3 1/2") and a self-addressed disk mailer to:

> Eve Paludan
> P.O. Box 24739
> Tempe, AZ 85285-4739

(Specify ScreenWright Professional shareware program.)

7

An Affaire of the Heart

*A*re you acquainted with *Affaire de Coeur* magazine?
In the current "battle of the romance trade magazines," editors at *Affaire de Coeur* have been quietly doing what they always do best: putting out a quality magazine with astute and succinct reviews, well-written and interesting articles, introspective interviews, personable profiles of authors, and insider news for writers about the romance novel market.

There is a dignity and reliable excellence about this magazine. It is a romance review and writer's trade magazine that treats the subject of romance literature with equal parts of respect and ardor.

Talking to Louise Snead, the publisher, is like talking to a best friend who likes all the things about romance that you do. Employed by the magazine for about five years before she recently became the publisher, Louise is candid—but modest—about the steadily growing success of *Affaire de Coeur,* which is now being distributed at Barnes and Noble, B.Dalton, and Waldenbooks stores, as well as by mail subscription. She is environmentally conscious, biting the bullet when it comes to paying for recycled paper and soy-based ink for the magazine (which is much more expensive than virgin paper and other inks). Louise wouldn't have it any other way.

She is also socially conscious about positive and negative themes in romance novels, as are her reviewers and her magazine article writers, and her advocacy for women and writers is an underlying theme of the magazine.

In a recent issue of *Affaire,* Hollie Dominano interviewed Pamela Goodfellow (of Goodfellow Press) about women's issues in romance novels, giving insight into the interviewer's search for books that empower women, as well as the concerns of the publisher to acquire and publish romances that will touch readers' hearts and affect their lives in positive ways.

This is the kind of interview you'll find in *Affaire:* Intelligent, meaningful, upbeat.

The reviewers at *Affaire* are the best in the business. Harriet Klausner is the most well-known of the reviewing staff. Her reviews transcend the usual "back-cover-blurb-blues." Readers won't go wrong if they rely on her keen sense of knowing what makes a book a good read. Harriet, along with the other 19 talented reviewers at *Affaire,* really digs into the inner messages of a book before passing judgment.

There are plenty of opportunities for romance authors and aspiring authors to get a piece published in *Affaire.* Writers who would like to be reviewers—yes, you can get paid to write book reviews!—should submit several reviews of books they have recently read, along with an SASE. Louise Snead will evaluate the reviews and decide if she wants to hire you on as a regular reviewer. (Reviewers' pay rate or salary will be negotiated individually. *Affaire* also reimburses expenses such as postage and phone calls that are incurred to the reviewer.)

If you have an idea for an article or an interview—a profile, writing tips, or news about a new publisher—send a query letter. Louise is always open to considering new ideas for the magazine and appreciates input from romance writers.

Authors should submit book galleys for review at least 4 months before the release date.

If you just want to write fiction, *Affaire* is also eager to consider your short romantic stories for publication.

What does Louise think are the coming trends for romance? She has great expectations that Zebra's ethnic romance line will hit the marketplace with a lively splash. It won't be the first time Zebra has led other publishers into unexplored territory in the mass market, and with the multitalented Monica Harris as the spearhead of these multicultural books, they are bound to make a positive impact that will be imitated by other romance publishers.

Louise Snead also notes that romance readers of the mid-90s are becoming quite avante garde in their tastes. Romances with paranormal, supernatural, and sci-fi elements are just now starting to get a firm hold on a steady readership, and she believes this trend will continue and spread, enthralling even more readers of other genres and bringing them into the romance marketplace. Which is good news for anyone reading this book!

By keeping an open line of communication at her magazine, and by hosting annual romance writers' conferences, *Affaire de Coeur* is truly looking toward the future of romance literature and meeting the needs of both romance writers and romance readers.

Affaire de Coeur has come a long way since the slender sixteen pages of the first issues. Currently, at about 60 pages per issue, there is plenty of information for the romance enthusiast to read, learn from, and reflect upon.

Being voted one of the top ten publications in the Bay area is an honor not easily earned. But to Louise and her staff, the effort reflects the finished product, and that's what counts.

Now—wouldn't you like to have an *Affaire*?

8

Directory of Non-Book Markets

This section was called MAGAZINE MARKETS in the first edition of *Romance Writer's Pink Pages,* but has been expanded here to include markets for short fiction, novellas, novelettes, and anthologies, as well as other markets related to the romance industry or the women's writing trade. These new listings are in addition to the magazine romance and confessional listings.

AFFAIRE DE COEUR

3976 Oak Hill Drive
Oakland, CA 94605
(510) 569-5675
FAX: (510) 632-8868

Acquisitions Editor: Louise Snead

Subscriptions: $30 yr/monthly issues by First Class mail, $55 Canadian. Samples copies are $5.

Submissions Policies

Don't query. Send the complete manuscript. Unsolicited manuscripts are OK, but simultaneous submissions are not. Don't forget SASE. Average response time is up to 6 months.

Pay Rate

Payment is on publication for First North American Serial Rights.

Actively Seeking
Fiction and Nonfiction
Contemporary romance	1,000–2,000 words
Historical	1,000–2,000 words
Inspirational Fiction	1,000–2,000 words
Ethnic Fiction	1,000–2,000 words

Romance Novel Industry News
How-to Articles for Writers

Tips

We are looking for articles about writing and authors, publishing, and author's bios. We would like manuscripts that are for (book) review only. No unpublished manuscripts for review.

AMELIA, SPSM&H, AND CICADA MAGAZINES
329 "E" Street
Bakersfield, CA 93304
(805) 323-4064

Editor: Frederick A. Raborg Jr.

Circulation: 1,500 quarterly

Subscriptions: $25 yr/4 issues or $48 for 2 yrs/8 issues. Single copies of *Amelia* are $7.95. $14 yr (each) for *SPSM&H* and *Cicada*. Combination subscriptions for all three for $48 per year.

Submissions

Queries are not necessary. Send the complete manuscript. Unsolicited manuscripts and simultaneous submissions are OK. Average response time is 2–12 weeks.

Pay Rate

Payment is on acceptance. $35 for story over 2,000 words, plus two contributor copies, less for shorter material. Publishing schedule is about 12 months after acceptance.

Actively Seeking
Romantic Fiction and Nonfiction

Contemporary Romance	to 5,000 words
Historical	to 5,000 words
Mainstream	to 5,000 words
Ethnic	to 5,000 words
Romantic Suspense	to 5,000 words
Mystery/Suspense	to 5,000 words
Western Fiction	to 5,000 words
Science Fiction	to 5,000 words
Alternate Lifestyle Fiction	to 5,000 words

Nonfiction—critical essays, interviews, articles of universal interest, etc.

Tips

Be professional; have something to say and say it well.

Amelia, SPSM&H, Cicada Writer's Guidelines

The best guidelines to any magazine's particular needs is, of course, a copy of the magazine itself. *Amelia* perhaps uses more traditional fiction and poetry than any other small press magazine published today, but we also look for the freshness and innovation as well. And neatness does count.

Fiction, Amelia: We look for depth of plot and strong character-ization in stories of any type to 4,500 words (a piece would have to be exceptional to exceed that length). We use science fiction, westerns, romance, and Gothic horror as well as mainstream. We like to have the feeling of the whole world in story lines. Payment of $35 on acceptance, plus two contributor copies, for stories over 2,000 words; less for shorter pieces. (Also accept poetry.)

Fiction, Cicada: We use stories with an emphasis on the Orien-tal, especially Japanese, though we have used stories set in China and other Asian locales. All types are welcome to 2,000 words maximum. Payment $10 on publication, plus one copy. (Also ac-cept poetry with Oriental emphasis.)

Fiction, SPSM&H (stands for Shakespeare, Petrarch, Sidney, Milton, & Hopkins): We use stories with romantic or Gothic themes, to 2,000 words maximum. Especially welcome are tales that somehow incorporate the sonnet. Payment $10 on publication, plus one copy. (Also accept sonnets and sonnet se-quences, experimental or traditional.)

We're also publishing Belle Lettres, book reviews, transla-tions, illustrations and well-constructed erotica.

AMELIA CONTEST DEADLINES AND GUILDELINES
All of our competitions are annuals. They may be entered at any time with the understanding that decisions are made 8–10 weeks following deadline date. All deadline dates are postmarks. Any number may be entered. Include SASE with all entries, one for each category entered, if return is desired. If no SASE is in-cluded, non-winning entries will be destroyed following an-nouncement of winners. Neither *Amelia* nor its staff can be responsible for materials lost in the mails. Except for the quar-terly Encore Awards, First North American serial rights will be required of all winners, otherwise the entry will be disqualified.

Be sure that name, address, and Social Security number appear on each entry. Telephone numbers may also be helpful.

Here are just a few of the contests:

Anna B. Jantzen Romantic Poetry Award. Deadline is January 2. $100 prize for best romantic poem, of any type, up to 100 lines. $4 entry.

Amelia Erotic Poetry Award. Deadline is May 1. $100 for best erotic poem, any form to 50 lines. Entry fee: $4 each.

Amelia Erotic Fiction Award: Deadline is July 1. $100 is offered for best short story, any type, to 3,000 words, with an erotic theme. Entry fee: $5.

Amelia Romantic Fiction Award: Deadline is October 1. $100 for best romantic fiction up to 2,000 words. Entry fee: $5.

Send SASE for complete writer's guidelines and details for more than 60 of our writing contests.

AMERICAN AUDIO LITERATURE, INC.
P.O. Box 1392
Cicero, NY 13039
(315) 676-7026

President: Joan Basile

Media Type: Audio Cassette (expect 20 titles/yr)

Submissions Policies

Send complete manuscripts with SASE. New authors are encouraged. Unsolicited manuscripts are OK. Unagented manuscripts are OK. No simultaneous submissions or electronic submissions. Agents may call after manuscript is approved. Usual response time is 1 month.

Pay Rate

Average advance is $500–$1,000. Average royalty is 65¢ after the first 2500 copies are sold. Normal publishing schedule is about 4 months after acceptance.

Actively Seeking

Contemporary	25,000–30,000 words
Women's Fiction	25,000–30,000 words
Mystery/Suspense	25,000–30,000 words
New Age	25,000–30,000 words

Tips

Romances are conservative stories read aloud and are three hours in length. Good writing makes manuscripts fit the editor's wish list. Violence is unacceptable. Audio cassettes are not adaptations of published books; they are original works of fiction. This concept sets American Audio Literature apart from other audio cassette companies, which buy rights to already published material. See guidelines below for more information.

American Audio Literature Writer's Guidelines

American Audio Literature is a company designed to produce audiotapes for the purpose of listening to original literature for pleasure.

There are at present several very successful companies who are recording books that have been previously published, including self-improvement tapes, instructional tapes, inspirational tapes, and fiction/nonfiction tapes.

Our intention is to deal primarily in fiction. However, there are two major differences between our concept and the recycled, pre-published books that are now on the market.

Our material will be specifically designed by the author for the 3-hour listening format that has proven to be so successful. We will not be paying a major publishing house for the rights to use their material and we will not be paying for a book that would take several hours to read aloud to be scaled down to three hours of reading time. These two items will save thousands of dollars and allow us to be highly competitive.

The stories are designed to be read aloud in 3 hours, (approximately 23,000 to 28,000 words.) They should capture the attention of adults in situations that can get monotonous (driving, jogging, etc.).

Interested writers should submit manuscripts for review. Our cash offering will be a maximum of $1,000. Royalties will be paid after the first 2500 copies are sold. Be assured that those writers who come with us initially will be highly rewarded as the company grows and expands.

Please notify us if you intend to begin work on a manuscript and give us an idea of the expected completion date.

The success of the audio business is irrefutable. The 10-year manager of one of the largest nationally known booksellers in the Syracuse area tells us that 5 years ago they carried less than a dozen audiotapes. Today they have in excess of 1,000 titles! And there is a tremendous demand for more.

We feel that with this concept we will be in a position to establish a whole new and exciting art form for the 21st century. We hope you will be a part of it with us.

AUDIO ENTERTAINMENT, INC.

P.O. Box 461059
Aurora, CO 80046
(303) 680-6020
FAX: (303) 680-6019

Acquisitions Editor: Connie Rinehold

Media Type: Audio Cassettes, 24/yr

Submissions Policies

Don't query. Send complete manuscript. New authors are encouraged. Unsolicited or unagented manuscripts are OK. Agents may call. See Writer's Guidelines for more information.

Pay Rate

When a synopsis is accepted one third payment is paid. When audioscript is completed, including any necessary revisions, two thirds of the advance is paid. $500–1,000 average advance for a 90-minute/16,000 word audioscript. A special 3-hour audioscript pays an advance of $1,500. Royalties are paid at 5% on the wholesale price after 50,000 units are produced. (A tape retails for about $6.99.) Although the guidelines say Audio Entertainment will own all rights, Audio Entertainment's Chief Financial Officer, Jeff Prager, said that specific rights could be negotiated into the contract to the satisfaction of both parties.

Actively Seeking
Scripts of 16,000 words.
Historical
Contemporary
Time Travel
Paranormal
Mystery/Suspense
Mainstream

Tips

Our romances are sweet. Heroine should be a strong female figure. The hero should be able to deal with his own vulnerability and show growth. Dialogue must be crisp, realistic, and lively. Need strong, well-motivated characters. Knowledge of location is a must. Any time period is welcome. The tone of your story is determined by the characters. Humor should be subtle. Exotic locales or a mystery subplot should enhance the story.

Turn-offs / Taboos

Not too many subplots or characters. Avoid slang, and avoid long blocks of either dialogue or narrative. Avoid tears on the heroine! Sex should not be used as reconciliation, but as an expression of love, trust, and commitment. No contrivances should be used to reconcile hero and heroine. Children and animals should not be used as plot devices.

Audio Entertainment Writer's Guidelines

Audio Entertainment, Inc. is currently accepting romances in the following formats:

Synopsis of 15–20 pages
Manuscript of approximately 16,000 words

In order to have a consistent quality product, we have established the following product guidelines.

THE PRODUCT
We produce 90-minute audio readings for the romance enthusiast. Each tape is made up of a novella, which will be read by a narrator, male voice, and female voice. Dividing the tape into chapters enables the listener to enjoy the tape in a number of different sittings. It is important that each chapter advances the story while keeping the listener's interest.

The story should contain the following basic elements:

The Encounter: The main characters and setting are introduced. The hero and heroine meet—an immediate physical attraction exists, which must develop quickly into an emotional and intellectual bond. However, there is apprehension and/or conflict on the part of the hero and/or heroine that should not rely on contrived plot devices, but rather elements within the characters' pasts, lifestyle, goals, interests, and/or personalities. Clichés should be avoided, but can work if fully motivated. The plot is established, the potential for conflict introduced, and the characterization developed.

The Chase: The romance progresses while the conflict accelerates. The listener finds out more about the hero and heroine and the apprehension that keeps them from committing to one another. At this point the hero and heroine should be gaining some knowledge and understanding of one another, which enhances or alters their initial perceptions. They should be showing growth within themselves. Provide information as needed rather than all at once, especially in introspection. The sexual tension continues to increase, but should focus on the sensual and be motivated by elements of friendship, respect, trust, and a growing love—reluctant or not. Love scenes—complete or interrupted—may occur, but only if the emotional bond has been established and lovemaking is a choice that is responsibly made by one or both parties. Lovemaking should be used to show depth of feeling and as a physical means of communicating emotion.

The Crisis: Conflicts reach the breaking point, driving a wedge between the hero and heroine. Any subplot or external conflict is also reaching its peak. Emotion should be strong and well-defined. Hero and heroine must now set priorities and make decisions/choices as to what they really want from life and what compromises each is willing to make to achieve the goal—namely a future with one another. Their character growth should be apparent rather than subtle at this stage, and they should be honest with themselves about their feelings. The listener should be in some suspense about how the hero and heroine will resolve the crisis. Subplots and external elements/conflicts begin to move toward resolution.

The Resolution: Subplots and external conflicts should be resolved. The hero and heroine confront one another and begin to communicate on a deeper level. Compromise is generally an essential element unless the conflict that keeps them apart is one-sided—then understanding and compassion is the element. Mutual realization/understanding is necessary. Sex should not be used as a means of reconciliation, but rather a consummation of their commitment to work together to build a future, and as an expression of love. External conflicts and/or situations can bring them together, providing opportunity for them to reach a resolution, but it should be well-motivated. It should not be contrived. The story should end on a note of hope, with faith in the strength and power of love, trust, and commitment.

ADDITIONAL POINTS

The Characters: Every good story begins with solid, well-defined, three-dimensional characters. The direction the plot takes, the conflict, and the development of the relationship and its resolution are determined by the characters, not the other way around. For instance, a shy character will react differently to a situation than a confident, aggressive character.

There are three types of characters: Primary (hero and heroine), Secondary (those who are pivotal to the plot), and Minor (only on a few pages, but still important to the story). In this (audio) format, there should not be too many characters, and the roles and motivations of each should be clearly defined by their mode of speech, habits, body language descriptions, etc. Quirky characters can be interesting as long as they are not caricatures. The heroine is a strong female figure, able to make it on her own, whether she believes it or not. The hero should be described with sensual details and there should be a sense of mystery or vulnerability about him, something the heroine must find out and understand.

Tone: Any story should have a balance of emotion, drama, and humor, with descriptions that establish atmosphere and enhance the story.

Dialogue: Every line of dialogue should either reveal character, reveal plot, or advance the plot. Avoid long blocks of dialogue without breaks for tags, emotion, action, etc.

Setting: Any location is acceptable. Make listeners feel they are there, but do not use description to excess. Establish time period early on, and make time passage clear. Any time period is OK.

Plot: Strong plot with simple and very few subplot complications.

Format: Double-spaced, 1" margins all around, header in upper left corner with title and author's last name, page number in upper right corner. Title page with author's name, address, and telephone number. Title page should also include setting of work and pseudonym, if applicable.

Submissions: Synopsis of 15–20 pages and/or a full manuscript of approximately 20,000 words is required. If writer chooses to sell rights to synopsis only, the full manuscript will be produced by Audio Entertainment, Inc. We prefer the writer complete the full manuscript. Editor will request revisions of accepted synopses and manuscripts.

BLACK CONFESSIONS/BLACK ROMANCE SECRETS/BRONZE THRILLS/JIVE

Sterling/Macfadden, Inc.
233 Park Avenue South, 5th Floor
New York, NY 10003
(212) 780-3500
FAX: (212) 780-3555

Acquisitions Editor: Tonia L. Shakespeare

Circulation: 250,000 bimonthly, combined

Submissions Policies

Don't query. Send the complete manuscript. Unsolicited and simultaneous submissions are OK. Usual response time is 2 months.

Pay Rate

$75–$100 per standard confession story, $100–$125 for special features and service articles, $50 for reprints. Payment is after publication. Buys First North American Serial Rights/All Rights.

Actively Seeking

Confessional	18–24 pages double-spaced
Contemporary Romance	18–24 pages double-spaced
Ethnic Romance	18–24 pages double-spaced

Also seeking nonfiction relationship/advice articles.

Tips

Follow the Writer's Guildelines below.

For *Jive, Intimacy,* and *Black Secrets* magazines, we strive for the stories to lean toward romantic lines. This does not mean that the stories should not have true-to-life experience plots. We simply want to project romance, love, and togetherness, rather than to overwhelm our readers with violence or anything too depressing.

Make the stories believable. We do not want to deviate from reality. All endings cannot be happy ones, but we want to try to cast an optimistic outlook whenever possible.

There is no limit to how many stories you may submit at one time. It is good to submit material as frequently as you can, so that outlines for upcoming months can be created. However, if you send us an excessive amount of manuscripts to evaluate, you must be patient, for it will take us longer to get back to you.

Black Confessions Writer's Guildelines

1. Stories must be written from a young, Black, female perspective with romance in mind. (This is not to discourage male writers.)
2. Stories must be true-to-life confessions with interesting plots.
3. Stories need to exude an aura of romance.

4. Stories should have at least two descriptive love scenes, each one page in length.

5. Stories must be written in the first person voice of the heroine.

6. Stories should be written in the past tense, but keep action current.

7. Stories must be typed and double-spaced, with each page numbered and identified either with your name or the title of the work.

8. Each manuscript should follow a professional manuscript format, including your name, address, and daytime phone.

9. Stories should be 18–24 pages.

   Allow at least 2 months for a response.

GUIDELINES FOR WRITING LOVE SCENES

All stories must have two love scenes. They should be romantic in nature and allude to the couple making love. Do not use graphic description. Decribe the feelings and thoughts of the heroine at that moment.

   Remember, less is best! Use tags to describe an act of love. Consult *The Romance Writer's Phrase Book* by Jean Kent and Candace Shelton. This is excellent workbook for obtaining romantic tags and getting an idea of how to keep love scenes more romantic than sexual. Love scenes should be light, romantic, and have an air of magic/fantasy about them.

BOHEMIAN CHRONICLE

P.O. Box 387
Largo, FL 34649-0387

Circulation: 500

Subscription:. $12 yr/monthly (USA). Samples for $1 and #10 SASE.

Submissions Policies

Don't query. Send the complete manuscript. Unsolicited OK, but no simultaneous submissions are accepted. Usual response time is 6 weeks.

Pay Rate

Payment is upon publication. Buys First North American rights, All Rights, or Reprint rights. $5 per story or article, plus five copies of that issue.

Actively Seeking
Experimental Ethnic Fiction   500–1,000 words
Experimental Fiction Primarily   500–1,000 words
Nonfiction Essays of Life Experiences (not the perils of writing
    romances!)

Tips

Not interested in anything mainstream. If you are a new writer in need of clips, *BC* may be the publication to help you get started. Try us.

Bohemian Chronicle Writer's Guidelines

Bohemian Chronicle is a publication that promotes sensitivity in the arts. Any pieces glorifying violence, racism, porn, and the like, will not be considered. We're looking for anything different— stories about people, circumstances, events, real feelings, etc. written in a conversational style that communicates color, humor, emotion, and personality. Satire and humor submissions should have a universal appeal. We would like to remain gender neutral if possible. Overt sexism will likely be rejected. Submit well written works and we will edit little or nothing. Don't forget SASE for response. Any works without SASE will be automatically shredded.

Fiction: 500–1,000 words. Anything different. Short stories, dialogue, surprise us!

Nonfiction: 800–1,500 words. First person life experiences written in a conversational style. Informative articles, essays, etc. Pays $5 and five copies.

Poetry: Short poems and verse. Pays $2 and two copies.

Art Work: Photos, pen and ink drawings, collages (no larger than 8½″ × 11″). Pays $3 and three copies.

BYLINE

P.O. Box 130596
Edmond, OK 73013

Acquisitions Editors: Kathryn Fanning, Managing Editor (fiction/nonfiction); Marcia Preston, Editor (poetry)

Circulation: 4,000+

Subscription: $20 yr/monthly (July/Aug is combined issue)

Submissions Policies

If you're not a regular reader and don't know what articles we've run, it's wise to query. Don't query for fiction, however. Send the complete fiction manuscript. You can send the complete fiction or nonfiction manuscript, but it's smarter to query for nonfiction if you're new to *ByLine*. We welcome the beginning writer as well as the pro. If your submission is a simultaneous one, please mention this at the upper right corner of page one of your manuscript. Usual response time is 6–10 weeks.

Pay Rate

Payment is on acceptance. $50 per story or article, less for filler length material. We buy First North American Serial Rights.

Actively Seeking
All types of fiction,
    except sexually explicit   2,000–4,000 words

Tips

We do not buy author profiles, but are looking for 1,500- to 1,800-word articles on how-tos for writers. We also buy fillers. We also have an annual romance fiction contest and genre fiction contest. Send #10 SASE for full contest list, deadlines, and rules, as well as requirements for other types of articles.

Turn-Offs/Taboos

No profanity.

COGSWELL PUBLISHING
Notable Novellettes
P.O. Box 840453-PP
Houston, TX 77284
(713) 859-6334

Publisher/Editor: Victoria P. Lawrence

Media Type: Short Paperback, 12–36 titles/yr

Submissions Policies

Query first, if manuscript is ready. Query letter must include a two paragraph synopsis of the story. Do not send synopsis and sample chapters. OK to send the complete manuscript with accompanying query letter (as described above). New authors are encouraged to send submissions. Your writing is what matters, not whether you're published or unpublished. Unsolicited manuscripts are OK, as are unagented manuscripts. Simultaneous submissions are OK, but please immediately inform us when it is picked up by someone else. Agents may call. Usual response time is 3–6 weeks. See Writer's Guidelines for additional information.

Pay Rate

No advance at this time. Average royalties for stories are 9% plus author copies and publication credit. Royalty is less for poetry.

Actively Seeking

Historical	10,000 words, any time period, preferred setting, Earth
Contemporary	10,000 words, any topics
Mainstream	10,000 words
Mystery/Suspense	10,000 words
Time Travel	10,000 words
Paranormal	10,000 words
Thriller	10,000 words
Adventure	10,000 words
Horror	10,000 words
Suspense	10,000 words
Occult	10,000 words
Fantasy	10,000 words
Futuristic	10,000 words
Science Fiction	10,000 words
Poetry	50 words maximum

Our romances are conservative, sweet, spicy, sensual, and sexy.

Tips

Notable Novellettes are sold mail order, subscription, and distributed through some national booksellers, as well as places with waiting rooms (doctor's offices, hair salons, etc.).

Editor's favorite romance novel is *The Wizard of Seattle* by Kay Hooper.

Editor's Wish List

First, a manuscript must include an SASE. If it doesn't, we won't even look at it. Subjects can include rags to riches, first date, knights and damsels, murder, ghosts, aliens, insanity, voodoo, werewolves, vampires, psychics, witchcraft/magic, etc. Time periods can be any: pre-history, historical, contemporary, futuristic. Romance can be included, but is not required to be the primary focus of the story. The locale of the story can be anywhere. The main character must be a human, human-like, or formerly human. The pace should be quick, the writing tight. Action and transition/flow are the key!

Turn-offs / Taboos

No explicit sex. No sex or gore for the sake of sex or gore—must fit story. No severely sacrilegious, racial-hate, mean pieces.

Notable Novellettes Writer's Guidelines

ABOUT COGSWELL PUBLISHING

Cogswell Publishing is an independent publisher in Houston, Texas. We want to help talented unpublished writers get publishing credits for their resumes.

The first line of fiction, Notable Novellettes, was founded to provide a quick read for a small price with a variety of genres . . . from horror to science fiction, from romance to mysteries. Some deal with the dark side of human nature; others, with romance or humor. Two novellettes and a poem per publication.

Future lines will include:

1. KVK Unusuals, a line of full length novels, all off the beaten track genres, word count of 85,000–125,000.

2. KVK Romances, a line of mid-length novels, straight romances, but not clichéd, word count of 60,000–85,000.

3. Rose Books, a line of children's books.

4. Daniel Books, a line of nonfiction books (self-help, home school aids, etc.).

Have you had trouble getting published? Been told by publishers that you have talent, but there's no market for your story? Is your forte short tales of around 10,000 words? Give Notable Novellettes a try. We might be interested!

SUBMISSIONS
Authors wishing to be considered for publication as a Notable Novellette (story or poem) should query the publisher first with a two-paragraph synopsis on the cover letter, resume/qualifications, and SASE. Story, 10,000 maximum word count; poem, 50 per poem maximum word count. If a story is accepted, a diskette version (text in ASCII) will be requested.

All submissions must include a complete SASE; those that do not will not be considered. Authors are not required to use pen names. Payment is in royalties, copies, and by-line pub/credit, and is discussed on an individual basis.

SUBJECT MATTER
Genres appropriate for publication under the Notable Novellettes line include, but are not limited to: thriller, adventure, horror, suspense, occult, time travel, paranormal, fantasy, mystery, futuristic, romance, science fiction. Please specify which genre in the query letter.

Subjects can include rags to riches, first date, knights and damsels, murder, ghosts, aliens, insanity, voodoo, werewolves, vampires, psychics, witchcraft/magic, etc. Time periods can be any—pre-history, historical, contemporary, futuristic.

Romance can be included, but is not required to be the primary focus of the story. The locale of the story can be any. The main character must be a human, human-like, or formerly human. The pace should be quick, the writing tight. Action and transitions/flow is the key! No explicit sex or gore/sex for the sake of gore/sex.

Take a look at our back publications. If you can't find them at a bookseller near you, send $3.75 to the address above and mark the envelope: N.N. Sample.

Novellettes are 5¹/₂″ × 8¹/₂″, folded, digest bound/stapled. Covers are glossy card stock.

COSMOPOLITAN
224 W. 57th Street
New York, NY 10019

Executive Editor: Helen Gurley Brown

Fiction and Books Editor: Betty Kelly

Subscriptions: $24 yr/monthly, or $1.95 per copy

Tips

Stories must have solid upbeat plots, and sharp characterization. They should focus on contemporary man-woman relationships. Sophisticated handling and sensitive approach is a must, and female protagonists are preferred since our readers most easily identify with them. Short-shorts range from 1,500 to 3,000 words, short stories from 4,000 to 6,000 words. Payment is $1,000 and up for short stories, from $300 to $600 for short-shorts. Previously published serious novels and mystery and suspense novels are sought for condensing and excerpting; payment is open to negotiation with the author's agent or hardcover publisher.

Please enclose an SASE or your submission cannot be returned.

FICTION WRITER'S GUIDELINE
P.O. Box 4065
Deerfield Beach, FL 33442
(305) 426-4705

Director/Editor: Blythe Camenson

Circulation: 1,000+ monthly

Submissions Policies

Query or send completed manuscript. Unsolicited manuscripts are OK, as are simultaneous submissions. See Writer's Guidelines for additional information.

Pay Rate

Pays $5–$100 upon publication. Usual response time is 1 month. Buys First North American serial rights, reprint rights or one-time rights.

Actively Seeking
Nonfiction
Author Profiles	200–1,500 words
How-to Articles for Writers	200–1,500 words
Interviews with Agents/Editors	200–1,500 words

Tips

Request a sample copy to see our format. Subscriptions are $39 a year, but newsletters are free to Fiction Writer's Connection members. (See the network section of this book).

FWG Writer's Guidelines

FWG is a membership organization providing practical assistance and information to writers pursuing the craft of fiction. Among the benefits to members is a monthly newsletter, *Fiction Writer's Guideline.*

Fiction Writer's Guideline is accepting freelance submissions covering the following topics: Success stories, Interviews with authors, agents, and editors (see below for required and suggested interview questions), how-to articles on the craft of fiction and getting published.

Submissions: Please query by letter or telephone before submitting manuscripts. All manuscripts will be considered on an "on spec" basis, but if the topic is approved first, chances are likely the article will be accepted.

Please submit all manuscripts typed and double-spaced, on one side of the page, with the exact word count typed in the upper right hand corner of the first page. Be sure to include your name, address, phone number and Social Security number. An SASE must accompany all articles submissions.

All submissions must be received by the fifth of the month in order to be considered for publication in the next month's issue.

Other Topics: In addition to articles, FWG is always on the lookout for new markets, upcoming contests, seminars, conferences, fillers, and any other events of interest to fiction writers. It is not necessary to write up these tips; you can submit clippings in bulk, once a month. Payment is 25¢ for each tip published. If more than one writer submits the same tip, the first one received will be credited.

INTERVIEW GUIDELINES

You are free to choose which authors you want to interview. The only requirements are that he or she is an author of fiction and has been at least moderately successful. The author can work in any genre, but FWG will vary the genres from month to month.

Please inform each author that the interview will be read by fiction writers, both new and published.

Below are required questions for the interview:

1. Ask authors how they became interested in writing as a profession—when they started writing, who inspired them, etc.
2. Ask authors to detail how they got started. How did they get
   their first book published—did they go through an agent, or
   submit to editors themselves? How many places did they
   submit their manuscript to until it was accepted—any interesting anecdotes, feedback, comments, about the process?
   How were they notified of their first sale—by phone, mail,
   etc.?
3. Ask authors if they are willing to reveal how much they
   advance/royalty they received for their first and latest
   sale.
4. Any advice to aspiring writers.
5. Next project in the works?

   Other questions might discuss how they got their ideas, how
they choose settings and characters, and questions related to their
specific books.

   Articles can be written in a fairly chatty style, laced liberally
with quotes and anecdotes.

Agent Interviews: Agents interviewed must handle fiction, be
open to new writers, have room to add new clients to their list,
and must not charge a reading fee. The following information
must be obtained during your interview: genres they are most
interested in; how they prefer to be approached (telephone or
query letter); what they want to see (synopses, first three chapters, fifty pages, etc.) response time; recent sales (if available);
commission charged; advice to writers. Read one of our interviews before submitting.

Editor Interviews: Editors interviewed must handle fiction and
be willing to accept unagented submissions. The following information must be obtained during your interview: genres they are
interested in; how they want to be approached initially, response
time, submissions dos and don'ts, advances, royalties, advice, etc.
Read one of our interviews before submitting to us.

In addition, agents and editors must supply information:

Turn-offs (pet peeves with either writing or how writers approach them).

First Novel Problems (difficulties with writing style or technique that they typically see first-time novelists succumbing to).

Advice (a line or two of quotable advice to aspiring writers).

Please feel free to call Blythe Camenson at (305) 426-4705 if you have any questions about these guidelines.

FIRST FOR WOMEN

270 Sylvan Avenue
Englewood Cliffs, NJ 07632
(no phone calls or faxes accepted from writers)

Managing Editor: Theresa Hagan

Circulation: 1.6 million, 16 issues per year

Submissions Policies

No queries. Send complete manuscript. Address to Fiction Department. Unagented and unsolicited manuscripts are OK. SASE is essential. One story at a time. Average response time is 1–2 months.

Pay Rate

$1,000 on acceptance. Publishes about 6 months after acceptance.

Actively Seeking

Mainstream with romance elements   about 2,000 words

Tips

No foreign settings. No mysteries or New York settings. SASE a must. Send one story at a time. See Writer's Guidelines for more information.

First for Women Writer's Guidelines

First is looking for quality fiction that will appeal to intelligent, thoughtful women in all walks of life. Many of our readers are working mothers between the ages of 24 and 45 with some college education; some have limited education and hold blue collar jobs. We believe they enjoy serious, sensitively told stories that leave the reader feeling she has been enriched as well as entertained.

The stories we publish will have memorable images, a style that expresses the writer's personal voice, and vivid realistic settings that provide a strong sense of place. They offer insights into relationships and suggest a positive movement in the lives of the characters through changes in circumstance or in perception. At the core of these stories is a vividly rendered female protagonist who is grappling with the important issues in her life.

We prefer dramatic narratives with a strong sense of emotional resolution, but the rich story that doesn't quite form a neatly tied package, leaving the reader with something to consider, has a chance here.

We do not publish mysteries, tales of the rich and famous, stories with foreign settings, or stories containing pat, moralistic messages. A strong regional flavor is okay as long as our readers can easily identify with the characters and situations. We use very few stories set in New York City. We may publish an occasional story from a male viewpoint if female characters are the true focus of the story.

GENRE PRESS DIGEST
c/o Bonnie Mumford, Fiction Editor
24 Roberts Way
Northeast, MD 21901

Genre Press Digest is a publication of the Small Press Genre Association (SPGA). Here are the fiction guidelines (excerpted):

Fiction manuscripts of 1,000–3,000 words submitted for publication should be in standard manuscript format: double-spaced, on one side of the paper with one inch margins all around.

Real name, address, phone number should appear single-spaced in the upper left hand corner of the first page. Indicate aproximate word count in the upper right corner of the first page.

Pseudonyms should be indicated on the byline.

Since not everyone shares an enthusiasm for erotica or violence, keep fiction R-rated or under.

Send #10 SASE for info on SPGA.

GOOD HOUSEKEEPING

959 Eighth Avenue
New York, NY 10019
(212) 649-2202
FAX: (212) 265-3307

Fiction Editor: Lee Quarfoot

Circulation: 5 million per month

Submissions Policies

No queries necessary for short fiction. Send complete manuscript. No SASE please. Rejections are not returned or acknowledged. Unagented and unsolicited manuscripts are OK. See Writer's Guidelines for additional information.

Pay Rate

Pays "market rates" on acceptance.

Actively Seeking

Contemporary Romance	1,000–3,000 words
Mainstream with Romance Elements	1,000–3,000 words

Short fiction of emotional interest to women.

Tips

We purchase first serial rights only on about-to-be-published novels. We do not accept submission of unpublished novels; therefore, there is no reason to send sample chapters or synopses. We do welcome short story submissions.

Good Housekeeping Writer's Guidelines

We look for stories with strong emotional interest, such as stories revolving around courtship, romance, marriage, family, friendships, personal growth, coming of age. The best way to gauge whether your story might be appropriate for us is to read the fiction in several of our recent issues. (We are sorry, but we cannot furnish sample copies of the magazine.)

Owing to the huge volume of submissions, those manuscripts not accepted for publication cannot be returned, so please *don't* include a self-addressed stamped envelope. We do assure you, however, that every submission is read. If in our judgment a story has possibilities for *GH,* you will hear from us within a month's time.

We prefer double-spaced typewritten (or keyboarded) manuscripts, accompanied by a short cover letter listing any previous writing credits. Make sure your name and address appear on the manuscript, and that you retain a copy for yourself.

HOUSEWIFE-WRITER'S FORUM
P.O. Box 780
Lyman, WY 82937

Acquisitions Editor: Diane Wolverton

Circulation: 1,000+

Subscriptions: $15 yr/bimonthly. Sample copy $4.

Submissions Policies
Submit complete manuscript with SASE and cover letter.

Actively Seeking

Short Fiction	less than 2,000 words (which will be reviewed in the magazine)
Nonfiction	less than 2,000 words
Poetry	

Also seeking entries for various contests.

Send SASE for complete contest rules and/or writer's guidelines.

MODERN ROMANCES
Macfadden Women's Group, Inc.
233 Park Avenue, South
New York, NY 10003
(212) 979-4800
FAX: (212) 979-7342

Acquisitions Editor: Cherie Clark King

Circulation: 200,000 monthly

Submissions Policies

Never query first. Send the complete manuscript with SASE. Unsolicited manuscripts are OK, but simultaneous submissions are not acceptable. Response time is about 9 months.

Pay Rate

Payment is upon publication at the rate of 5¢ per word. We buy all rights.

Actively Seeking
Confessional   3,000–9,000 words
Recipes

Modern Romance Writer's Guidelines

Thank you for your interest in *Modern Romances* magazine. We would like to see your work. However, we do not issue "official" guidelines. As an alternative, we suggest that you read several issues of the magazine for an idea of the style of stories we print.

Manuscripts should be typed, double-spaced, and between 2,500 and 12,000 words. Only those stories offering us all rights and written in the first person will be considered.

Subject matter can be anything from light romance to current social concerns that would be of interest to our readers.

Each manuscript we receive will be considered and a reply will be sent to you between 3–9 months after we receive your work. We do not acknowledge receipt of manuscripts. Please enclose a stamped self-addressed envelope for your manuscript's return.

We also accept light romantic poetry, such as love poems or poems with a holiday/seasonal theme. Maximum length, 24 lines. Payment of poems is based on merit.

We look forward to reading your story. Best of luck!

MYSTERY TIME
Hutton Publications
P.O. Box 2907
Decatur, IL 62524

Acquisitions Editor: Linda Hutton

Subscriptions: sample copies $3.50

Actively Seeking

Rotten Romance Contest—Annual deadline February 14th post-mark. Cash prize for the best or worst opening sentence (original) of a romance novel you *never* wrote, no length limit. Submit typed with SASE. No entry fee, one entry per person. Type all envelopes.

Mystery Mayhem Contest—Annual deadline Agatha Christie's birthday, September 15th. Cash prize for best or worst opening sentence of the mystery novel you *never* wrote, no length limit. Submit typed, with SASE. No entry fee; one entry per person. Winner will be published in *Mystery Time.* Type all envelopes.

Also needed are mysteries of up to 1,500 words for *Mystery Time,* a semi-annual anthology of short fiction with a mystery or suspense theme. 1/4¢ per word paid for first rights. Type all envelopes.

NEW READER'S PRESS
c/o Laubach Literacy International
1320 Jamesville Avenue, Box 131
Syracuse, NY 13210

No response to questionnaire or follow-up letter. Publishes short romances (and other genre fiction) for adults who are reading at about a fourth grade level, 6,500–9,500 words. Query first with synopsis and sample chapters (and SASE).

NEW WRITING
Box 1812
Amherst, NY 14226
(716) 286-8627

Acquisitions Editor: Pamela Wayne, Executive Editor; S. Meade, Co-Editor

Submissions Policies

Don't query. Send the complete manuscript. Simultaneous submissions are OK. Usual response time is 1 month. Payment is upon publication.

Actively Seeking
Confessional
Contemporary Romance
Historical
Inspirational
Mainstream
Ethnic
Mystery/Suspense
Other
Word counts not specified.

Tips

We sponsor contests and are part of a literary agency seeking talent.

NOTABLE NOVELLETES
(See COGSWELL PUBLISHING.)

OVER MY DEAD BODY!
THE MYSTERY MAGAZINE
P.O. Box 1778
Auburn, WA 98071
(206) 473-4650

Acquisitions Editor: Cherie Jung

Circulation: 1,000

Subscriptions: $12 yr/quarterly

Submissions Policies

Query or submit complete typed (double-spaced) manuscript
with SASE. Unsolicited manuscripts are OK, as are simultaneous
submissions. Usual response time is 4–6 weeks. For electronic
submissions, please query first. Address Fiction Editor or Feature
Editor, as appropriate.

Pay Rate

Payment is within 30 days of publication, at the rate of one cent
per word for fiction, about $10–$25 per nonfiction article. Payment also includes two contributor copies. We buy First North
American Serial Rights. All rights revert to the author upon publication.

Actively Seeking
Mystery/Suspense   250–4,000 words
Author Profiles

Tips

We look for stories our readers will want to read more than once.

Over My Dead Body! Writer's Guidelines

Over My Dead Body! The Mystery Magazine publishes a wide variety of mystery-related manscripts, from cozy to hard-boiled and everything in between. We don't discriminate on the basis of content, subgenre, or author recognition. Send us your best.

Fiction: We want to see taut, absorbing, original work. Keep dialogue and narrative consistent with characterization unless you're using discrepancy as a plot point. Don't waste words, and don't ignore facts to faciliate your plot. Most importantly, if you're going to break the rules, do it well. 750–4,000 words.

Nonfiction: We're looking for mystery-related author interviews/profiles and articles. Mystery-related travel pieces will also be considered (for example, travel pieces about the Reichenbach Falls of Sherlock Holmes fame). 500 words.

PUBLISHERS SYNDICATION INTERNATIONAL
1377 K Street, N.W., Suite 856
Washington, D.C. 20005

Editor: A. P. Samuels

Media Type: Paperback, Hardcover, *The Post*, Novelettes

Submissions Policies

Send complete manuscripts, including word count and SASE. (Sleuth Editor is Mary Straub.) Unsolicited and unagented manuscripts are OK. New authors are encouraged. No simultaneous submissions. No phone calls from agents. Specify computer type, disk size and density, and word processing program used, in case a disk copy of the story is requested. Usual response time is 4–6 weeks, sometimes longer. SASE is required for return.

Pay Rate

Upon acceptance; 1–4¢ a word, plus royalty. Byline is given. (Sleuth novelettes pay ³/₄–3¢ a word.)

Actively Seeking

Romance Adventures	9,250 words (approximately)
Mystery/Suspense	9,250 words (approximately)
Romance	30,000 words (approximately)
Miscellaneous Subjects	30,000 words (approximately)
Mystery	30,000 words (approximately)
"Sleuth" Novelettes	10,000 words

Tips

Romances should not contain explicit sex, as they are for a general audience. Mysteries should be similar to Sherlock Holmes. No blood and guts violence.

"Sleuth" novelettes are solved by the reader, who has a choice of multiple suspects. Solution and justification for solution should be typed on a separate page. Include pencil sketches of floor plans or street maps that will involve the reader.

We buy 12 romantic adventure *and* 12 mystery/suspense stories per year.

Publishers Syndication Writer's Guidelines

Will buy first time manuscripts if good enough. Photocopies are OK. No simultaneous submissions please. Prefer letter quality printing.

THE POST
Looking for Mystery/Suspense of 9,250 words and Romantic Adventure of 9,250 words.

No explicit sex, gore, sadism, or horror. Manuscripts must be for a general audience. Just good plain storytelling with a unique plot. Constant booze, chain smoking or swearing are not necessary to a well-written, action filled story.

Some stories of 4,500 words are considered if they are exceptional.

Post pays 1–4¢ per word on acceptance, plus royalty.

NOVELETTES

Looking for Romance of 30,000 words, Mystery of 30,000 words, and Miscellaneous Subjects of 30,000 words.

Novelettes pays ³/₄–3¢ per word on acceptance. Show word count on submissions. (The type of mystery we are looking for is devoid of references which might offend. Sherlock Holmes would be a good example of the type of mysteries we require.) No explicit sex in Romance stories.

If you use a computer, please specify kind, disk size, density, and the name of the word processing program you are using. In some cases we may request disk copy of your story.

SLEUTH

Editor: Mary Straub

Sleuth requires mysteries that involve the reader. A story may contain one or two pencil diagrams: a street map with placement of figures pertinent to the story, floor plans, seating arrangements, etc. The reader must solve the mystery. Your solution to the mystery and reasoning should be on a separate page. Remember, you need multiple obvious suspects.

Submit the entire manuscript. Reports in 4–8 weeks. Byline is given. SASE please. Pays on acceptance, length is 10,000 words and pay is ³/₄–3¢ per word. No simultaneous submissions please. Show word count. No blood and gore. Looking for good mysteries that convert the reader into a detective.

RADIANCE, THE MAGAZINE FOR LARGE WOMEN

Box 30246
Oakland, CA 94604
(510) 482-0680

Editors: Alice Ansfield, Publisher/Editor; Catherine Taylor, Senior Editor; Carol Squires, Editiorial Assistant

Circulation: 10,000 quarterly

Submissions Policies

Authors may query first, or send synopsis and sample chapters or send complete manuscript. Unagented and unsolicited manuscripts are OK. Average response time is 6 weeks. See Writer's Guidelines for additional information.

Pay Rate

$50–$100. Payment is on publication at this time.

Actively Seeking

Contemporary Romance	800–2,000 words
Ethnic Romance	800–2,000 words
Romantic Suspense	800–2,000 words
Mainstream with Romance Elements	800–2,000 words
Inspirational	800–2,000 words

Other topics include women coming to awareness of their own strengths, dealing with careers, standing up for themselves.

Tips

Read a copy of *Radiance* to get our point of view before sending us your story. We like stories about women who are intelligent, thoughtful, sensitive, strong, vulnerable, sensual beings. We want more than woman-hates-self, woman-meets-man, woman-likes-self stories! We welcome unpublished writers. We want stories about women from all walks of life, of all ethnic groups, ages, and sizes. Stories from both women and men desired.

Radiance Writer's Guidelines

Radiance is a quarterly magazine now celebrating its seventh year in print with more than 100,000 readers worldwide. Its target audience is the one woman in four who wears a size 16 or over—an estimated 30 million women in America alone. *Radiance* brings a fresh, vital new voice to women of all sizes with our positive images, profiles of dynamic large women from all walks of life, and our compelling articles on health, media, fashion, and politics. We urge women to feel good about themselves now—whatever their body size. *Radiance* is one of the leading resources in the "size acceptance movement," linking large women to the network of products, services, and information just for them.

Radiance has the following departments:

Up Front and Personal—Interviews or first person accounts relating to life as a large woman from all walks of life. We like strong, intimate, in-depth profiles about a person's life and philosophy.

Health and Well-Being—Articles on health, fitness, emotional well-being related to women in general and large women in particular. Also profiles of healthcare professionals sensitive to the needs of large women.

Perspectives—Cultural/historical/social views of body size and female beauty attitudes worldwide.

Expressions—Interviews with artists who are either large themselves or whose work features large-sized women.

Getaways—Articles on vacation spots, getaways of all types anywhere in the world. Prefer if article somehow includes ideas or special tips for the woman of size.

Women on the Move—Articles about plus-sized women who are involved in some sort of sport or physical activity.

Images—Interviews with designers or manufacturers of plus-sized clothing or accessories. Prefer if the store/designer caters to women all sizes of large, i.e., includes "supersize" women. Can also be article on color, style, wardrobe planning.

Inner Journeys—Articles on personal growth and inner-directed approaches to feeling better about oneself. Can be profiles of people doing this work or general info.

Book Reviews—Books relating to women, body image, health, eating, politics, psychology, media, fashion, cultural attitudes, and so on.

Short Stories & Poetry—Related to body size, self-acceptance. Especially want fiction or poetry that is more than the "woman hates self until meets man to love her" type writing.

Deadlines for submission are July 1 (Winter issue), October 1 (Spring issue), January 1 (Summer issue), and April 1 (Fall issue).

We recommend you read at least one issue of *Radiance* prior to writing anything for us. Query us far in advance of the deadline if you want assurance that your articles will be considered for a particular issue. Our usual response time is 6–12 weeks. Include your name, address, and phone number on the title page and type your name and phone number on subsequent pages. Keep a copy of anything you submit to us. Remember to indicate availability of photos, artwork, illustrations (or ideas for them) in your query or with your article. Pertinent, high-quality photos or art can greatly enhance an article's desirability. If you do send photos, make sure they are marked with a caption and the photographer's name, phone, and address.

At this time, payment is made on publication. We intend to pay upon acceptance in the near future. And as we grow, we will continue to increase payment to writers, photographers, illustrators, etc. We appreciate and value your work. Payments are as follows:

Book reviews: $35–$100
Features/Profiles: $50–$100
Fiction: $50–$100

Poetry, Short Articles: $15–$50
Color Cover Photos: $50–$200
B & W Inside Photos: $15–$25
Illustrations/Artwork: $25–$100

Once we develop a working relationship with the writer, artist, or photographer and we can count on your professionalism, service, quality, and reliability, payment can increase. We will always send the contributor a copy of the magazine she/he is in. The contributor needs to send us an invoice after the work is completed with details of the service.

ROMANTIC INTERLUDES

P.O. Box 760
Germantown, MD 20875

Romantic Interludes is a bi-monthly digest-sized magazine of about 100 pages with full-color cover.

Acquisitions Editor: Wilma Leber

Editorial Consultant: Barbara Cummings

Subscriptions: $18 yr

Submissions Policies

Cover letter and manuscript with SASE.

Pay Rate

Varies from $25 to $100.

Actively Seeking
Short Romantic Fiction
   (no confessionals)   1,500–12,500 words

All subgenres of romance, including Time Travel, Ethnic, Paranormal, Historical, Regency, Gothic, Suspense, stories with
older heroines, etc.

Also buys romantic poetry (15¢/word)

Also seeking romantic fiction in which holidays provide a back-
drop for the story (New Year's Day, Valentine's Day, Mardi
Gras, Passover, Easter, Mother's Day, Halloween, Thanks-
giving, Christmas, etc.).

Sponsors ongoing writing contests (consult current issue for current contest).

SINGER MEDIA CORPORATION

(See listing in Chapter 5, Directory of Publishers.)

THE TALISMAN

P.O. Box 1641
Humble, TX 77347
(713) 277-1392

Editor: Glenna Volesky

Circulation: 500+ bimonthly

Submissions Policies

Query first with synopsis for short stories. For nonfiction send
complete manuscript. Don't forget SASE on all submissions.

Pay Rate

Usually $20 plus one copy. We buy reprint rights.

Actively Seeking

Short Stories   4,000–6,000 words
Also Author Profiles   200+ words
Romance Novel Industry news
How-to Articles for Writers/Open Forum

Tips

We are dedicated to romance with a twist and love elements of
the paranormal, supernatural, fantasy, futuristic, etc.

TRUE CONFESSIONS

Macfadden Women's Group, Inc.
233 Park Avenue, South
New York, NY 10003
(212) 979-4800
FAX: (212) 979-7342

Editor: Jean Sharbel

Circulation: 300,000 monthly

Submissions Policies

Queries are not necessary. Please do not send synopsis and partials—send the complete manuscript. Unagented and unsolicited
are OK. Usual response time is up to 6 months. See Writer's
Guidelines for additional information.

Pay Rate

Pays 5¢ a word. Pays on last day of publication date. Publishes
about 1–6 months after acceptance.

Actively Seeking

Confessional stories	1,500–8,000 words
Contemporary romances	1,500–8,000 words
Mainstream with romance elements	1,500–8,000 words
Inspirational stories	length depends on whether it's a story or an article

All stories are based on true incidents. No fiction.

Tips

If you don't have a typewriter or the money to pay a typist, this market is one that will accept neatly hand printed stories!

True Confessions Writer's Guidelines

All the stories in *True Confessions* are true.

If you would like to send us your story on speculation, we would be happy to read it. Write it in the first person, as you would tell it to a friend, and type it on one side of each sheet of paper, leaving double spaces between the lines. If you do not have a typewriter, please print neatly on one side of each sheet of lined paper.

If we publish your story, we will buy all world rights and pay you at our regular rate of 5¢ a word. Payment is made during the last week of the month of issue. For example, checks for stories printed in our June issue are mailed out during the last week of June.

Please include a stamped self-addressed envelope with your story so that we may return it to you if it does not meet our needs. If we decide not to publish your story, you should expect to hear from us only if you have enclosed a return envelope and sufficient postage. It is advisable for you to keep a copy of your story in case anything should happen to the original.

Because of the vast number of stories we receive, it usually takes at least 6 months for us to give you a report about your story.

Please enclose a self-addressed stamped envelope with any correspondence to *True Confessions*. Otherwise, we cannot guarantee a reply.

TRUE EXPERIENCE

Macfadden Women's Group, Inc.
233 Park Avenue, South
New York, NY 10003
(212) 979-4903

Fiction Editor: Jean Press Silberg, (212) 979-4896 (direct line)

Associate Editor: Cynthia Di Martino

Submissions Policies

All stories are written in first person, past tense. Submit the complete typed, doublespaced manuscript with SASE. Unsolicited and unagented manuscripts are OK. Average response time is 1–2 months.

Pay Rate

Pays 3¢ a word, upon publication. Publishes about 3 months after acceptance. No byline, buys all rights.

Actively Seeking
Confessional   7,000–20,000 words

Tips

Cynthia Di Martino reports, "We're looking for true-to-life stories about current topics women are interested in, although we're glad to accept a good love story." Publication is monthly.

TRUE LOVE
Macfadden Women's Group, Inc.
233 Park Avenue, South
New York, NY 10003
(212) 979-4895
FAX: 979-7342

Acquisitions Editor: Kristina M. Kracht

Circulation: 218,000 monthly

Subscriptions: $9.97 yr/11 issues

Submissions Policies

Don't query. Send the complete manuscript. Unsolicited manuscripts are OK, but no simultaneous submissions are accepted. The usual response time is 6–9 months. Please be patient with us! We get to stories as soon as we can. We love timely stories and lots of modern romance. No historicals.

Actively Seeking

Confessional	1,000–10,000 words
Contemporary Romance	1,000–10,000 words
Inspirational	1,000–10,000 words
Mainstream	1,000–10,000 words
Ethnic	1,000–10,000 words
Mystery/Suspense	1,000–10,000 words

Pay Rate

We buy all rights. Payment is upon publication at 3¢ per word.

True Love Writer's Guidelines

True Love is a women's magazine written for women and by women, although we also welcome male writers. Each month we print between 10 and 12 stories, several poems, and features such as "How I Know I'm in Love" and "The Life I Live." The best way to learn our editorial styles is to read the magazine itself and study the range of possibilities.

We look for modern, well-written stories that involve real people and real emotions. Our subject matter ranges from light romance to inspirational to current social concerns. Some aspect of love and romance will usually figure in, but it need not be the primary focus of the story. Characters will often face a conflict or solve a problem in their lives that can inspire *True Love* readers.

All stories should be typed, double-spaced. Include your phone number in case we have any questions.

No byline is offered. We buy all rights to the story. A large envelope with sufficient postage must be included for the manuscripts to be returned.

Thank you for your interest in *True Love*. Please call us if you have more questions. Good luck; we hope to be reading your *True Love* story soon!

TRUE ROMANCE
233 Park Avenue South
New York, NY 10003
(212) 979-4898
FAX: (212) 979-7342

Acquisitions Editor: Pat Byrdsong

Submissions Policies

Don't query first. Send the complete manuscript. Unsolicited manuscripts are OK, but simultaneous submissions are not. Usual response time is 3–6 months. See Writer's Guidelines for additional information.

Pay Rate

We buy all rights. Payment is on publication at the rate of 3¢ per word.

Actively Seeking

Confessional	2,000–10,000 words
Inspirational	2,000–10,000 words
Ethnic	2,000–10,000 words
Mystery/Suspense	2,000–10,000 words
Other	2,000–10,000 words

All stories are confessions only!

Tips

True Romance is an excellent market for beginning writers. I read all manuscripts and often work with writers. I suggest that writers read three or four issues before sending submissions. Do not talk down to our readers. Contemporary problems should be handled with insight and a fresh angle. We always need good romantic stories. Stories featuring ethnic characters are accepted, but stay away from stereotypical plots and characteristics. Our greatest need is for stories from 2,000 to 4,000 words.

True Romance Writer's Guidelines

True Romance features first-person narratives written for average, high-school-educated women, women who are juggling family and work responsibility, but always put their family first. After a long day she wants to read a compelling, realistic story about people she can identify with. Our readers do not want to read stories about men and women who lead glamorous loves. Stories must be set in towns, cities, and neighborhoods where hardworking Americans live.

Emotionally charged stories with a strong emphasis on characterization and well-defined plots are preferred. Stories should be intriguing, suspenseful, humorous, romantic, or tragic. The plots and characters should reflect the average American's values and desires.

"I want stories that cover the wide spectrum of America. A good story will have a well-defined plot and characters. I want to feel as though I intimately know the narrator and his/her motivation. If your story is dramatically gripping or humorous, you have an excellent chance of making a sale. Realism is the key to a sale at *True Romance*," says Pat Byrdsong, editor.

Do not send query letter; send completed manuscripts. Seasonal materials should be sent six months in advance and marked "seasonal material" on the outside of the envelope. No multiple submissions or photocopies of stories. We buy all rights. Manuscripts should be typed double-spaced. Letter quality printed word processed manuscripts are also acceptable. Dot matrix is OK if letter quality. Send SASE for response and return of your manuscript.

TRUE STORY
Macfadden Women's Group, Inc.
233 Park Avenue, South
New York, NY 10003
(212) 979-4800

Nonfiction Editorial Director: Sue Weiner

Circulation: 1 million monthly

Submissions Policies

No query letters. Prefers to see entire manuscript with large SASE. Unsolicited and/or unagented manuscripts are OK. Average response time is 6 months. Stories are written in first person, past tense.

Pay Rate

Pays 5¢ a word. Publishes about 3 months after acceptance. Pays 1 month after publication.

Actively Seeking
True Confessional
Contemporary Romance
Romantic Suspense
Mainstream with Romance Elements
Inspirational
No word count was specified.

Tips

True Story only publishes true stories—no fiction.

WOMAN'S WORLD
270 Sylvan Avenue
Englewood Cliffs, NJ 07632
(201) 569-0006
FAX: (201) 569-3584

Fiction Editor: Jeanne Muchnick

Circulation: 1.4 million weekly

Submissions Policies

Don't query. Send the complete manuscript. Unagented and unsolicited stories are OK. Average response time is 6–8 weeks.

Pay Rate

Buys First North American Serial Rights. Payment is on acceptance. $500 mystery, $1,000 contemporary romance.

Actively Seeking

Contemporary Romance   2,400 words

Mini-mystery   1,100 words

Tips

No phone queries. No faxes. No response without SASE. No excerpts from novels. No foreign locales in stories.

Woman's World Writer's Guidelines

SHORT STORY

Our feature fiction each week is a short story with a light romantic theme, at a length of approximately 2,400 words. The stories can be written from either a female or male point of view. Women characters may be single, married, divorced, or widowed. I like to see strong, interesting characters. Plots must be fast moving, emphasizing vivid dialogue and plenty of action. The problems and dilemmas should be contemporary and realistic, handled with warmth and a sense of humor. The stories must have a positive resolution.

We are not interested in science fiction, fantasy, historical romance, or foreign locales. We do not want explicit sex (although a strong attraction between the main characters should be apparent, early on), graphic language, or steamy settings. Stories slanted for a particular holiday should be sent at least 6 months in advance.

Please specify "short story" on the outside of your envelope. And always enclose a stamped, self-addressed envelope. We purchase North American rights for 6 months at a standard rate of $1,000 paid on acceptance.

MINI-MYSTERY

The mini-mysteries, at a length of 1,100 words, may feature either a "whodunnit" or "howdunnit" theme. The mystery may revolve around anything from a theft to a murder. However, we are not interested in sordid or grotesque crimes. Emphasis should be on the intricacies of the plot rather than gratuitous violence. We don't print horror or ghost stories, science fiction, fantasy, or foreign settings. Stories slanted for a particular holiday should be sent at least 6 months in advance.

We purchase North American rights for 6 months at a standard rate of $500 paid on acceptance. Sorry, no manuscripts will be returned without SASE or International Postal Coupons. Label the envelope "mini-mystery."

We strongly urge you to examine a sample copy before submitting your manuscript.

WRITER'S WORKSHOP REVIEW
511 W. 24th Street
Vancouver, WA 98660
(206) 693-6147

Circulation: 500 monthly

Subscriptions: $20 yr. Samples are $3.

Acquisitions Editor: Rhia R. Drouillard

Submissions Policies

Don't query. Send the complete manuscript. Simultaneous submissions are OK. Usual response time is 1–4 weeks.

Pay Rate

We pay one copy upon publication and acquire First North American Serial Rights or reprint rights.

Actively Seeking
Contemporary Romance	1,500 words
Historical Romance	1,500 words

Mainstream	1,500 words
Mystery/Suspense	1,500 words
Humor	1,500 words
Also actively seeking Nonfiction:	
Author profiles	1,500 words
Romance Novel Industry News	500 words
How-to Articles for Writers	500–1,500 words
"My First Publication"	500 words
"My Worst Rejection"	500 words

Writer's Workshop Writer's Guidelines

Writer's Workshop Review will consider mysteries, horror, romance, science fiction, fantasy, essays, humor, poetry that rhymes, personal experiences, and articles of interest to writers.

My First Publication and My First Rejection should not be over 500 words. Words of Wisdom is a column by writers and editors containing submissions tips, market tips, organizational tips . . . anything that will help other writers become better or more productive at their craft.

Be sure to include SASE for response and return of submissions. Even if you don't want your submission returned, enclose a #10 envelope with SASE, in case our editor would like to contact you personally.

9

Directory of Networks

International Networks

Australia

ROMANCE WRITERS OF AMERICA (SOUTH AUSTRALIA CHAPTER #131)

22 Glen Eagles Road
Mt. Osmond, South Australia
(08) 379-0517

Contact Person: Diane Beer, President

Annual Dues: $50

Benefits of Membership

Network support; critique service; brainstorming workshops; marketing advice.

Other

Affiliated with Romance Writers of America. Annual conference in August in Adelaide. $200 includes accommodations, speakers, workshops. Contest is being planned.

Canada

GREATER VANCOUVER CHAPTER OF ROMANCE WRITERS OF AMERICA (GVCRWA)
22412 Morse Crescent
Maple Ridge, B.C. V2X 9G6
CANADA

Advisor: Barbara Briggs

Annual Dues: $25

Benefits of Membership

Monthly meetings and speakers; critique service; monthly newsletter; daylong workshops; networking and support from fellow writers.

Other

Affiliated with Romance Writers of America. No annual conference or contest. Hosts daylong workshops twice a year.

RWA ONTARIO
P.O. Box 2221, 5334 Yonge Street
North York, Ontario M2N 6M2
CANADA

Annual Dues: $35 Canadian

Benefits of Membership

Lectures by published authors and editors; workshops; tape library; reference library; market news.

Other

Affiliated with Romance Writers of America. No annual conference is planned at this writing.

Contests

Write for more info on contest or membership.

WINNIPEG RWA CHAPTER

4-468 Carpathia Road
Winnipeg, Manitoba R3N 1Y5
CANADA
(204) 488-6370

Contact Person: Shirley Alton

Annual Dues: None

Benefits of Membership

Free; critique each other's work; offer support and a friendly ear. Group is very small and members become good friends.

Other

Affiliated with Romance Writers of America. No annual conferences or contests at this writing.

USA National and Regional Networks

ANNUAL AFFAIRE DE COEUR
ROMANCE CONVENTION

Call *Affaire de Coeur* at (510) 569-5675 or check the magazine for the latest conference information.

ANNUAL ROMANTIC TIMES
BOOKLOVERS CONVENTION

Check the latest issue of *Romantic Times* magazine for details or call the magazine at (718) 237-1097.

ASSOCIATION OF AUTHOR'S
REPRESENTATIVES (AAR)
10 Astor Place, Third Floor
New York, NY 10003
(212) 353-3709

Formerly ILAA and SAR, this new, merged association is for literary agents. For $5, AAR will send a brochure, a list of members, and a "Code of Ethics." Enclose SASE with 52¢ postage.

THE AUTHORS GUILD
330 W. 42nd Street
New York, NY 10036-6902
(212) 563-5904

Annual Dues: First year is $90. Thereafter, dues are based on income from writing, on a graduated scale.

Benefits of Membership

Over 6,500 members have a collective power to voice opinions on professional issues. Members receive a copy of *Recommended Trade Book Publishing Contract and Guide.* The Guild issues reports and even offers call-in help for members who need guidance with contract negotiations and other issues related to the business of writing. Periodic symposia provide opportunities to get expert answers to questions on libel, publicity, editors, book reviews, and more. Transcripts are circulated. The Guild publishes the *Authors Guild Bulletin,* a periodical. Health insurance may be obtained through the Guild (at an extra charge).

Requirements for Membership

Active (voting) membership requires publication of one book within the last seven years, by an established American publisher, *or* three magazine works within the last 18 months, *or* approval by the membership committee for authors who otherwise have professional standing. Associate (nonvoting) memberships are available for contracted authors who have not yet met the above requirements and Member-at-large status is available for persons interested in supporting the Guild and its services. Write for an informative précis regarding membership requirements and benefits.

Other

Not affiliated with Romance Writers of America. The Authors Guild and The Dramatists Guild are component organizations of The Authors League of America, representing American writers in the battle to reform copyright laws, which resulted in the 1976 Copyright Revision Act. The Authors Guild has an active lobbying campaign to protect the interests of all writers. The *Authors Guild Bulletin* keeps members up-to-date on professional writer's topics such as contracts and royalty statements, libel, taxes, Guild activities and more.

FICTION WRITER'S CONNECTION
P.O. Box 4065
Deerfield Beach, FL 33442-4065
(305) 426-4705

Contact Person: Blythe Camenson

Annual Dues: $59 ($54 for students and senior citizens). Professional memberships are $65. (Newsletter is free to members or $39 a year for non-members.)

Benefits of Membership

Monthly newsletter. Free critiquing service includes (per membership year) the first fifteen pages of a novel and a one or two page synopsis *or* two short stories of up to fifteen pages. (Additional critiquing services available at reasonable rates.) Discounts on seminars. Toll-free member hotline provides help, advice, and information, and assistance with publisher/agent/editor problems. Discount on *Writer's Digest* books. Annual contest with cash prizes.

Other

FWC is for beginning writers who may have questions about writing technique or submissions, are in search of an agent or publisher, need feedback on their work or help with synopses, or want info on contests and new markets. FWC is also for the seasoned writer, who may need help on a book contract, publicity tips, or perhaps a critique to get the next book project underway. FWC is even for agents and editors who may be looking for new talent and want to stay in up-to-date touch with the industry. FWC is not affiliated with Romance Writers of America.

INTERNATIONAL WOMEN'S WRITING GUILD

Box 810, Gracie Station
New York, NY 10028
(212) 737-7536

Contact Person: Hannelore Hahn

Annual Dues: $35

Benefits of Membership

Founded in 1976, IWWG is a network for the personal and professional empowerment of women through writing. Any woman may join, regardless of portfolio. List of over twenty literary agents is made available to members. Subscription to the bi-monthly 28-page newsletter. Access to health insurance and other benefits at group rates. Opportunity to participate in regional and national writing conferences, open houses, IWWG clusters, and round-robin manuscript exchanges. Year-round supportive networking with writing-related women for an exchange of ideas and information, contacts, and conversation.

Other

Not affiliated with Romance Writers of America. Send SASE for conference brochure and membership information.

NATIONAL WRITER'S ASSOCIATION

1450 S. Havana, Suite 424
Aurora, CO 80012
(303) 751-7544
FAX: (303) 751-8593

Executive Director: Sandy Whelchel

Annual Dues: $50 Regular members, $60 Professional members

Benefits of Membership

Services specifically geared to writers at all levels, all kinds of writing. Advocate for writers' rights.

Other

Not affiliated with Romance Writers of America.

Conferences

Well-known published writer for keynote speaker; editors and agents from both coasts; and panels, Q & A sessions, workshops. Covers all facets of writing, fiction and nonfiction.

Contests

Novel Writing Contest, an annual contest, is open to all genres. Runs December 1 to April 1. Three cash awards of $500, $250, and $150. (Write for details.)

PSYCHIC WRITER'S NETWORK
62 Main Street
High Bridge, NJ 08829
(908) 638-4426

Contact Person: Christina Lynn Whited

Benefits of Membership

A psychic newsletter network for professional psychics and writers who want to promote the positive aspects of psychic subjects (joy, health, and well-being) in romance novels and in everyday life. Newsletter offers book reviews, upbeat articles by informed psychic professionals, and editorials that are positive and do not delve deeply into dark subjects (such as vampires), but focus on the goodness of psychic power in romances and the writing life. Six issues for $15.

Other

Not affiliated with Romance Writers of America. No contests or conferences.

ROMANCE WRITERS OF AMERICA
(RWA NATIONAL)
13700 Veterans Memorial, Suite 315
Houston, TX 77014
(713) 440–6885
FAX (713) 440–7510

Contact Person: Linda Fisher, Office Supervisor

Annual Dues: $60

Benefits of Membership

Bimonthly 72-page magazine; published authors network; RITA contest for published novels; Golden Heart Contest (unpublished manuscripts); medical insurance available; local chapters; Agent Handbook; Rate the Publishers Survey; and more.

Other

RWA National has over one hundred regional, local and outreach chapter affiliates. Outreach chapters support romance writers who live in remote areas or who cannot attend meetings.

Conferences

RWA holds an annual national conference in June or July and sponsors contests for members. Please call or write for conference brochures.

1995 Conference: Honolulu, Hawaii (July 19–23, 1995)

1996 Conference: Dallas, TX (July 10–14, 1996)

Approximate cost: $265 (subject to change).

Workshops for the beginner through multi-published, agent and editor appointments, networking, Awards ceremony to honor the contest winners.

Contests

RITA—Best published romance in eleven categories.
Golden Heart—Best manuscript by an unpublished writer in ten
     categories.

ROSE PETALS AND PEARLS

115 Eastmont Drive
Jackson, TN 38301
(901) 422-6223

Contact Person: Diane Kirk

Annual Dues: $20

Benefits of Membership

This non-profit organization is dedicated to the preservation of the romance genre. They also sponsor a romance author cruise every year to promote the positive and professional aspects of authors and their novels. Members can be readers or writers. The quarterly newsletter (which will be monthly starting January '95) has information on events and also articles by romance authors. Sponsors humanitarian projects and performs community services for women, as well as supporting literacy programs. $20 annual fee includes newsletter and membership.

Other

Not affiliated with Romance Writers of America. Yearly cruise. (Romance authors who are invited on the cruise as speakers have their travel costs covered.)

THE SCENE & UNSEEN

250 N. 36th Street
Springfield, OR 97478
   or

1210 Woodside Drive
Eugene, OR 97401

A Network for "Writers Who are Not Afraid of the Unbelievable or Things That Go Bump in the Night."

Editor/Publisher: Laura Hoscoe Spinder (send to 1st address)

Researcher: Sue Greenlee (send to 2nd address)

Annual Dues: $15

Benefits of Membership

Bi-monthly newsletter containing market news and trends, articles, author contributions regarding market trends and personal experiences, free advertising for member authors' new releases, member editorial and article contributions, and a list of upcoming titles with paranormal themes.

Other

Not affiliated with Romance Writers of America. No annual conferences or contests.

SMALL PRESS GENRE ASSOCIATION
2131 S. 227th Drive
Buckeye, AZ 85326-3872
(602) 386-3634

Contact Person: Cathy Hicks, Secretary

Annual Dues: $25 U.S. and Canada, $30 International. Publishers may join for $35 (includes American Bookseller Association Extras from COSMEP).

Benefits of Membership

Subscription to bimonthly *Genre Press Digest,* which includes articles, reviews, art, poetry, how-to, market news, some fiction; Prose, Poetry and Art Commentary Services (free with membership); Grievance Arbitration; Info-Swap/Collaboration Service; COSMEP membership; etc.

Other

Not affiliated with Romance Writers of America. No conference or contests planned as yet, although perhaps in the future.

WOMEN'S NATIONAL BOOK ASSOCIATION
1115 Grandview Drive
Nashville, TN 37204
(615) 269-1000 ext. 2441

Contact Person: Carolyn T. Wilson, National President

Annual Dues: Dues are paid through individual chapters and they vary. About $25 is average.

Benefits of Membership

WNBA is an umbrella organization of 1,000+ women and men who work with and value words. Provides a focus for exchange of information, ideas, contacts and support in eight chapters across the country. Members are publishers, librarians, booksellers, writers, editors, agents, illustrators, designers, and book and magazine producers. Members are both experienced and young, in-house staff and freelancers building connections with colleagues through WNBA. Offers chapter activities, national periodical, *The Bookwoman,* chapter newsletters, networking opportunities throughout the book industry, educational programs, seminars, workshops, career programs, job listings, etc.

Other

Not affiliated with Romance Writers of America. No national annual conferences or contests at this writing, but WNBA sponsors educational programs at American Bookseller's Association (ABA) and American Library Association (ALA) conventions. Individual chapters may offer seminars and workshops. Sponsors awards for booksellers and for bookwomen who have made extraordinary contributions to the book industry. There are chapters of WNBA in New York City and Binghamton, NY; Boston; Detroit; San Francisco and Los Angeles; Nashville; and the Washington D.C. area. Write to Carolyn T. Wilson at the above address for chapter contact names and addresses, or for a brochure about WNBA.

THE YOUNG ADULT NETWORK
700 Malaga Drive
Ukiah, CA 95482

Contact Person: Diane Crawford, Membership/Treasurer

Annual Dues: $12

Benefits of Membership

Bimonthly newsletter; Big Sister/Little Sister Mentor Program.

Other

Affiliated with Romance Writers of America. No conferences or contests.

Local Networks

Alabama

HEART OF DIXIE

720 Lily Flagg Road, S.E.
Huntsville, AL 35802
(205) 881-9193

Contact Person: Gail Froelich, President/Advisor

Annual Dues: $20

Benefits of Membership

Fellowship of our published and unpublished writers; critiquing groups; monthly meeting featuring writing help and published authors from the Southeast area.

Other

Affiliated with Romance Writers of America. Annual conference. No annual contests.

Conferences

Heart of Dixie Conference

When: Usually in the fall (write for info)

Where: Huntsville, Alabama

Cost: About $50

The conference will feature authors Linda Howard, Beverly Barton, Theresa DiBenedetto, Patricia Potter, Vernita Hilton, and Linda Winstead Jones.

Alaska

ALASKA CHAPTER OF ROMANCE WRITERS OF AMERICA

P.O. Box 870009
Wasilla, AK 99687
(907) 376-4117

Contact Person: Cheryl Johnson, President

Annual Dues: $15

Benefits of Membership

Education; critiquing; networking; moral support.

Other

Affiliated with Romance Writers of America. No chapter conference. No annual contests.

Arizona

ARIZONA AUTHORS ASSOCIATION

3509 E. Shea Boulevard, Suite 117
Phoenix, AZ 85028
(602) 942-4240

Contact Person: Gerry Benniger, President

Annual Dues: $40

Benefits of Membership

Newsletter; seminar discounts; book discounts; critique groups; networking with other writers.

Other

Not affiliated with Romance Writers of America. No annual conference. Holds annual contest. (Send SASE for rules.)

DESERT ROSE CHAPTER—PHOENIX RWA #60

2553 S. Playa Avenue
Mesa, AZ 85202-6926
(602) 917-8041

Co-Presidents: Dawn Creighton and Pat Jennings

Annual Dues: $18 plus membership in National RWA

Benefits of Membership

Monthly chapter meetings with time for networking and bi-monthly guest speaker; monthly newsletter that includes local happenings, member achievements, articles, and national market news; monthly meeting sale of used books; lending library of tapes; quarterly workshops; Mentor Programs; critique groups. These programs have all evolved with the writer's needs in mind. Despite the impressive expansion over the last 10 years (to more than 100 members), this is still a group which welcomes each individual with the hope that each can achieve his or her full potential in the writing profession.

Other

Affiliated with Romance Writers of America. No annual contest. Annual conference with top authors, editors, and literary agents. This chapter supports adult literacy programs.

Conferences

Annual Desert Dreams Conference

When: September

Where: Phoenix Area (usually a Tempe hotel)

Cost: About $120 for non-members, $100 for chapter members

Guests and speakers include bestselling authors in all areas of romance. Agents will be taking appointments and leading round-tables. Editors will talk about their lines and scout out new talent. The don't-miss workshops have topics such as synopsis preparation, writing sensual romance, humor in historicals, characterization, and more. Events include a no-host cocktail party (Friday night), a Continental breakfast (Saturday A.M.), Saturday workshops, Saturday lunch, Saturday night "Walkabout" in Old Towne Tempe, Sunday Book Fair and autograph party, and a Sunday brunch with editors and agents.

NORTHERN ARIZONA ROMANCE WRITERS OF AMERICA

1911 E. Rainier Loop
Flagstaff, AZ 86004
(602) 774-7629

Contact Person: Joyce Reid, Newsletter Editor

Annual Dues: $12

Benefits of Membership

Communication and fellowship with other writers of romance—both published and unpublished.

Other

Affiliated with Romance Writers of America. No conferences or contests as yet. Offers 148-page book written by national best-selling authors, and edited by Joan Elliott Pickart. *See the Elephant, Lotsa Stuff 'bout Writing Romance* is $15 postpaid.

SOCIETY OF SOUTHWESTERN AUTHORS
P.O. Box 41897
Tucson, AZ 85717

Write for information on membership, conferences, and events.

TUCSON RWA #58
681 N. Hearthside Lane
Tucson, AZ 85748
(602) 751-9141

Contact Person: Evelyn Marie Snover

Annual Dues: $15

Benefits of Membership

Support each other; critique each other's work; networking.

Other

Affiliated with Romance Writers of America. No annual conferences or contests at this writing.

VALLEY OF THE SUN ROMANCE WRITERS
4918 W. Torrey Pines
Glendale, AZ 85308
(602) 439-3535
FAX: (602) 843-2924

Contact Person: Christine Jones, President

Annual Dues: $15

Benefits of Membership

High quality networking; weekend mini-workshops; outstanding contest.

Other

Affiliated with Romance Writers of America. No annual conference.

Contests

Annual Hot Prospects Contest—open to all unpublished writers. Send SASE for rules.

WRITERS OF THE PURPLE PAGE— YUMA, AZ CHAPTER OF RWA
P.O. Box 228
Winterhaven, CA 92283
(619) 572-0876

Contact Person: Pinkie Paranya

Annual Dues: $15

Benefits of Membership

Support; mutual knowledge of craft; newsletters.

Other

Affiliated with Romance Writers of America. No annual contest or conference.

California

GOLD COAST CHAPTER RWA

P.O. Box 6118
Santa Barbara, CA 93160
(805) 683-6340

Contact Person: Margaret Dear

Annual Dues: $15 plus membership in National RWA

Benefits of Membership

Monthly newsletter; monthly meetings with interesting speakers; critique groups available; networking.

Other

Affiliated with Romance Writers of America. No annual conferences or contests are planned as of this writing.

RWA/MONTERREY BAY CHAPTER

137 Rustic Lane
Santa Cruz, CA 95060
(408) 427-2275 (evenings and weekends)

Contact Person: Suzannne J. Barrett, President

Annual Dues: $20 plus National RWA membership fee

Benefits of Membership

Hands-on programs on varied writing topics; published authors network; critique groups; reference library; tapes on all aspects of writing and publishing.

Other

Affiliated with Romance Writers of America. No annual conferences are planned at this writing.

Contests

Annual Silver Heart Competition—Entries consist of synopsis (10 page maximum) and first chapter, not to exceed 30 pages. Send SASE for rules.

SACRAMENTO CHAPTER RWA

Call RWA National at (713) 440-6885 for current contact address.

Annual Dues: $20

Benefits of Membership

Newsletter; conferences; workshops.

Other

Affiliated with Romance Writers of America. Annual One-Two-Three Step Synopsis Workshop and Contest. Send SASE for more.

RWA SAN DIEGO CHAPTER

P.O. Box 22805
San Diego, CA 92192
(619) 425-3093

Contact Person: Carol Heflin

Annual Dues: $25

Benefits of Membership

Monthly newsletter; monthly workshops and meetings ($5 meeting fee); special events including editor dinners.

Other

Affiliated with Romance Writers of America. No annual conference. Holds annual contest.

Contests

Annual ChEMistry Test—Focuses on Conflict, Emotion and Motivation. Send long SASE for rules, or watch *Romance Writer's Report* magazine for details.

WOMEN WRITERS WEST

P.O. Box 1637
Santa Monica, CA 90406
(818) 841-1193

Contact Person: Betty Payton, President

Annual Dues: $25

Benefits of Membership

Monthly newsletter lists events; contests and other information of interest to writers; monthly meetings feature excellent speakers, and opportunities to read work in progress or to present published work. We have not had a conference for the last six years, and will probably not do so in the foreseeable future. (Our monthly meetings have almost replaced the need for a conference.)

Other

Not affiliated with Romance Writers of America.

Colorado

PIKE'S PEAK ROMANCE WRITERS
P.O. Box 16976
Colorado Springs, CO 80935
(719) 392-1505

Annual Dues: $21

Benefits of Membership

Networking; education; motivation; promotion for published members; unpublished and published contest; critique groups; workshops; library.

Other

Affiliated with Romance Writers of America. Holds annual weekend retreat in a serene mountain setting, bringing writers together to rediscover their creativity. Write for dates and other information.

Contests

Top of the Peak Contest—This contest is for members only who are unpublished. First prize is registration fee to RWA's Annual National Conference.

Pike's Peak Romance Writer of the Year Contest—This contest is for published members who want to enter books eligible for the annual RITA contest. Winner receives entry fee to the RITA, including all costs, and the title "Pike's Peak Romance Writer of the Year."

Connecticut

CONNECTICUT CHAPTER/ROMANCE WRITERS OF AMERICA

140 River Road
Thomaston, CT 06787
(203) 283-6330

Contact Person: Judith Odiorne, Membership

Annual Dues: $25

Benefits of Membership

Monthly programs featuring editors, published romance writers, and "elements of fiction writing" series; monthly newsletter; library of "How to Write" books for rental by members; networking with other writers.

Other

Affiliated with Romance Writers of America. No annual conference.

Contest

Annual Contest—This contest is for unpublished writers of historicals (past), contemporaries (present), and futuristic or time travel (future) romances. Judges will critique first chapter and a synopsis. Entrants receive a critique. Finalists are judged by an editor.

Florida

FLORIDA ROMANCE WRITERS, INC.

2000 N. Congress Avenue, #6
West Palm Beach, FL 33409
(407) 684-3651

Conference Chair: Susan McConnell Koski, Vice President

Annual Dues: $20

Benefits of Membership

Newsletter; writing programs; monthly luncheons; summer seminar.

Other

Affiliated with Romance Writers of America. No annual contests at this writing.

Conferences

When: February 24–26, 1995

Where: Hilton Airport Hotel (Ft. Lauderdale)

Cost: $125 (approximate)

Conference will feature six to nine romance editors; four agents, keynote speaker, Friday orientation, all-day Saturday workshops and seminars, Sunday breakfast with editors and agents, plus manuscript evaluation service. Don't miss special guests Bertrice Small and Eileen Dreyer. Saturday night, instead of a banquet, we are throwing the Ultimate Pajama Party! Please write for ore information

SOUTHWEST FLORIDA ROMANCE WRITERS

P.O. Box 420028
Naples, FL 33942

President: Kristine Hughes

Annual Dues: $20

Benefits of Membership

Writer's support and meetings with guest speakers (whenever possible) with time allotted for question and answers, followed by critique group sessions and idea exchange. This chapter has planned annual "Joint Chapter Luncheons" with other writers groups. Contact this RWA chapter for info on membership or current events.

Other

Affiliated with Romance Writers of America. No annual contests. Holds one day events with other Florida chapters.

Note: Kristine Hughes has a regular column in *Romantic Times* magazine and reviews fiction for *Publisher's Weekly*. Ms. Hughes is the author of six historical reference books.

SARASOTA FICTION WRITERS
Sarasota, FL
(813) 923-3047

Contact Person: Deanne C. Miller

Annual Dues: $12

Benefits of Membership

Latest market and agent news; published author networking; how-to classes; guest speakers; critiques.

Other

Not affiliated with Romance Writers of America. No annual conferences or contests at present.

TAMPA AREA ROMANCE WRITERS, (TARA) INC. #100
P.O. Box 370159
Tampa, FL 33697
(813) 961-8136

Contact Person: Susan Brown

Annual Dues: $25

Benefits of Membership

Monthly meetings; bimonthly newsletter; monthly workshops; annual summer seminar; critique groups. Provides support for those experiencing the joys, sorrows, and concerns of a working writer.

Other

Affiliated with Romance Writers of America.

Conferences

Annual One-Day Seminar

When: Summer, usually in June

Where: Tampa Airport Marriott Hotel

Cost: $45 for TARA members, $55 for non-members (1994 rate) (includes luncheon)

Agents and editors from major publishing houses speak. An authors' panel speaks on subjects related to writing. Writers may schedule appointments with editors.

Contests

First Impressions Contest—Entries consist of the first 25 pages of an unpublished manuscript. Send SASE for more information.

Georgia

GEORGIA ROMANCE WRITERS
P.O. Box 142
Acworth, GA 30101
(404) 974-6678
   or

4128 Manson Avenue
Smyrna, GA 30082
(404) 432-4860

Contact Person: Marian Oaks (contact at 1st address)

Current President: Sandra Chastain (contact at 2nd address)

Annual Dues: $15

Benefits of Membership

Access to writing/marketing info; informative newsletter; monthly meetings and networking with other writers; reduced annual conference rate for members.

Other

Affiliated with Romance Writers of America. Annual Conference and also annual contests for both published and unpublished writers.

Conferences

Moonlight and Magnolias Annual Conference

When: Fall

Where: Atlanta

Cost: Send SASE for complete conference details. Editor/Agent appointments, published author suite, assorted workshops and panels for all levels of writing skill, unique programs. Agents and editors are from the major publishing houses.

Contests

Annual Published Division Contest—RWA Region 3 members, published authors only, send your list of books, pen names and publishers to Ann White, 440 Dogleg Court, Roswell, GA 30076.

Annual Maggie Awards for Unpublished Romance Novelists—
Eligibility: RWA members, unpublished romance novelists
only. Professional fiction authors (full-time income producing) are ineligible. First 110 entries only. One entry per
contestant. Entry must not have won a Maggie Award/
certificate in this contest previously.

Projected lengths and categories are Short contemporary
series romance (50,000–70,000 words), Long contemporary
series romance (70,000+ words), Historical romance and
Regencies (50,000 words minimum), and Mainstream-
contemporary or historical (50,000 words minimum).

The Maggie prize is a magnolia design engraved on a silver pendant, which will be awarded to the best work of published and unpublished writers in each category.

Entry fee is $20 for GRW members, $25 for nonmem-
bers. To enter, include a cover sheet with author's name,
address, phone number, title of entry, and entry category.
Author's name should be on the cover sheet *only,* or the
entry will be disqualified! Send 3 copies of a synopsis that is
no longer than 10 pages, and first 50 pages of manuscript.

For more specific rules and an entry form, write to Ann
White at the address on page 287.

Hawaii

ALOHA CHAPTER—HAWAII RWA #72
P.O. Box 240013
Honolulu, HI 96824-0013

Contact Person: Lynde Lakes, President

Annual Dues: $15 plus national dues of $60

Benefits of Membership
Market info; sharing; writer support.

Other

Affiliated with Romance Writers of America. No annual chapter conferences. Occasionally holds contests.

Idaho

COEUR DU BOIS CHAPTER RWA

1462 W. Merganser Drive
Meridian, ID 83642
(208) 887-1295

Contact Person: Stef Ann Holm, President

Annual Dues: $20

Benefits of Membership

Coeur Du Bois Chapter meets monthly and provides networking, information about markets, and the chance for writers to learn more about their craft.

Other

Affiliated with Romance Writers of America. May organize conference if funds and coordinators are available. No contest.

SOUTHERN IDAHO CHAPTER OF RWA

2125 Midway
Idaho Falls, ID 83406
(208) 523-0363

Contact Person: Sherry Roseberry

Annual Dues: $15

Benefits of Membership

Bimonthly educational meeting; conference tapes; annual contests, conferences; used books sold at half price; encouragement; networking; critique groups available; etc.

Other

Affiliated with Romance Writers of America. Annual conference and contest. Write for conference details.

Contests

Annual "When Hearts Meet" Contest—First 20 pages of manuscript are judged on the first meeting between the main characters. First place is $20, plus manuscript read by an agent.

Illinois

CHICAGO NORTH CHAPTER RWA

411 E. Roosevelt Road
Wheaton, IL 60187
(708) 668-3316

Contact Person: Susan Donahue

Annual Dues: $25

Benefits of Membership

Monthly newsletter; group critique; networking.

Other

Affiliated with Romance Writers of America. No annual conferences or contests at this time.

LOVE DESIGNERS WRITERS CLUB, INC.
1507 Burnham Avenue
Calumet City, IL 60409
(708) 862-9797

Contact Person: Nancy McCann, President

Annual Dues: $20

Benefits of Membership

Support group: We encourage each other and share our knowledge with each other.

Other

Affiliated with Romance Writers of America. No annual contest at this time. Nancy McCann writes ". . . we do publish *Rendezvous,* a monthly review magazine of about 38–40 pages each month and we seem to be appearing on [back covers of] more and more releases. 1994 marked *Rendezvous'* tenth birthday."

Conferences

Annual Autumn Authors Affair Conference

When: October 1995

40–70 authors share their expertise in workshops covering every aspect and all areas of writing.

PRAIRIE HEARTS RWA #43

607 W. Park
Thomasboro, IL 61878
(217) 333-4397 (daytime), (217) 643-2592 (evening)

Contact Person: HiDee Ekstrom, President

Annual Dues: $12

Benefits of Membership

Bimonthly newsletter; critiquing; support.

Other

Affiliated with Romance Writers of America. No annual conferences.

Contests

Dark and Stormy Night Annual Contest—Send SASE for information.

Louisiana

COEUR DE LOUISIANE, INC.

P.O. Box 109
Marksville, LA 71351
(318) 253-6553 (daytime), (318) 253-8754 (evening)
FAX: (318) 253-0027

Contact Person: Donna Caubarreaux

Annual Dues: $15/Newsletter subscription only is $10

Benefits of Membership

Monthly newsletter; monthly mini-contest; annual writing awards; monthly programs; published author support.

Other

Affiliated with Romance Writers of America. Holds conference and contest.

Conferences

When: May 1995

Where: Alexandria, LA

Cost: About $70, includes three meals

Workshops are geared to benefit authors at all stages, agent and editor appointments, press conferences for published authors, autograph tea.

Contests

Writing 101: The Synopsis Annual Contest—Ten pages maximum. Three preliminary round judges (usually published authors); the final round is judged by an agent, an editor, and a multi-published author.

Note: FYI, Debbie Hancock (aka Elizabeth Leigh), a member of this RWA chapter, has information for published authors about an independent quotes service she coordinates. There is no charge for this service. For details, send #10 SASE to Debbie at 43 Westwood Boulevard, Alexandria, LA 71301.

NORTH LOUISIANA ROMANCE WRITERS, INC.
1333 Pecan Square
Bossier City, LA 71112
(318) 747-5124

Contact Person: Debra Shelton, President

Annual Dues: $20

Benefits of Membership

Bimonthly newsletter, monthly meetings, annual March "Romance and More" Conference, October workshop.

Other

Affiliated with Romance Writers of America. Holds conference and contest.

Conference

When: March 1995 and 1996

Where: Shreveport, LA

Cost: about $65

Agent and editor appointments; writers presenting workshops on publishing in fiction.

Contests

Annual Novel Beginnings Contest—first chapter of a novel. Entry fee is $20. Deadline is 12/1/94. Write for details.

Maryland

MARYLAND ROMANCE WRITERS
P.O. Box 435
Hunt Valley, MD 21030–0435
(410) 584-2862

Contact Person: Jo Anne Dreyfus, President

Annual Dues: $24

Benefits of Membership

Monthly meetings (speakers include published authors, editors, agents, and individuals with areas of expertise); monthly newsletter; critique groups; networking with other writers.

Other

Affiliated with Romance Writers of America. No annual conferences or contests.

Massachusetts

NEW ENGLAND CHAPTER, INC. RWA #2
P.O. Box 1000
Attleboro, MA 02703
(508) 226-8205

Contact Person: Linda Murphy

Annual Dues: $20 (must also be a member of RWA National)

Benefits of Membership

Education; support; access to critique service; information/marketing news about publishers and agents; conferences/seminars.

Other

Affiliated with Romance Writers of America. Conference information is not available at this time. This chapter holds an annual contest.

Contests

Annual First Kiss Contest—The First Kiss Contest is for authors unpublished in book length fiction. Finalists will be judged by an editor. Please write for details and entry form.

Michigan

MID-MICHIGAN RWA #2
930 Lincoln Lake
Lowell, MI 49331
(616) 897-5500

Contact Person: Laurie Kuna

Annual Dues: $15

Benefits of Membership

Monthly meetings; speakers; monthly newsletter containing market news; annual spring retreat with outside speakers.

Other

Affiliated with Romance Writers of America. No annual contest at this writing. Holds annual retreat.

Annual Retreat: Usually held in May in the Kalamazoo area. The cost is about $15 for program only. Does not include meals or overnight accommodations.

Authors will be speaking on romance writing topics. This is informal, very laid-back, "kick off your shoes" type of thing, with ample time to talk about the writing industry.

Call or write for information.

UPPER MICHIGAN CHAPTER RWA

436 W. Bluff
Marquette, MI 49855
(906) 226-8493

Advisor: Carol Anne Smith

Annual Dues: $15

Benefits of Membership

Bimonthly meetings; bimonthly newsletter (alternates with meeting); meeting programs; critique sessions; chapter critique-by-mail.

Other

Affiliated with Romance Writers of America. No annual conferences or contests are planned yet.

Minnesota

MIDWEST FICTION WRITERS
16101 125th Avenue North
Dayton, MN 55327
(612) 422-9639

Advisor: Lois Greiman

Annual Dues: $20

Benefits of Membership

Informative monthly meetings; interaction with many well-known published authors; monthly newsletter.

Other

Affiliated with Romance Writers of America. Annual conferences are held. Contact the Midwest Fiction Writers for more info on the conference or current contests.

Missouri

OZARKS ROMANCE AUTHORS
1902 E. Bennett
Springfield, MO 65804
(417) 886-2289

Contact Person: Weta Nichols

Annual Dues: $15

Benefits of Membership

Support and encouragement for all writers; annual seminars and great speakers; mentor program.

Other

Affiliated with Romance Writers of America. Holds conference. Contest plans are in the works.

Montana

HEART OF MONTANA RWA CHAPTER

1809 Mountain View Drive
Great Falls, MT 59405
(406) 454-3003
FAX: (406) 727-9613

Contact Person: Rita Karnopp, President

Annual Dues: $15

Benefits of Membership

Newsletter; meetings; guest speakers; critiquing round robin.

Other

Affiliated with Romance Writers of America. No conferences or contests. This relatively new chapter formed in 1993.

Nebraska

CAMEO WRITERS
1864 Eldorado Drive
Omaha, NE 68154
(402) 493-0322
FAX: (402) 493-0322

Contact Person: Karon Petersen/Pauline Hetrick

Benefits of Membership

Motivation; education; support.

Other

Affiliated with Romance Writers of America. Conference co-sponsored with Readers & Writers, but no contest.

ROMANCE AUTHORS OF THE HEARTLAND
2568 Crown Point Avenue
Omaha, NE 68111
(402) 453-3889

Contact Person: Cheryl Ludwigs

Annual Dues: $15

Benefits of Membership

Critique groups; critique by mail; promotion for published authors; support and encouragement for aspiring authors; bimonthly newsletter; new member packet.

Other

Affiliated with Romance Writers of America. Annual conference and contest.

Conferences

Heartland Conference (co-sponsored with university of Nebraska at Omaha)

When: March 25, 26, 27, 1995

Where: Peter Kewitt Conference Center

Cost: $99

Combined Scholar/Writer/reader panels and workshops

Contests

Annual Hot Stuff Contest—Five page scene of sexual tension, judged by published authors. Send SASE for rules.

Nevada

CACTUS ROSE RWA

4615 Faircenter Parkway, #285
Las Vegas, NV 89102
(702) 293-3039

Contact Person: Carol C. MacLeod

Annual Dues: $15

Benefits of Membership

Critique groups; speakers; monthly meetings.

Other

Affiliated with Romance Writers of America. No annual conference or contest yet. Brand new group in 1994 intends to offer workshops and contests.

RWANN (ROMANCE WRITERS OF NORTHERN NEVADA)

315 Cliffview Drive
Reno, NV 89523
(702) 345-6344

Contact Person: Bobbie Hill, President

Annual Dues: $15

Benefits of Membership

RWANN provides a strong network of published and unpublished writers sharing their knowledge and expertise. Our members benefit from guest lecturers, writer's workshops, critique sessions, as well as developing a knowledge of the publishing industry.

Other

Affiliated with Romance Writers of America. No annual conference or contest.

New Jersey

NEW JERSEY ROMANCE WRITERS

P.O. Box 646
Old Bridge, NJ 08857

Annual Dues: $45

Benefits of Membership

Monthly workshops featuring editors, agents, and professional speakers; monthly newsletter; access to writer's library; critique programs; fall conference; special events.

Other

Affiliated with Romance Writers of America. Annual conference and contests.

Conferences

When: October 6–7, 1995

Includes workshops for all levels of writing; national best-selling authors as speakers; book signing; networking; and appointments with agents and editors. Write for complete details.

Contests

"Put Your Heart in a Book" Contest—for unpublished writers, and open to all RWA members.
Golden Leaf Contest—for published authors in Region One only.

New York

HUDSON VALLEY CHAPTER RWA #80
224 S. Broadway
S. Nyack, NY 10960
(914) 358-7141

Advisor: Janet Walters

Annual Dues: $15 plus National Membership dues

Benefits of Membership

Critiques; support; specialized knowledge of members (i.e., medicine, astrology, etc.); and more.

Other

Affiliated with Romance Writers of America. No annual conferences at this writing.

Contests

Hook, Line and Sinker Annual Contest—The first three pages of a novel. The contest runs from June to the deadline, October 31st. There is a $10 entry fee for each entry. SASE is required. Write or call for more info.

ROMANCE WRITERS OF AMERICA/ NEW YORK CITY, INC.

Bowling Green Station, P.O. Box 1719
New York, NY 10274-1133
(718) 441-5214

Chapter President: Maria C. Ferrer

Annual Dues: $20 (all members must also be members of RWA National)

Benefits of Membership

Monthly meetings; network dinners; optional outings; annual contest; workshop and wine and cheese reception for editors and distributors. New! RITA/Golden Heart contest lottery in which four members win their entry fees to one of these national contests. For published authors there's a chapter ad in *Romantic Times* magazine, book signings, and quarterly dinners with professional speakers.

Other

Affiliated with Romance Writers of America.

Conferences

Annual Workshop/From Dream to Reality

When: Last weekend in February

Where: Skyline Hotel in New York City

Cost: $75 (price subject to change)

From Dream to Reality Workshop starts Friday evening with a "Meet the Speakers" reception. Saturday is full of writing workshops with professional speakers, published authors, editors, agents, and other industry professionals. There are also popular one-on-one sessions with published authors and roundtable discussions on various topics. On Sunday there are more dynamic speakers, sessions, etc. Great place to network and meet other writers.

Contests

Annual Love and Laughter Contest—Open to all unpublished writers. Submission is a humorous scene from a romance novel manuscript. $15 entry fee. Grand prize is $50 plus a critique by an editor. Multiple entries are permitted (three maximum). Write for more info.

WESTERN NEW YORK ROMANCE WRITERS, INC.

135 Colony Street
Depew, NY 14043
(716) 685-1425

Contact Person: Vera M. Hodge

Annual Dues: $25. Also available are annual $18 long distance memberships.

Benefits of Membership

Monthly meetings and workshops; access to tape library; reference materials; critique groups; annual conference. (Membership in Romance Writers of America is required.)

Other

Affiliated with Romance Writers of America. No annual contests are planned at this time. Conference planned.

Conferences

When: October 22, 1994

Where: Sheraton Inn (Airport) in Buffalo, NY

Cost: $45 for members, more for non-members

One-day event features published authors as guest speakers, as well as editors and agents attending (speaking).

North Carolina

CAROLINA ROMANCE WRITERS

P.O. Box 470761
Charlotte, NC 28226

President: Peg Robarchek

Annual Dues: $20

Benefits of Membership

Monthly newsletter, annual conference, monthly meetings with speakers/programs, critique groups.

Other

Affiliated with Romance Writers of America. Write for information on annual conference.

Ohio

NORTHEAST OHIO RWA

1497 Clarence Avenue
Lakewood, OH 44107
(216) 221-4962

Contact Person: Donna Stuart, President/Chapter Advisor

Annual Dues: $15, plus membership in National RWA

Benefits of Membership

Monthly meeting; newsletter; critique partners.

Other

Affiliated with Romance Writers of America. Annual conference. Annual contest.

Conferences

Annual "Reach for the Stars" Conference

When: Mid-September

Where: Cleveland, Ohio

Cost: $45 members

National Star author and Star Editor. Ohio Stars. Includes luncheon and meet the author forum and book signing to benefit Cleveland's Literacy "Project: Learn."

Contests

Annual Romancing the Novel Contest—Deadline is June 1st. Entry Fee $20. Send #10 SASE for rules.

OHIO VALLEY ROMANCE WRITERS OF AMERICA
P.O. Box 58077
Cincinnati, OH 45258
(513) 598-1240

Contact Person: Robin L. Wiete

Annual Dues: $20

Benefits of Membership

Information and support; meetings; conferences; contests; networking; plus the benefits of national RWA membership. This is an active, professional, committed organization of 60+ writers.

Other

Affiliated with Romance Writers of America. Reading, Writing and Romance Conference and Spice of Life Contest. Contact the chapter for detailed information.

WOMEN FICTION WRITERS ASSOCIATION
715 San Moritz Drive
Akron, OH 44333
(216) 867-5786

Contact Person: Debra Moser

Annual Dues: $15 (Must also belong to RWA, National)

Benefits of Membership

Support; critiques; accessibility to workshops; seminars; conferences; contests; networking; benefits of national RWA membership.

Other

Affiliated with Romance Writers of America.

Contests

Annual Great Beginnings Contest—RWA members only may enter the first ten pages of an unpublished manuscript. The pages will be judged and scored for $10 and critiqued for an additional $5. Write for exact contest rules and details.

Oregon

CASCADE CHAPTER RWA #59
7218 NE Sandy #3
Portland, OR 97213
(503) 284-2021

Contact Person: Janet L. Brayson

Annual Dues: $20

Benefits of Membership

Monthly meetings; workshops; reference library; a friendly group
of writers who are always willing to help. An active chapter of 70+
members.

Other

Affiliated with Romance Writers of America. Annual contest and
annual conference.

Conferences

Annual Retreat and Recharge Conference

Every year R & R brings together authors, aspiring writers,
agents, and editors in a relaxed country setting. We bring out at
least one New York editor (often more) and some very knowledgeable speakers. Topics are aimed to provide help and encouragement to beginning and advanced writers. Call or write for
exact dates and other info.

Contests

Our contest is open *only* to members and those attending our annual conference. This year's contest is a synopsis and a pivotal
scene. Call or write for more info.

HEART OF OREGON RWA

1140 Waverly Street
Eugene, OR 97401-5235
(503) 485-0583

President and Publicist: Ann Simas

Annual Dues: $15

Benefits of Membership

Monthly educational/informational meetings; monthly newsletter (awarded 1992 best by RWA); annual writing contest; annual writing conference; periodic writing workshops.

Other

Affiliated with Romance Writers of America. Annual conference and contest.

Conferences

Annual Conference

Where: Eugene, Oregon

Cost: approximately $120–$135

Editors, authors and agents gather to exchange information and discuss "breaking in." There will be a focus on general writing with emphasis on theme topics, as well as other published and unpublished authors to "network with."

Contests

Annual Contest—Twilight Shadows is the theme. Send query letters (up to 2 pages), prologue/first chapter (up to 25 pages) and synopsis (up to 5 pages). There will be five finalists with final judging to be done by an editor. Contest guidelines are available with SASE. Contest entry fee is $15 for RWA members or $20 for non-members. Critiquing will be done and score sheets and entries will be returned.

MID-WILLAMETTE VALLEY RWA (SALEM)
490 Lochmoor Place
Eugene, OR 97405
(503) 687-8879

Contact Person: Sharon Morris, President

Annual Dues: $12

Benefits of Membership
Every third Thursday of the month, we meet in the Salem Public Library from 7:00–9:00 P.M. to listen to speakers, usually published authors in the romance field. Every 3 months we have a group critique for manuscripts. Monthly member newsletter.

Other
Affiliated with Romance Writers of America. Annual conference. No annual contests at this writing.

Conferences
Annual Conference

When: April (all day Saturday)

Where: Salem, Oregon

Cost: $35, including lunch

Our all day workshop includes multi-published authors from the Northwest. Our workshops have always been informative, informal, and friendly. It's open to the public.

PORTLAND/VANCOUVER CHAPTER
ROMANCE WRITERS OF AMERICA

19900 N.E. Dopp Road
Newberg, OR 97132
(503) 538-4196

Contact Person: Barbara Rae Robinson

Annual Dues: $21

Benefits of Membership

Monthly meetings featuring knowledgeable speakers; networking with other writers, including published writers; market information; workshops.

Other

Affiliated with Romance Writers of America. No annual conference or contest.

Pennsylvania

CENTRAL PENNSYLVANIA ROMANCE WRITERS (CPRW)

Judy C. Kiner, President
R.D. #1 Box 303
Port Royal, PA 17082
(717) 527-2510
or
Janice Costello, Secretary
24 E. Manor Avenue
Enola, PA 17025
(717) 732-2454

Annual Dues: $15

Benefits of Membership

As a newly formed organization, CPRW is establishing goals, both long term and short term, at this point. Members will be able to benefit from lectures, guest speakers, group and/or individual critiquing—all associated with romance writing. CPRW is planning a conference for the group early in 1994. Members will be able to participate in the preparation, carrying out and any such benefits (meeting contact persons, other writers, gaining valuable insight from workshops) a local conference will be able to provide, especially when financial realities limit members from travelling to many other state conferences.

Other

Affiliated with Romance Writers of America.

Conferences

We are hoping to have one main speaker at our conference. We also have a three- to four-time published author who is currently serving as CPRW's Vice-President, who will, most likely, be giving a seminar. We are hoping to include agents and editors. Write or call Janice Costello during the day for additional information.

Tennessee

RIVER CITY ROMANCE WRITERS
RWA #23 (OF MEMPHIS, TN)
Call (901) 757-9301

Contact Person: Denise Hawkins Camp, Newsletter Editor

Annual Dues: $24

Benefits of Membership

Networking; publishing information; guest speakers; and newsletter to help the published and unpublished romance writer.

Other

Affiliated with Romance Writers of America. Annual conference and contest.

Conferences

Annual Duel on the Delta Conference

When: March

Where: Memphis, Tennessee.

Cost: $65–$70

Editor/Agent appointment available. Published authors and editors speak on the craft of writing romance.

Contests

Annual Duel on the Delta Contest—Deadline October. Call for
details.

Texas

AUSTIN ROMANCE WRITERS
905 Sweetwater Cove
Round Rock, TX 78681
(512) 218-9183

Contact Person: Coral Smith Saxe

Annual Dues: $15

Benefits of Membership

Local critique groups; professional programs; local PAN groups; contacts; local hands-on conference.

Other

Affiliated with Romance Writers of America. Annual conference. No contest.

Conferences

One-Day Hands-On Workshop

When: April or May each year

Where: Austin, Texas

Cost: $20

Presentations by mutiple-published authors on all aspects of romance writing.

BAY AREA (HOUSTON) CHAPTER 30 RWA
10904 Scarsdale #270
Houston, TX 77089
(713) 481-3425

Contact Person: c/o Sharon Murphy/Paperback Trader

Annual Dues: $15

Benefits of Membership

Support group for all writers.

Other

Affiliated with Romance Writers of America. No annual conference. Query-Synopsis Contest entitled "Show Me More."

DALLAS AREA ROMANCE AUTHORS (DARA)

P.O. Box 803201
Dallas, TX 75380
(903) 874-1952

Contact Person: Diane Anderson, President

Annual Dues: $18

Benefits of Membership

Monthly newsletter; pre-meeting writing workshops; free critique services; networking and active published authors network group.

Other

Affiliated with Romance Writers of America. Annual conference. No contest.

Conferences

Annual All-Day Seminar

When: Fourth Saturday in September

Where: Garland's Women and Business Center in Downtown Garland

Cost: $25

Three published authors present an all day, how-to writing workshop.

GREATER DALLAS WRITERS' ASSOCIATION
4201 Nightfall
Plano, TX 75075

Not affiliated with Romance Writers of America. (214) 596-5335 or call the University of Texas at Dallas Center for Continuing Education (214) 690–2204.

NORTH TEXAS ROMANCE WRITERS OF AMERICA
923 Golden Grove Road
Lewisville, TX 75067
(214) 316-1818

President: Shelley Bradley

Annual Dues: $21

Benefits of Membership

Meetings are held each month to discuss the craft of writing and share fellowship with peers. Monthly newsletter with articles for writers at all levels, including a calendar of events containing other chapter contests and conferences. Offers support for aspiring writers with a critique exchange program. Supports the needs/concerns of published authors with PARTners (for published authors only). Provides information in all aspects of writing via monthly workshops and programs by experts and authors. Maintains a tape library of seminars and instructional lectures devoted to writing and publishing. Annual contest is judged by published authors and editors. Bookmarks are printed annually listing the names of all the published authors in this chapter.

Other

Affiliated with Romance Writers of America. Contact the chapter by mail for a conference brochure.

Contests

An annual contest is judged on a first chapter of up to 30 pages and a query letter targeted at agent or editor. Finalists judged by editors, agents, or multi-published authors. Details are available by writing to chapter.

NORTHWEST HOUSTON
ROMANCE WRITERS OF AMERICA
2507 Woodvale
Kingwood, TX 77345
(713) 361-3603

Advisor: Laura Powell

Annual Dues: $15

Benefits of Membership

Monthly newsletter; monthly meetings with informative speakers; yearly one-day workshop; manuscript critiquing.

Other

Affiliated with Romance Writers of America. Annual conference but no contest.

Conferences

Contact Mica Kelch, 4426 Algernon Drive, Spring, TX 77373 or call (713) 350–2844.

The speakers will be Candace Camp, Sally Hawkes, Penny Richards, Erica Spindler and Gina Wilkins.

ROMANCE WRITERS OF AMERICA— EAST TEXAS CHAPTER

P.O. Box 56
Tyler, TX 75710
(903) 531-0104

Contact Person: Vince Brach, President

Annual Dues: $20, plus current member of national RWA

Benefits of Membership

Monthly meetings where professionals speak; critique sessions with members; monthly newsletter; great fellowship!

Other

Affiliated with Romance Writers of America. Annual conference and short romance contest, usually in late summer. Send SASE for details.

ROMANCE WRITERS OF THE TEXAS PANHANDLE

P.O. Box 1343
Amarillo, TX 79105
(806) 372-2447 (day) or 655-1675 (evening)
FAX: (806) 345-2299

Contact Person: Vanessa Reeves

Annual Dues: $15

Benefits of Membership

Monthly meetings; monthly newsletter; fellowship, support and understanding as well as contact with published writers and the chance to hear interesting speakers.

Other

Affiliated with Romance Writers of America. Annual Conference and contest. (Call or write for more information.)

WEST HOUSTON RWA #28
1302 Crystal Hills
Houston, TX 77077
(713) 496-5263

Contact Person: Anne Dykowski

Annual Dues: $21

Benefits of Membership

We are a very focussed writer's group providing education, motivation, and networking opportunities for our members.

Other

We are affiliated with Romance Writers of America, but have writers of all genres in our group. Annual chapter conference and two writing contests.

Conferences

When (probably March), where, and cost details for '95–'96 conferences had not been finalized, as of this book's printing. Write to the chapter for current information.

West Houston RWA sponsors a conference designed for every stage in a writer's career to achieve optimum success. Our conference offers practical information on the business aspects of a writer's career, as well as the craft of writing. The 1994 conference featured eight editors, two agents, two *New York Times* bestselling author speakers plus twenty published authors and eight related professionals offering workshops in concurrent sessions.

Contests

Annual Honey of a Heroine Contest—Submit a five page scene showing heroine in action (can be accompanied by a one-page setup). Judges will be looking for strong writing and a heroine who comes alive—one they like and with whom they can identify. $10 entry fee. One winner. Send SASE for complete rules and official entry blank.

Annual Emily Contest and Award —Second only to the Golden Heart, the Emily runs in conjunction with our conference. $25 entry fee. Four categories consisting of Short Contemporary (under 70,000 words), Long Contemporary (over 70,000 words), Historical (includes Time Travel), and Mainstream. Complete contest guidelines and information are available by sending an SASE to the Contest Chair: Brenda Young, 711 Studewood, Houston, TX 77007.

Utah

ROMANCE WRITERS OF AMERICA, UTAH CHAPTER

416 E. 3075 N.
Ogden, UT 84414
(801) 782-8336

Treasurer and Conference Chair: Isolde Carlsen

Annual Dues: $20

Benefits of Membership

Informative programs on writing skills; critique of work; Annual
Golden Pen contest and conference; plain old support.

Other

Affiliated with Romance Writers of America. Annual tricks of the
trade conference is usually held in October in Salt Lake City. Annual Golden Pen Contest.

Conferences

Annual Tricks of the Trade Conference

In attendance will be Lane Ferguson, children's and YA author;
Debbie Bedford, Region IV Advisor; Pat Collinge, Region IV
Representative; local Harlequin author Rebecca Winters; Danise
Allen (aka Emily Dalton and Betina Lindsay). Sessions include
creativity, what to do before you start writing, characterization,
synopsis preparation, and more!

Contests

Annual Golden Pen Contest—Unpublished writers (of book-
length fiction) may enter this annual contest. Entries *must*
be submitted with the official entry form, (obtainable from
Isolde Carlsen) and entry fee.

Vermont

GREEN MOUNTAIN ROMANCE WRITERS

P.O. Box 89
Greensboro, VT 05841

Contact Person: Krissie Ohlrogge

Benefits of Membership

Support and encouragement; advice and critiquing for fellow writers of romance and romantic suspense; etc.

Other

Affiliated with Romance Writers of America. Write to Krissie Ohlrogge at the above address for detailed information about this writer's group.

Virginia

VIRGINIA ROMANCE WRITERS

P.O. Box 35
Midlothian, VA 23112
(804) 748-0343 or (804) 741-5384
FAX: (804) 355-8008

Contact Person: Vicki Lojek, President

Annual Dues: $20

Benefits of Membership

Monthly newsletter; monthly meetings; reduced rate at conferences and workshops; support of fellow writers; market news.

Other

Affiliated with Romance Writers of America. Holds annual conference and contests.

Conferences

Annual Step Back In Time Conference

When: Friday, March 31, 1995 through Sunday April 2, 1995

Where: Williamsburg, Virginia at the Ft. McGruder Inn/Conference Center

Cost: VRW Members $100, Non-members $130 (plus $72 night hotel rate for single or double)

The conference will offer editor and agent appointments, workshops for beginning writers, of general interest, for the writer who is almost there, author signings, book fair, Friday night reception, luncheon and dinner on Saturday.

Contests

Fool for Love Contest—First chapter (send SASE for entry form/rules).
First Line Contest—Opening line for a novel (send SASE for entry form/rules).

Washington

RWA PENINSULA CHAPTER 84

P.O. Box 3208
Bremerton, WA 98528
(206) 372-2836

Contact Person: Karen Speece, President

Annual Dues: $18

Benefits of Membership

Great programs for little or no cost; newsletter; meetings and programs held on Saturdays at 10:00 A.M.

Other

Affiliated with Romance Writers of America. No annual conference or contest.

SEATTLE CHAPTER ROMANCE WRITERS OF AMERICA

P.O. Box 5845
Bellevue, WA 98006

Contact Person: Angela Butterworth, President

Annual Dues: $20 local (plus national)

Benefits of Membership

Monthly meetings; newsletter; market news; support; networking with fellow writers.

Other

Affiliated with Romance Writers of America. Holds annual conference and contests.

Conferences

Annual Emerald City Romance Writers Conference

When: Usually held in October

Where: Bellevue, Washington

Cost: $145 (Does not include lodging)

Authors, agents and editors will attend. Contact this chapter for details.

Contests

Annual Emerald City Opener Contest—The first five pages of a manuscript may be entered for a $10 fee. Send #10 SASE for rules.

TACOMA CHAPTER RWA
12922 SE 278th
Kent, WA 98031
(206) 630–2217

President: Lisa Wanttaja

Annual Dues: $18 (may go up to $20)

Benefits of Membership

Monthly meetings; monthly newsletters; workshops; editor dinner.

Other

Affiliated with Romance Writers of America. No annual conferences or contests at this writing, but a one day workshop is normally held in January or February.

Wisconsin

WISCONSIN ROMANCE WRITERS OF AMERICA (WISRWA)

6940 S. Timber Ridge #10308
Oak Creek, WI 53154
(414) 761-9780

Contact Person: Leslie J. Parker, President

Annual Dues: $15 plus $45 in National RWA

Benefits of Membership

Critique groups; networking and support meetings for published and unpublished writers; bimonthly newsletter; writer's contest; fall workshop and spring conference.

Other

Affiliated with Romance Writers of America.

Conferences

Annual Romance Writer's Conference

When: May 1995

Where: Milwaukee, Wisconsin

Cost: Approximately $85

Friday is Specialty Day. Talk with the experts or focus on theme. Three workshops every hour on Saturday.

Contests

Annual Fabulous Five Contest—The entry is the first 5–10 pages of a manuscript, from unpublished writers. The top three winners will be announced at our conference. The top three entries will be critiqued by an editor. Write for complete rules/conference information.

West Virginia

WEST VIRGINIA ROMANCE WRITERS OF AMERICA #106

403 Fairview Drive
Charleston, WV 25302
(304) 343-2793

Contact Person: Lynn Eldridge, President

Annual Dues: $25

Benefits of Membership

WVRWA is dedicated to education, support, market news, networking, and getting published in the romance field. We offer a monthly meeting, monthly newsletter, and workshops.

Other

Affiliated with Romance Writers of America. No annual conferences or contests at this time.

Note: Some writer's associations did not respond in time to meet the publication deadlines of this reference book.

10

Directory of Writer's Publications

AFFAIRE DE COEUR

3976 Oak Hill Drive
Oakland, CA 94605-4931
(510) 569-5675

Affaire de Coeur is a well-recommended magazine for writers of romance fiction. Circulation is 150,000 monthly. Contains articles about writing romance fiction, publishing news, author bios, and reviews. This magazine is also listed in the non-book market section of this book. A subscription is $30 per year.

CANADIAN WRITER'S JOURNAL

c/o Gordon Smart Publications
Box 6618, Depot 1
Victoria, B.C. V8P 5N7
CANADA

Quarterly Digest. $15 for four issues. 64 pages of Canadian, U.S., and foreign market info; writing technique and advice articles; copyright info; book reviews; computer help; contest news; and resource information. Well-written and useful for all genres.

THE GILA QUEEN'S GUIDE TO MARKETS
P.O. Box 97
Newton, NJ 07860

Highly recommended for current market listings (for all types of writing), this thematic magazine is 28 pages packed tightly with markets, news of what editor left what house and where she went, market guidelines, book reviews, agent news, dead markets, slow markets, etc. Write to Kathryn Ptacek, Editor. Monthly. $28 yr/12 issues (USA), $32 (Canada).

GOTHIC JOURNAL
Publisher: Kristi Lyn Glass
19210 Forest Road North
Forest Lake, MN 55025

Bimonthly reviews Gothic and romantic suspense novels, author bios, articles, upcoming titles, market news. $18 yr/ 6 issues.

HEART TO HEART

A bimonthly romance newsletter with book reviews, author interviews and a check off shopping list of new titles. It's available free at B. Dalton Bookstores.

HOUSEWIFE-WRITER'S FORUM
P.O. Box 780 Dept RWPP
Lyman, WY 82937

Nonfiction book reviews, articles on writing and writers, varied market listings, fiction (critiqued also), and well-written nonfiction articles about women and the writing life. Inspiring and useful with info you won't find elsewhere. $15 yr/6 issues ($4 Sample Copy).

LADY'S GALLERY
P.O. Box 1761
Independence, MO 64055
(800) 622-5676

Full color magazine of antique clothing, old recipes, art, Victorian customs, history of items (example, purses), historical research resources, and much more. Very helpful for writers of Americana/British historical romances. Bimonthly, $23.95 yr (USA), $32 yr (Canada).

LITERARY TIMES
P.O. Box 516
Moultonboro, NH 03254
(603) 476-5692

Circulation 1,000. (90% of readers are authors.) This quarterly has book reviews, author profiles, romance novel industry news, how-to articles for writers, feedback from readers, and concerns of writers. Offers advance quotes from author's galleys. Query or send completed articles etc. to Diana Potwin, Editor. Disk Submissions (PC) are also welcome. (Low density disks only.) No payment, but author's book titles are promoted in a bibliography with articles. $28 yr/4 issues.

LOVE LETTERS
c/o Maudeen Wachsmith
P.O. Box 756
Gig Harbor, WA 98335
(206) 858-6830

Monthly newsletter packed with information about authors, romances, and the industry. (Send galleys for review.) $15 yr.

MANDERLEY
P.O. Box 880
Boonville, CA 95415-0880
(800) 722-0726 for questions or book orders.

This is a review magazine and book catalog. Also sells nonfiction of interest to romance writers.

THE MEDIAEVAL CHRONICLE

P.O. Box 1663, (Dept. RWP)
Carlsbad, CA 92018-1663

Contains articles about Dark Ages, Middle Ages, and Tudor period, as well as info on upcoming Medieval romances. Meet new authors and discover hard-to-find research resources. A subscription to this is a must for mediaeval writers. Bimonthly. $10 yr/6 issues (USA), $14 Canada.

PAPERBACK PREVIEWS MAGAZINE

P.O. Box 6781
Albuquerque, NM 87197

Lists new releases with mini-"blurbs." Several reviews. Not a book club, no purchase required. Call (800) 872-4461 to request a free sample copy. Monthly newsletter/book catalog $15 yr.

POETS & WRITERS MAGAZINE

72 Spring Street
New York, NY 10012
(212) 226-3586

Published 6 times a year, this magazine has interesting interviews with poets and literary writers, grants and awards info, news about legislation that affects authors, etc. A literary/arts focused magazine that is helpful to all types of writers. $18 yr/ 6 issues.

PSYCHIC WRITER'S NETWORK
62 Main Street
High Bridge, NJ 08829
(908) 638-4426

Editor Christina Lynn Whited is a professional psychic who wants to promote the positive aspects of psychic subjects (joy, health, and well-being) in romance novels and in everyday life. Book reviews, upbeat articles by informed psychic professionals, editorials that are positive and do not delve deeply into dark subjects (such as vampires) but focus on the goodness of psychic power in romances and the writing life. $15 yr/6 issues.

PUBLISHER'S WEEKLY
P.O. Box 1979
Marion, OH 43302
(800) 842-1669 inside the continental U.S. (614) 382-3322

Most large libraries subscribe to this magazine. *Publisher's Weekly* is the info-track magazine of the entire publishing industry. Contains bestseller lists, reviews, publisher's staff changes, and other insider tidbits.

THE READER'S VOICE
2646 Wyoming Avenue, S.W.
Wyoming, MI 49509-2370
FAX: (616) 532-9042 (After January '95)

All material accepted for publication relates to reading, writing, or selling romance novels. Authors, avoid sending dated promo pieces; we are interested in the personal side of your life. Actively seeking author profiles (500 words), romance novel industry news of conferences, book signings, press releases, etc. personal or humorous anecdotes, inspirational pieces, and editorials up to 700 words. Acquires first time rights, one time rights, some reprints considered. Also seeking bookmarks. Bimonthly, $15 yr/6 issues. Sample issue $3 (USA).

THE REGENCY PLUME NEWSLETTER
Marilyn Clay, Editor
711 D. Street Northwest
Ardmore, OK 73401

This newsletter is for Regency devotees, readers, and writers. Market news, upcoming titles, book reviews, historical articles, market news, and more. Highly recommended. $10 yr/6 issues.

RENDEZVOUS
1507 Burnham Avenue
Calumet City, IL 60409
(708) 862-9797

This monthly is published by the Love Designers Writer's Club. It is 32 pages of very candid reviews of current romance, fantasy, gothic, mystery, and women's fiction. There is also a market news column by Nancy McCann. Totally staff written (no freelance articles). A subscription is six months for $18 or one year for $36. Single copies are $3. Recommended.

ROMANCE WRITERS' REPORT (RWR)
Romance Writers of America
13700 Veterans Memorial Drive, Suite 315
Houston, TX 77014

A well-done bimonthly publication of Romance Writers of America for members. Members of the RWA receive the magazine as one of the benefits of membership. For current fees and membership application, write or phone (713) 440-6885.

ROMANTIC READER
This free bimonthly newsletter is distributed next to the cash registers at Waldenbooks chain stores. They run out quickly, though, so find out when they are usually delivered.

ROMANTIC TIMES
Romantic Times Publishing Group
55 Bergen Street
Brooklyn, NY 11201
(718) 237-1097

A monthly publication, RT has with helpful articles on romance writing, convention news, industry gossip, and current trend info. New books are previewed and reviewed. Multimedia romances (on tape, videos, etc.) are also reviewed. $42 yr/12 issues (4th Class Mail), or $60 yr/12 issues (1st Class Mail).

ROSE PETALS AND PEARLS
c/o Diane Kirk
115 Eastmont Drive
Jackson, TN 38301
(901) 422-6223

This non-profit organization sponsors a quarterly newsletter (which will go monthly in January '95) that includes information about events and articles by romance authors.

THE TALISMAN
Glenna Volesky, Editor
P.O. Box 1641
Humble, TX 77347-1641

Dedicated to Romance with a twist, this 72-page magazine features at least eight author profiles per issue (not necessary to buy ads), travel info about paranormal and supernatural places, New Age articles, and information on the latest mystery/romance, romantic intrigue, supernatural romances, futuristic, fantasy, and time travel romances. Bimonthly. $25 yr/ 6 issues (USA). Samples $4. Circulation: 500.

TRENDS
Darlene Roger, Editor
P.O. Box 297
Lacombe, LA 70445-0297

A historical research newsletter for writers, *Trends* includes articles on clothing (illustrated), customs, folklore, writer's tips, and more. Also does historical research. Monthly. $25 yr/12 issues (USA).

WGA JOURNAL
8955 Beverly Boulevard
Los Angeles, CA 90048

Published by Writers Guild of America, this $5.00 monthly magazine gives an up-to-date list of television series in current production, and names/phone numbers of contact people accepting submissions.

WRITE ON NEWSLETTER
P.O. Box 5438
Street Louis, MO 63147

Bimonthly, $6 yr/6 issues. Sample copy $1.

WRITER'S DIGEST
1507 Dana Avenue
Cincinnati, OH 45207

All types of writing and markets are discussed in how-to articles.
Monthly market information is usually related to nonfiction articles needed for magazine markets. Writer's Digest is a general
purpose magazine for the writer who is interested in more than
romance writing.

WRITER'S EXCHANGE
Box 394
Society Hill, SC 29593

Publishes markets, money-saving articles for writers, author bios,
book reviews, etc. Quarterly—$10 yr.

WRITER'S GUIDELINES
Box 608
Pittsburg, MO 65724
FAX: (417) 993-5544

Writer's Guidelines has fiction and nonfiction market news, helpful advice and articles about writing, plus roundtable discussions,
book reviews, and free messages for subscribers.

WRITER'S JOURNAL

Published bimonthly by Minnesota Ink, Inc.
27 Empire Drive
Street Paul, MN 55103

How-to articles combined with quality gems of fiction, poetry, book reviews, contests, monthly columns and more. Format and tone of magazine is somewhere between the literary-type Poets and Writers magazine and the slick commercial presentation of *Writer's Digest* magazine. $18 yr/6 issues.

WRITER'S REPORT

Karel Juhl, Editor
P.O. Box 27614
Lansing, MI 48909

Monthly, $21 for 12 issues. A review publication of products and services for writers, including books, videos, workshops, etc.

WRITER TO WRITER NEWSLETTER

P.O. Box 1003
Wickenburg, AZ 85358

Unique ideas to aid writers; feature articles; conference and contest news; first sales for authors; comments and opinions from a writer's slant.Circulation: 300+ quarterly.

Electronic Networks for Writers

You can debate and schmooze, get conference, contest, and market news, category cruise, and find friends to chase away those writing blues. There are plenty of writer-friendly networks whose members will welcome your input and be glad to share what they know. With a computer, a modem, communications software, and a phone line, you can gain access to gigabytes of information at reasonable on-line hourly rates (if a local number is available).

America Online, (800) 827-6364. Real-time chats and conferences, e-mail, writers' message boards, etc.

Compuserve, (800) 848-8199. Many services offered.

Delphi, (800) 695-4005. Less-expensive Internet route.

GEnie Electronic Network, (800) 848-8199. Many interests including RomEx (Romance Writer's Exchange), Writers, and SciFi/Fantasy message boards, real-time roundtable discussions, libraries. You can e-mail author Eve Paludan at this electronic address: R.Paludan1.

Prodigy, (800) 776-3449. Books and Arts/Writers message boards, e-mail, conferences, etc.

Z-Talk, Sandra the sysop is at (212) 889-2299 (for questions). Z-talk (run by Zebra) has more than 150 message boards, all about reading and writing romance.

APPENDIX 2

Book Publisher's Quick Reference Guide

Merline Lovelace

Imprint	# Words (in thous.)	Submission Requirements	Characteristics
Avalon			
Hardcover			
Contemp.	40–50	Synop. + 1st ch.	Wholesome adult fiction, kisses only
Avon			
Contemp.	100–125	Synop. + 3 ch.	Mainstream, no category types
Historical	100–125	Synop. + 3 ch.	Sensual, no rape, 1100–1900
Treasure	100–125	Synop. + 3 ch.	Established authors only
Regency	50–55	Synop. + 3 ch.	Strong sexual tension/woo with words
Woman's Fic.	100–125	Synop. + 3 ch.	Sensual/sexy, established auths.
Myst./Susp.	60	Synop. + 3 ch.	Psychological/woman in jeopardy/cozy/straight
Ballantine			
Fantasy	60–100	Synop. + 3 ch.	Del Rey Ed. Barb. Dicks/ McCaffrey fan
Regency	70–75	Synop. + 3 ch.	Fawcett/Ballantine
Historical	100–125	Prefer full ms.	Try Sr. Editor Barbara Dicks
Women's Fic.	—	Pam Strickler says not buying now	

Imprint	# Words (in thous.)	Submission Requirements	Characteristics
Bantam			
Loveswept	55	2–3 pg. query if not an agent	h/h meet as close to p. 1 as poss.
Fanfare	80	2–3 pg. query if not an agent	Hist. and Contemp., no rape
Spectra	—	Agented only	Sci-fi, fantasy (downplay romance)
Barbour & Company: Heartsong Presents *(Christian Romances)*			
Historical	45–50	Synop. + 3 ch.	Pre-WWII, biblical messages
Contemp.	45–50	Synop. + 3 ch.	No drinking, divorce, nudity
Bethany House *(Christian Romances)*			
Prairie	—	Synop. + 3 ch.	Read Janette Oke/ Marian Wells
Historical	—	Synop. + 3 ch.	Hist. settings/conservative
Young Adult	—	Synop. + 3 ch.	Read Judy Baer
Dare to Dream *(Personalized Books)*			
Historical	50	Synop. + 3 ch.	Don't traumatize hero/heroine
Contemp.	50	Synop. + 3 ch.	No heroines as writers
Mainstream	50	Synop. + 3 ch.	One lover/no past lover in book
Myst./Susp.	50	Synop. + 3 ch.	Movie stars, sports figs., CEOs
Time Travel	50	Synop. + 3 ch.	No religion or controvers. subs.
Dell			
Historical	110–120	Agented only	Need strong emotion
Contemp.	110–120	Agented only	Need strong emotion
Dutton/Signet			
Onyx	125–150	Query first	Mainstream
Signet Regncy	75	Query first	Typical Regencies
Topaz Hist.	110–125	Query first	Newer historical line
Thrillers	100	Agents, please	Suspense/female protaganist
Goodfellow Press			
Women's Fic.	85–120	Query first	Five major scenes—see listing
Harlequin			
American	70	Query (pubs. send ms.)	Upbeat, lots of action, dialogue
Historical	95+	Query or synop. + 3 ch.	1700–1900 England, France, N. America
Intrigue	70–75	Query + 1–2 pp. synop.	Murder, whodunnit, suspense, time travel
Regency	50–60	Query + 1–2 pp. synop.	4/yr., Eng./Scot., 1811–1820

Imprint	# Words (in thous.)	Submission Requirements	Characteristics
Superromance	85	Query + 1–2 pp. synop.	Focus on issues, mainstream tone
Temptation	60	Query + 1–2 pp. synop.	Fast-paced, glitzy, humorous
Harper			
Historical	—	Synop. + 3 ch.	USA/Eur. settings/read Wiggs
Time Travel	—	Synop. + 3 ch.	New or est. authors
Contemp.	—	Synop. + 3 ch.	Romantic suspense/ read Macomber
Leisure			
Historical	115	Synop. + 3 ch.	Spunky heroine, untouched before hero
Gothics	90	Synop. + 3 ch.	Virginal heroine, brooding tone
Futuristics	100	Synop. + 3 ch.	Historicals from the future
Time Travel	100	Synop. + 3 ch.	Hist. seen through modern eyes
Paranormal	100	Synop. + 3 ch.	No hard sci-fi
Mills & Boon			
Harlequin Presents	50–55	Query + 1–2 pp. synop.	Contemp. category/ conservative
Harlequin Romance	50–55	Query + 1–2 pp. synop.	Contemp. category/ conservative
Legacy of Love	75–85	Query + 1–2 pp. synop.	Hist. setting/no bodice rippers
Love on Call	50–55	Query + 1–2 pp. synop.	Medical professionals fall in love
MIRA			
(Established authors preferred but will consider new authors)			
Contemp.	—	Query first	Mainstream/big concepts
Historical	—	Query first	Very few historicals needed
Pocket			
Historical	90–120	Synop. + 2 ch.	Agents only
Contemp.	90–120	Synop. + 2 ch.	Agents only
Archway YA	35	Synop. + 2 ch.	Young adult, esp. romantic comedies
Putnam/Berkley/Jove			
Wildflower	90–100	No unsolic. ms.	Western historical w/passion
Homespun	90–110	No unsolic. ms.	Midwest/less sexy
Diamond	90–100	Query first	
Tea Rose	—	Query first	
Harmony	—	Query first	New line/late '94/sweeter romances

Imprint	# Words (in thous.)	Submission Requirements	Characteristics
Paranormal	90–100	Query first	
Time Travel	90–100	Query first	Believable
Myst./Susp.	60–90	Query first	Read current offerings
St. Martin's Press			
Historical	—	Synop. + 3 ch.	Research well
Contemp.	75–100	Synop. + 3 ch.	Try Women's Fiction
Silhouette			
Desire	55–60	Query first	Emotional conflict, no light-hearted sex
Int. Mom.	80–85	Query first	Category w/flash of mainstream
Romance	53–55	Query first	Modern relationships
Shadows	70–75	Query first	Dark side of love, brooding
Spec. Ed.	75–80	Query first	Sophisticated, explores issues
Written Wd.	50	Query/part/all	"Meeting hinges on written word"
TOR-Forge			
Historical	60	Synop. + 3 ch. (or all)	Any time period
Contemp.	60	Synop. + 3 ch. (or all)	Range of topics, strong heroine
Women's Fic.	60	Synop. + 3 ch. (or all)	Wide range of topics
Myst./Susp.	60	Synop. + 3 ch. (or all)	Any great plot considered
Warner			
Historical	125	Query or synop.	Interesting subplots/characters
Contemp.	120	Query or synop.	No glitz, no glamor, no Hollywood
Zebra/Pinnacle/Kensington/Z-Fave			
Historical	130	Synop. + 3 ch.	Research setting and hist. events
Magnolia Rd.	120	Synop. + 3 ch.	Plantation setting
Regency	60–90	Synop. + 3 ch.	Passion, humor, adventure
Love Again	110	Synop. + 3 ch.	Heroine is 45+, starting over
Suspense	100	Synop. + 3 ch.	Contemporary Gothic/ no trad. Gothic
Time Travl	110–130	Synop. + 3 ch.	Believable, no sci-fi explanations

(This information was compiled by Merline Lovelace and reprinted here with permission.)

Index

About the Author

Eve Paludan became interested in the romance genre at age eight, when she watched Christopher Plummer kiss Julie Andrews in *The Sound of Music*. Her own version of happily-ever-after occurred when she answered a personals ad in 1987. She and Ron were married within the year.

A full-time writer, Eve has been published in *Writer's Journal, Writer's Digest, Kumquat Meringue* literary magazine, and many other publications. She also finds time for travel and patent research for her inventions and is an active member of Romance Writers of America. She is currently working on a romance novel and a screenplay.

Eve and her husband Ron live with their two children in Arizona.